The Mailbox® 2010–2011 Kindergarten Yearbook

Managing Editor, *The Mailbox* Magazine: Lynn Drolet

Editorial Team: Becky S. Andrews, Diane Badden, Jennifer Bragg,
Kimberley Bruck, Karen A. Brudnak, Kimberly Ann Brugger, Pam Crane,
Chris Curry, Amy Erickson, Pierce Foster, Tazmen Hansen, Marsha Heim,
Lori Z. Henry, Troy Lawrence, Debra Liverman, Kitty Lowrance,
Tina Petersen, Gary Phillips (COVER ARTIST), Mark Rainey, Greg D. Rieves,
Kelly Robertson, Hope Rodgers, Rebecca Saunders, Hope Taylor Spencer,
Donna K. Teal, Rachael Traylor, Zane Williard

ISBN 978-1-61276-139-8
ISSN 1088-5552

Printed in the United States of America.

The Mailbox® *Yearbook*
PO Box 6189
Harlan, IA 51593-1689

HPS 232520

The
Education
Center®

The MAILBOX
IDEA MAGAZINE FOR TEACHERS®

2010–2011 YEARBOOK

The Education Center, Inc.
Greensboro, North Carolina

Contents

Math Units

Seasonal Units

www.themailbox.com

Arts & Crafts

Arts & Crafts

Caramel Apples

To showcase these tasty treats, display them on your classroom door with the title "Welcome to Our Sweet Kindergarten!" 🖥

Materials for one caramel apple:

child's photo, trimmed	glitter
red construction paper apple cutout	paintbrush
brown construction paper scrap	scissors
craft stick	glue

Steps:

1. Glue the craft stick to the top of the apple.
2. Trim the brown paper so it looks like dripping caramel; then glue it to the apple.
3. Brush glue on the caramel and sprinkle it with the glitter, shaking off the excess.
4. Glue the photo to the apple.

Sue Fleischmann
Sussex, WI

T Is for Tiger

Plan to complete these "*T*-rific" projects over two days to allow time for drying between steps. 🖥

Materials for one tiger:

9" x 12" orange construction paper	2 sticky dots (eyes)
black paper scraps	black pom-pom (nose)
T template, smaller than the 9" x 12" paper	black marker
shallow container of black paint	scissors
paintbrush	glue

Steps:

1. Paint thin black horizontal stripes across the paper.
2. When the paint is dry, trace the *T* template onto the paper and cut out the letter.
3. Use the leftover paper to cut out two ears, four paws, and a tail.
4. Glue the pieces to the *T* cutout as shown.
5. Attach the eyes and draw pupils.
6. Cut whiskers from the black paper and glue them in place.
7. Glue the nose in place.

Phyllis Prestridge
West Amory Elementary
Amory, MS

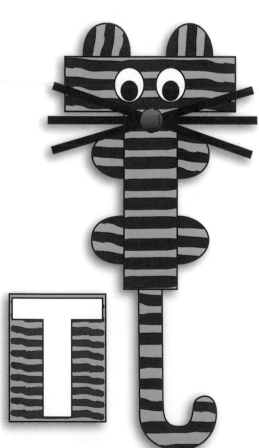

Arts & Crafts

Peekaboo Mask

Repeat this idea whenever you need a cute prop for a seasonal song or rhyme. 🖥

Materials for one mask:

construction paper scraps

large paper plate with precut
   slit (for viewing)

assorted craft supplies

jumbo craft stick

masking tape

crayons

scissors

glue

Steps:

1. Choose a seasonal object, such as a pumpkin, cat, squirrel, or goblin. Then color the paper plate accordingly.
2. Decorate the plate so it resembles the object you chose.
3. Tape the craft stick (handle) to the back of the plate.

Amy Rodriguez
Public School 212
Brooklyn, NY

A Terrific Turkey

These projects are so cute you'll want to show them off! Display them with the title "Our Gorgeous Gobblers!" 🖥

Materials for one turkey:

4 pieces of double-sided foam tape

construction paper circles: 8½" brown, 6½" red, 5" orange, 4" yellow, 3" brown

2" x 5" construction paper strips in assorted colors (feathers and legs)

construction paper scraps

scissors

glue

Steps:

1. Use the tape to join the circles from smallest to largest as shown.
2. Trim several paper strips to make feathers and legs; then glue them in place.
3. Cut a beak, a wattle, and two eyes from the paper scraps and glue them in place.

Rosemary Cliburn, Christian Home and Bible School, Mount Dora, FL

Arts & Crafts

Colorful Ornament

Hang these festive projects on a classroom tree before sending them home as a holiday gift. 🖥

Materials for one ornament:

tagboard circle
colorful tissue paper squares
construction paper scrap
diluted glue
paintbrush

glitter
ribbon
scissors
tape

Steps:

1. Brush diluted glue on the circle (ornament) and cover it with tissue paper squares. Then brush diluted glue over the tissue paper.
2. While the glue is still wet, sprinkle glitter on the ornament. Shake off the excess.
3. After the glue dries, repeat Steps 1 and 2 on the other side of the ornament.
4. When both sides are dry, trim any excess tissue paper from the edges.
5. Cut a small rectangle (ornament topper) from the construction paper scrap and tape it to the ornament.
6. Tape a ribbon loop to the ornament topper for hanging.

Chonna Parker, Maryvale Elementary, Mobile, AL

Simple Santa

These jolly fellows are sure to create a "ho-ho-whole" lot of holiday cheer! 🖥

Materials for one Santa:

flesh-color construction paper rectangle
red construction paper triangle
   (sized to fit the rectangle)
cotton balls

red pom-pom
2 white sticky dots
glue
crayons

Steps:

1. Glue the triangle to the top of the rectangle. Fold down the tip of the triangle (hat) and glue a cotton ball on it.
2. Glue several stretched-out cotton balls on the bottom edge of the hat.
3. Draw pupils on the sticky dots (eyes) and attach them to the rectangle.
4. Glue on a pom-pom nose and draw a mouth.
5. Glue several stretched out cotton balls to the bottom of the rectangle so they look like a beard.

Shirley A. MacDonald
Troy, MI

Roly-Poly Penguin

Mount these critters on a snowy background for an adorable winter display. 🖥

Materials for one penguin:

9" paper plate

two 3" black paper circles

3 orange paper triangles

construction paper scraps

black crayon

scissors

glue

Steps:

1. To make the body, color the rim of the plate.
2. Cut the construction paper scraps to make eyes. Glue the eyes and an orange triangle (beak) to one of the black circles (head).
3. Glue the head to the body.
4. Cut the other black circle in half to make wings. Glue one wing to each side of the body.
5. Cut notches in each of the remaining orange triangles (feet) and glue them to the body.

Lisa Igou
Silbernagel Elementary
Dickinson, TX

Snazzy Snowpal

Plan on allowing these cool projects to dry overnight. 🖥

Materials for one snowpal:

tagboard rectangle

equal-part mixture of
  nonmentholated shaving
  cream and white glue (snow)

construction paper scraps

craft stick

pipe cleaner

scissors

Steps:

1. Draw a pencil outline of a snowpal on the rectangle.
2. Cut desired features (hat, scarf, eyes, mouth, buttons) from the construction paper scraps.
3. Use the craft stick to spread a thin layer of snow inside the pencil outline.
4. While the snow is still wet, gently press the cutouts on the snowpal.
5. Cut the pipe cleaner in half and press one half on each side of the snowpal's body to make arms.

Sandra W. Burchette, Newport Grammar School, Newport, TN

Arts & Crafts

Personalized Pocket

Provide time for each youngster to sort her valentines into this cute cardholder. 🖳

Materials for one pocket:

tagboard heart tracers (various sizes, none larger than 7")
12" x 18" sheet of construction paper
construction paper scraps
glue
scissors
crayons

Steps:

1. Fold the paper leaving about two inches at the top. Glue the sides to make a pocket.
2. Trace several hearts on the construction paper scraps and cut them out.
3. Arrange the hearts on the front of the pocket in the shape of an animal. (Trace and cut out more hearts as needed.) Glue the hearts in place.
4. Use the crayons to write your name and add desired details.

adapted from an idea by Marieca Pilcher
Lee Elementary
Oklahoma City, OK

Stand-Up Lion

Adding a staple to the body of this project allows it to easily stand on a tabletop or bookshelf, making an adorable beginning-of-March display. 🖳

Materials for one lion:

tagboard copy of the patterns on page 13
5" brown construction paper circle
scissors
crayons
stapler
glue
unsharpened pencil

Steps:

1. Color and cut out the patterns.
2. Fold the body in half and staple it near the fold.
3. Glue the face atop the circle (mane) to make the head.
4. Fringe-cut the mane. Then gently use the pencil to curl some of the pieces inward.
5. Glue the head to the body.
6. Glue the tail to the body.

Trish Davis, Poplarville Lower Elementary, Poplarville, MS

Arts & Crafts

Tweet, Tweet!

These baby birds are just in time for spring! 🖥

Materials for one nest:

6 cotton balls
7" brown paper circle
3 yellow paper diamonds
black paper scrap

blue marker
glue
hole puncher
scissors

Steps:

1. Cut one-inch slits around the brown circle and fold the edges up to make a nest.
2. Color the cotton balls blue. Glue pairs together (one cotton ball atop the other) in the nest to form the body and head of three birds.
3. Hole-punch six circles in the black paper to make eyes. Glue two eyes to each bird's head.
4. Fold the diamonds in half to make beaks and glue them on to complete the birds.

Sue Fleischmann, Sussex, WI

Fluffy Flower

This colorful bloom is perfect for Mother's Day or other springtime occasions. 🖥

Materials for one project:

copy of the vase pattern on page 14
12" x 18" construction paper
3 coffee filters
watercolor paints
chenille stem
paintbrush

hole puncher
crayons
scissors
tape
glue

Steps:

1. Paint the coffee filters.
2. When the paint is dry, stack the coffee filters and fold them in half and then in half again. Punch a hole through the filters about an inch above the fold.
3. Thread the chenille stem through the hole and twist it. Open the filters and fluff them to look like a flower.
4. Color and cut out the vase pattern.
5. Tape the chenille stem ends to the back of the vase.
6. Glue the vase and back of the flower to the construction paper.

Michele Smith, Central Fine Arts Academy, Sand Springs, OK

Step 3

Arts & Crafts

Scented Strawberry

This painted fruit brings a sweet summer smell into your classroom! 🖥

Materials for one strawberry:

strawberry gelatin powder
tagboard strawberry and cap tracers
9" x 12" sheet of red construction paper
4" x 7" piece of green construction paper
diluted glue
scissors
paintbrush
glue

Steps:

1. Trace the strawberry on the red paper and cut the tracing out.
2. Brush a thin layer of diluted glue on the strawberry cutout.
3. Sprinkle the gelatin powder on the glue.
4. Trace the strawberry cap on the green paper and cut the tracing out.
5. Glue the cap to the strawberry.

Gina Glenn
Fish Hawk Learning Center
Lithia, FL

Editor's Tip:
To freshen the scent, simply spritz the strawberry with water.

Buzzin' by the Flowers

The flight of a bumblebee is the main attraction of this 3-D craft. 🖥

Materials for one project:

waxed paper scrap
9" x 12" sheet of construction paper
three 3" construction paper circles
2" yellow oval
construction paper scraps
glitter glue
scissors
glue
cotton ball
black marker

Steps:

1. Fringe-cut the edges of the circles. Then fold up the edges to make 3-D flower heads.
2. Cut three sets of stems and leaves from the construction paper scraps. Glue the stems, leaves, and flower heads along the bottom of the construction paper sheet to make flowers.
3. Draw bee details on the yellow oval. Then cut out and glue on paper antennae and waxed paper wings.
4. Drizzle glitter glue on the paper above the flowers to show a bee's flight path. Glue the bee to one end of the path.
5. Pull apart the cotton ball to make clouds. Glue the clouds to the paper.

Janet Boyce
Cokato, MN

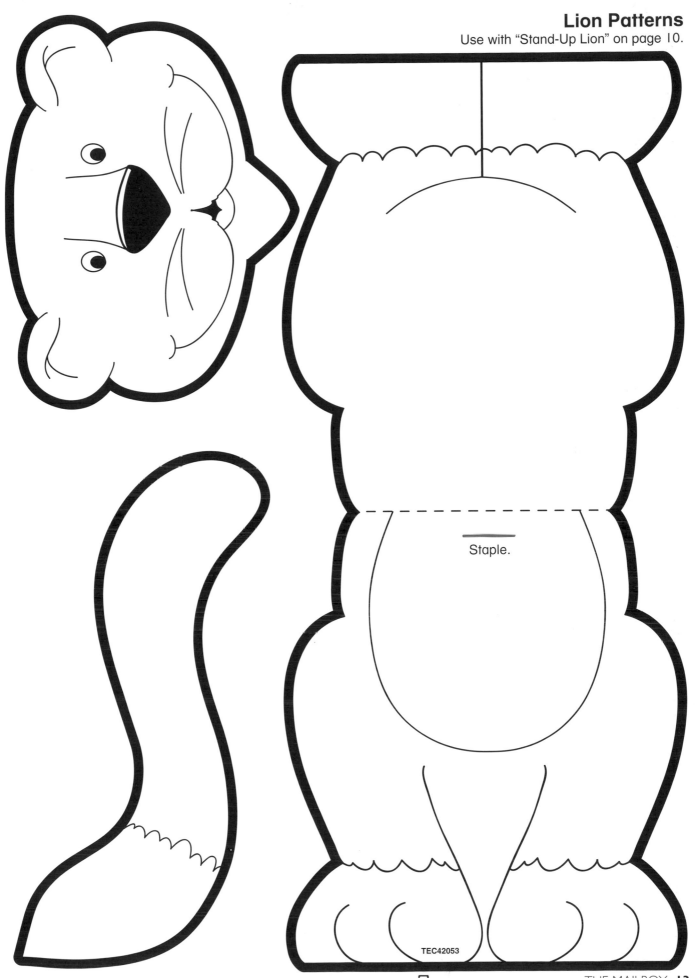

Staple.

TEC42053

Vase Pattern

Use with "Fluffy Flower" on page 11.

A special flower
From me to you
To thank you
For all you do!

TEC42054

THE BOOK CORNER

The Book Corner

Literacy Ideas for Teachers®

THE LITTLE ENGINE THAT COULD

by Watty Piper

with new art by Loren Long

The Little Engine That Could

Written by Watty Piper
Illustrated by Loren Long

When a little train engine breaks down, the toys it carries are in despair. They appeal to larger engines for help, but the engines ignore the plight of their fallen comrade. Fortunately, the little engine is helped by an equally small blue engine. The familiar refrain of "I think I can, I think I can," will resonate with your little ones.

Teach youngsters the power of positive thinking and get an overview of their fine-motor abilities with a booklet showing a victorious little engine! For each child, stack a copy of the booklet cover (page 22) and four 4½" x 8½" booklet pages with the programming shown. Staple the resulting booklet. Then have her complete each page. Finally, compliment her on the wonderful things she can do! 💻

Kiva English, Cato-Meridian Elementary, Cato, NY

Brown Bear, Brown Bear, What Do You See?

Written by Bill Martin Jr.
Illustrated by Eric Carle

A series of colorful sightings begins when Brown Bear spies a bird in this rhythmic and classic read-aloud.

When youngsters are familiar with this story, take them on a scavenger hunt to find all of the colorful critter characters! Make a copy of the cards on page 23. Place the card showing the bear in your classroom, along with a letter similar to the one shown. Then place the remaining cards in different locations throughout your school, leaving a hint with each card to lead youngsters to the next location. To begin, read the letter from Brown Bear. Then guide youngsters to the next location and help them find the card and hint. Continue until all the story characters have been found. 💻

Lori Morgan, Woodrow Wilson Elementary, Hays, KS

The Book Corner

Literacy Ideas for Teachers®

The Very Busy Spider
by Eric Carle

A very busy spider spends her day weaving her web, ignoring the invitations of several farm animals. But in the end, the spider shows what a good friend she is when she traps a pesky fly in her web.

Have youngsters sit in a circle for this unique reading and retelling of the story. As you read the story aloud, slowly unwind a ball of black yarn to make a simple web shape inside the circle. Gauge your web-making so it coincides with the length of the story. After a question-and-answer session, challenge youngsters to retell the spider's story in their own words. Each time a child contributes to the story, he rewinds a portion of the yarn until the web is gone or the story is retold. ***Retelling a story*** 🖥

Cindy Schumacher, Prairie Elementary, Cottonwood, ID

Jungle Halloween
by Maryann Cocca-Leffler

When jungle animals celebrate Halloween, they have jungle treats, jungle prizes, and jungle dancing. Halloween is full of fun when you're in the jungle!

Halloween in the jungle sounds like loads of fun, but Halloween outside the jungle is fun too! There's even an excellent chance your youngsters enjoy some of the same activities that these jungle animals do! As you reread the book, pause for students to study the book's illustrations and recognize familiar Halloween objects and activities. Next, have each child glue a copy of the sentence strip shown to a sheet of drawing paper, draw and color a jungle activity he enjoys, and write a caption for his drawing. ***Making connections*** 🖥

What is fun in the jungle is fun for me too!

I Krv a pupKn.

The Book Corner
Literacy Ideas for Teachers®

Gingerbread Friends
By Jan Brett

The Gingerbread Baby enjoys his time with Mattie, but when Mattie is not able to play, the Gingerbread Baby is lonely. While he searches a bakery for some friends, Mattie is baking up a special surprise!

The Gingerbread Baby has a lot of qualities one looks for in a friend. Help your youngsters name other desirable qualities with this simple activity! After a read-aloud of the story, revisit the Gingerbread Baby's repetitive chants. Lead students to notice the positive words the baby uses to describe himself, such as *clever* and *peppy*. Have youngsters name other positive descriptive words the Gingerbread Baby could use. Write each child's suggestion on your board. Then prompt students to recite the chant several times, substituting a different descriptive word each time. (For added excitement, have students dance enthusiastically like the Gingerbread Baby as they recite the chant!) *Descriptive words* 🖥

smart
kind
nice
funny
silly

Snow
By Uri Shulevitz

Snow-free forecasts don't hamper a boy's enthusiasm as he and his dog watch tiny snowflakes fall from the sky. One snowflake leads to another, and soon the boy and his dog are frolicking in the snow with magical friends.

Youngsters turn a city white with snow just like the city in the book. Make a gray construction paper copy of page 24. Place the page at a table along with a die and white pom-poms (snowflakes). Two youngsters visit the table. A child rolls the die and counts the dots. Then she counts that number of snowflakes. Her partner repeats the process. Next, they combine their snowflakes and count the total number. Then they place the snowflakes on the city. Youngsters continue until the city is covered with snow! *Addition with manipulatives* 🖥

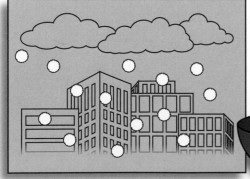

The Book Corner
Literacy Ideas for Teachers®

Miss Bindergarten Celebrates the 100th Day of Kindergarten
Written by Joseph Slate
Illustrated by Ashley Wolff

Miss Bindergarten and her menagerie of youngsters celebrate the 100th day of school! As Miss Bindergarten gets ready for the celebration, each student collects "100 of some wonderful, one-hundred-full thing!"

Give youngsters the opportunity to make collections of 100 items just like Miss Bindergarten's students! Attach ten sheets of paper to a tabletop and provide collections of manipulatives, such as craft sticks, craft foam shapes, linking cubes, and plastic animals. Also attach a larger sheet of paper labeled "100" to the table. A child chooses a manipulative and then counts ten onto each blank sheet of paper. When she is finished, she slides all of her sets onto the paper labeled "100." Now that's a lot of manipulatives! *Counting* 🖥

Corduroy
By Don Freeman

Corduroy, a toy bear in a store, goes on a search for his lost button. He is eventually found by the night watchman and taken back to the toy section where he belongs. The next morning, Corduroy is bought by Lisa, who takes him home and gives him a new button.

Give each child a colorful copy of page 25 and have her write about her favorite part of the story on the overalls. Next, have her attach a craft foam circle (button) to the overalls. If desired, display the overalls with a bear cutout and the title "We Love Corduroy 'Overall' Other Bears!" *Making connections* 🖥

adapted from an idea by Felice Kestenbaum
Goosehill Primary School
Cold Spring Harbor, NY

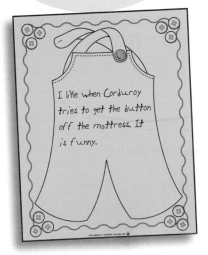

I like when Corduroy tries to get the button off the mattress. It is funny.

The Book Corner

Literacy Ideas for Teachers®

Clara Caterpillar

Written by Pamela Duncan Edwards
Illustrated by Henry Cole

Clara is not a gorgeous caterpillar. In fact, she will turn into a common cabbage butterfly. But she proves to her attractive friends that she is both cute and courageous!

Follow up this engaging story with the ideas below.

Beginning sound hard *c*: Place green paper ovals decorated to look like caterpillars at a center along with the book. Youngsters write words that begin with /k/ on the caterpillars, using the book as a reference if needed. Have students attach their caterpillars to an oversize leaf cutout.

Developing vocabulary: Cornelius the caterpillar says Catisha is conceited. Ask students what they think *conceited* means and their reasoning. Continue with a discussion of other words from the story, such as *captivating, camouflaged,* and *colossal.*

Beginning, middle, and end: Give each child a 6" x 18" strip of paper folded as shown. Help youngsters determine what happens in the beginning, middle, and end of the story. Then encourage them to write about or illustrate the sections of the story on the strip. Finally, have them round the edges and decorate the strip so it resembles a caterpillar. 🖥

Splash!

By Ann Jonas

A little girl and an assortment of creatures spend time in and out of her pond. Splash!

Count on this splashy activity to give youngsters plenty of math practice! After a read-aloud of the story, give each child a personal whiteboard (or a piece of white tagboard in a page protector), a dry-erase marker, and a paper towel. Show youngsters the first page of the story and have them count to find the number of creatures in the pond. After deciding there are six creatures in the pond, turn the page and note that the turtle jumps in. Then ask, "What is six plus one more?" Encourage students to write their answers on their boards and then hold their boards in the air. After you have checked their answers, have youngsters erase their boards. Then continue through the book, having youngsters add and subtract as needed to determine the pond population on each page. *Addition, subtraction, writing numbers* 🖥

Barb Denlinger, Ephrata Area School District
Ephrata, PA

See page 41 for a pond-related **addition practice page**.

The Book Corner
Literacy Ideas for Teachers®

Green Wilma
By Tedd Arnold

One morning, Wilma wakes up green, begins to croak, and starts to eat flies for breakfast! When Wilma goes to school, her new froggie character causes chaos as she hops, jumps, and chases flies. In this action-packed story, the surprise ending is not that Wilma's adventure is a dream but that the true dreamer is really a young frog!

For this story-related questioning activity, youngsters catch flies just as Wilma does! Cut out a copy of the fly cards on page 26 and attach a piece of Velcro fastener to the back of each card. Paint a jumbo craft stick red so it resembles a tongue. When the paint is dry, attach a corresponding piece of Velcro fastener to the tongue. Next, place the cards facedown and have a child use the tongue to pick up a fly. Then help the youngster read the question aloud. Invite a different student to answer the question and then encourage her to use the tongue for the next round. *Comprehension* 🖥

Jennifer Reidy, Halifax Elementary, Halifax, MA

The Relatives Came
Written by Cynthia Rylant
Illustrated by Stephen Gammell

The happiness and laughter of this annual reunion reveals the closeness of this family. When the relatives come in an old station wagon, they stay for several weeks. They laugh, hug, talk, eat, and hug some more! When the relatives leave, they drive back home to eventually fall into bed and dream of next summer's trip.

What would your students pack for a trip to visit relatives? You'll find out with this simple writing activity! After the read-aloud, give each youngster a sheet of paper with the sentence starter shown. Instruct him to name three items he would pack and help him complete the sentence. Then have him draw pictures to match his writing. For added fun, encourage students to share their work and then place it in a suitcase. To conclude the activity, zip up the suitcase with great fanfare! *Writing* 🖥

Janice Burch, Tri-Valley Elementary, Downs, IL

Booklet Covers
Use with *"The Little Engine That Could"* on page 16.

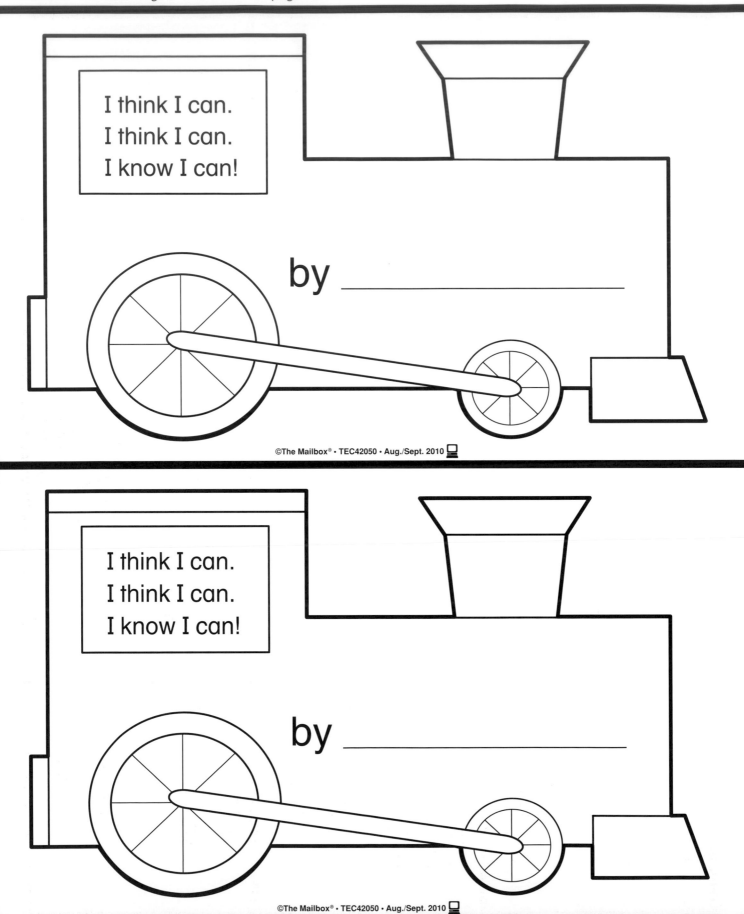

I think I can.
I think I can.
I know I can!

by _____

©The Mailbox® • TEC42050 • Aug./Sept. 2010

I think I can.
I think I can.
I know I can!

by _____

©The Mailbox® • TEC42050 • Aug./Sept. 2010

Character Cards

Use with *"Brown Bear, Brown Bear, What Do You See?"* on page 16.

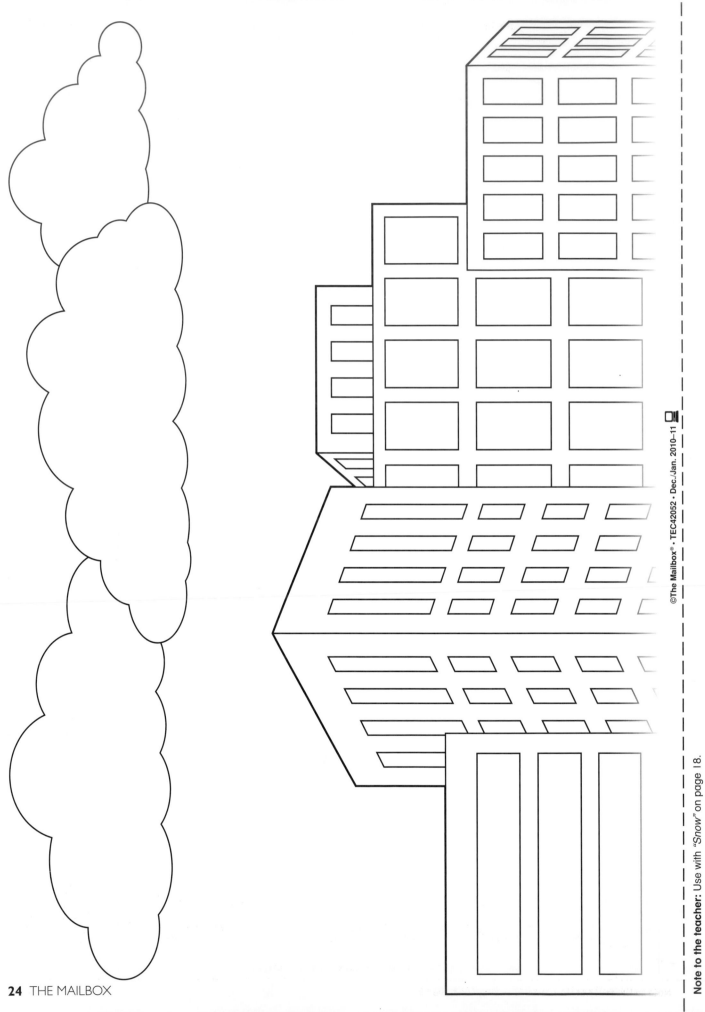

©The Mailbox® • TEC42052 • Dec./Jan. 2010–11

Note to the teacher: Use with "*Snow*" on page 18.

Fly Cards

Use with "*Green Wilma*" on page 21.

Who is the main character?

TEC42055

Is this story real or make-believe?

TEC42055

Where does the story take place?

TEC42055

What is your favorite part of the story?

TEC42055

Why does Wilma eat flies?

TEC42055

How do Wilma's parents feel? How do you know?

TEC42055

Why does the teacher think Wilma turned green?

TEC42055

What are three things that happen at Wilma's school?

TEC42055

What does Wilma chase around the school?

TEC42055

Do you think Wilma's classmates like her? Why or why not?

TEC42055

What is the surprise at the end of the story?

TEC42055

Do you like the story? Why or why not?

TEC42055

BUILDING MATH SKILLS

Building Math Skills

Dot by Dot

Counting

In your calendar area, post a black paper rectangle with a white line drawn down the center to represent a blank domino. During calendar time each day, add a white sticky dot to the domino. After it has five dots on one side, begin adding dots to the other side. Continue posting new dominos and making sets of five dots. Use the dominos to practice counting by ones and then by fives and tens.

Mary Ann Craven
Fallbrook United Methodist Christian School
Fallbrook, CA

Count, Count, Go!

Rote counting

Get students moving with a twist on the game Duck, Duck, Goose! To begin, gather youngsters in a circle and announce a number. Then play as in the traditional game, designating a student to—instead of saying, "Duck, duck, goose"— count from one to that number as he walks around the circle. Continue with more rounds, as desired. **To vary the activity,** review other skills, such as skip-counting or reciting the alphabet.

Kimberly Smith, Hunter Street Elementary, York, SC

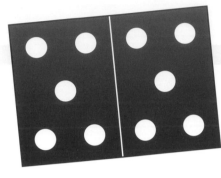

...four, five, six, seven!

In a Row

Patterning

Seasonal cutouts are perfect manipulatives to use at a patterning center. To prepare, glue seasonal cutouts to paper strips to begin several different patterns. Set the pattern starters in separate rows of a pocket chart. Set out additional cutouts by the pocket chart. A child places cutouts in each row to continue the patterns. If desired, have the child draw on a paper strip one or more of the patterns she extended. 🖥

Heather Brooner
West Englewood Elementary
Kansas City, MO

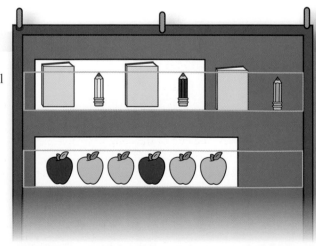

Building Math Skills

"Just-Write" Graphing

Data collection and analysis

In advance, ask each child to bring an ink pen from home. (Have some extras on hand for youngsters who forget.) Have students gather around a floor graph with their pens. Identify different ways the pens could be graphed, such as by pen color, ink color, or how the pen opens. Prepare appropriate labels for the graph and invite each child, in turn, to place his pen on the graph. Lead youngsters in discussing the results.

Jodi Darter, Cabool Elementary, Cabool, MO

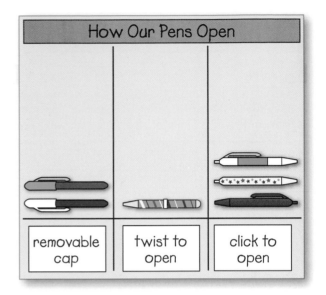

How Our Pens Open		
removable cap	twist to open	click to open

Estimation Bonus

Number sense

Improve your students' estimation skills with this investigation of *more* and *fewer*. After completing a guess-and-check activity, return the objects to the estimation jar. Next, remove a handful of objects from the jar. Ask the group whether the jar contains *more* or *fewer* objects. Count the objects again to check the answer. Repeat the activity over the course of several days. On some days remove objects and on other days add objects. Each time, have students determine whether objects were added or removed before they give new estimates.

Janice Sutherland, Louisiana Schnell Elementary, Placerville, NC

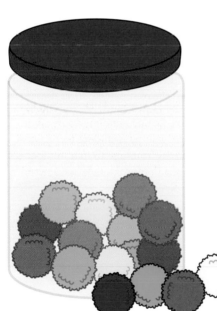

First, Last, or Between

Ordinal numbers

For this idea, ask several students to stand single file. Call the name of a student in line and then lead the group in singing the song shown. At the end of the song have a volunteer name the youngster's ordinal position. If the volunteer is correct, ask the students to switch places. Continue in this manner until math time is over or it's time for everyone to line up! 🖥

Jodi Darter

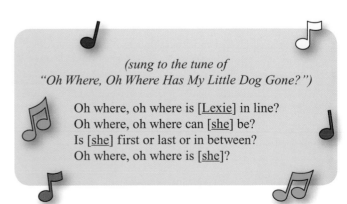

(sung to the tune of
"Oh Where, Oh Where Has My Little Dog Gone?")

Oh where, oh where is [Lexie] in line?
Oh where, oh where can [she] be?
Is [she] first or last or in between?
Oh where, oh where is [she]?

See the **practice pages**
on pages 35 and 36.

Building Math Skills

Cutting Cookies

Equal and unequal parts

For this small-group activity, give each child a ball of play dough (cookie dough), a symmetrical cookie cutter, and a plastic knife. Direct him to flatten the dough and cut out a cookie. Then announce "equal" or "unequal" and have each child cut his cookie to match. Ask group members to check each other's work before balling up their dough. Then have students trade cookie cutters and continue with another round.

Stella Loveland
Russell Cave Elementary
Lexington, KY

Roll It!

Number identification, comparing numbers

Youngsters roll into number sense skills with this group game. To prepare, program each side of a large die with a different number. Begin by writing a number on the board. Then invite a child to roll the die; name the number rolled; and tell whether the number is greater than, less than, or equal to the number on the board. If students agree with the answer, have them show approval by giving the thumbs-up signal. **For an easier version,** post a number line for youngsters to use.

Pamela Ballingall
Gossler Park Elementary
Manchester, NH

Editor's Tip:
Make a large die by covering a square tissue box with paper and writing a different number on each face.

A Colorful Lineup

Ordinal numbers

Give each of five or more youngsters a different-color bear cutout. Designate one color bear to be first and direct the students to stand in a line facing the group. Then give each seated student Unifix cubes to match the colors of the bears. Ask an ordinal number related question, such as "Which bear is third in line?" Encourage students to answer the question by holding up the corresponding-color cube. Have students hold the bears in a different order to play again.

Mary Ann Craven
Fallbrook United Methodist Christian School
Fallbrook, CA

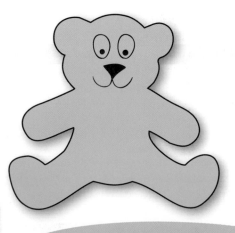

See page 37 for a **practice page** on nonstandard measurement.

Building Math Skills

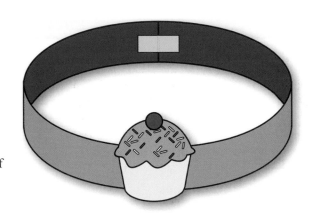

Counting Cupcakes

Concept of subtraction

Students are the main attraction at this bakery! For each student, glue a cupcake cutout to a paper strip and secure the ends of the strip to make a headband. To begin, have several youngsters stand in front of the group pretending to be cupcakes at the bakery. Lead seated youngsters to count the cupcakes. Next, invite a child to be the customer and point to the cupcakes he would like to "purchase." Instruct the corresponding students to sit by the customer. Then lead students to count and tell how many cupcakes are left. Continue modeling subtraction with different numbers of cupcakes. 💻

Amy Rodriguez, Public School 212, Brooklyn, NY

Domino Lineup

Nonstandard measurement

Here's a small-group activity that takes measurement to a higher level. Set out several objects and a supply of dominoes. Choose an object and direct a child to arrange a line of dominoes next to the object. Guide youngsters to notice whether the end of the object is closer to the end of the last domino or its midline, emphasizing the concept of one-half. Then have the group count the dominoes to determine the length of the object. **To extend the activity,** encourage students to predict objects' lengths to the nearest half of a domino prior to measuring.

Jodi Darter, Cabool Elementary, Cabool, MO

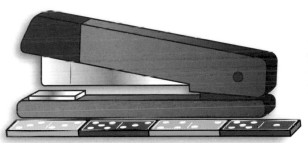

Timely Movements

Time

Add a new twist to telling time with this unique clock. Glue 12 library pockets, each labeled with a different number from 1 to 12, to a large tagboard circle. Use a brad to attach a pair of paper arrows (clock hands). Then write 12 different exercises on separate slips of paper and tuck one in each pocket. To begin, announce a time and invite a student to move the clock hands to show that time. When the correct time is displayed, direct the child to remove the slip from the pocket and help him read the words. Then have him lead the group in performing the action the number of times that matches the clock hour. Repeat the activity with different times. 💻

Donna Fugate
Whitesburg Elementary
Whitesburg, TN

| Jumping Jacks | Tummy Twists | Touch your elbow to your knee. |

See page 38 for a **practice page** on graphing.

Building Math Skills

Human Scales

Measurement

Students tip their hands like balance scales when comparing weights for this hands-on activity. Set out several objects that vary in weight. Then lead youngsters in the action poem shown to demonstrate the mechanics of a scale. After sufficient practice, invite a volunteer to take an object in each hand and tip as a balance scale. Encourage classmates to determine the lighter or heavier of the two objects. Continue with more comparisons as time permits.

Light as a feather	
Or heavy as a whale?	
Which way will weight tip the scale?	*Shrug.*
Heavier pushes down,	*Lower one hand.*
And lighter pops up.	*Raise other hand.*
Equal weight means both sides line up.	*Hold both hands at the same height.*

Jennifer Reidy, Halifax Elementary, Halifax, MA

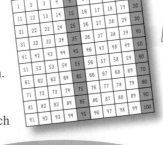

Graph It!

Solid figures

Incorporate a home-school connection for this solid-figure review. Create a floor graph similar to the one shown. Ask each child to bring an object from home that is a sphere, cube, cylinder, or cone. The next day, invite each child, in turn, to show her object, name the figure, and place it on the appropriate column of the graph. (Be sure to have solid-figure objects available for students who do not have one.) Use the completed graph to name similarities and differences in the figures, such as whether the objects slide or whether the number of faces match. **To extend the activity**, lead youngsters in discussing the graph's results.

Jodi Darter, Cabool Elementary, Cabool, MO

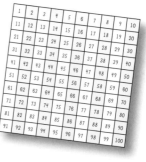

Color-Coded Counting

Skip-counting

Counting by twos, fives, and tens is a snap with these number charts. Gather three large hundred charts and highlight them as shown. Then use the charts to lead students in skip-counting. When a student demonstrates mastery, invite him to lead the group in counting as he points to each number. **To encourage independent practice**, have each child highlight his own copies of the charts. 💻

Tammy Shanks, Stepping Stones Learning Academy, Fruitland, MD

See the **practice sheets** on pages 39 and 40.

Building Math Skills

"Woof!" o' Clock

Time

Transform a CD into an adorable puppy clock with this idea! To make a clock, cut out the patterns and cards on a copy of page 42 and set aside the dog bone cards. Glue the clock cutout to a CD. Next, use paper or craft supplies to add facial details and ears as shown. (Use a water bottle cap to make the nose 3-D.) Then use a long brad to secure the clock arrows to the nose and CD. To use the clock, choose an activity below. 🖥

Small group: Distribute the dog bone cards. Then show a time to the hour on the puppy clock. The youngster with the matching card "woofs" for each hour like a cuckoo clock. If correct, she pretends to feed the dog her bone. Continue as time permits.

Center activity: Set out the puppy clock, the dog bone cards, a clock stamper, an inkpad, and paper. A child uses the supplies to record the analog and digital times for each hour.

Janice Burch, Tri-Valley Elementary, Downs, IL

Woof, woof!

2:00

8:00

Story Problem Productions

Subtraction

Your students are the performers for these subtraction-themed plays. Choose several students to be in a "Take-Away Play." Then have them act out the parts as you tell a simple subtraction story problem. After the play, lead youngsters to name the corresponding number sentence. Continue with different story problems as time permits. **For more advanced students,** have youngsters write each number sentence on a sheet of paper.

Kate Wonders, Carlisle Elementary, Carlisle, Iowa

Size and Weight

Measurement

Try this artistic twist to compare one object to other objects. Give each child an object such as a wooden block. After examining the object's size and weight, have her fold a sheet of paper to make four sections and label it as shown. Then instruct her to draw an object in each section to match the labels. 🖥

Tracy Shaner
Eastside Christian School
Marietta, GA

Block

bigger

heavier

smaller

lighter

See page 43 for a **practice page** on addition.

A Yummy Snack

Count.

Write the number.

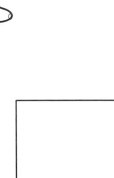

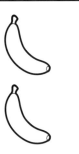
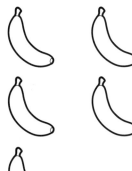

Bunches of Bubbles

✏️ Write the missing numbers.

1, ◯, 3   3, 4, ◯

8, ◯, ◯   ◯, 6, ◯

10, ◯, 12   18, ◯, ◯

◯, 5, ◯, ◯

14, ◯, ◯, ◯

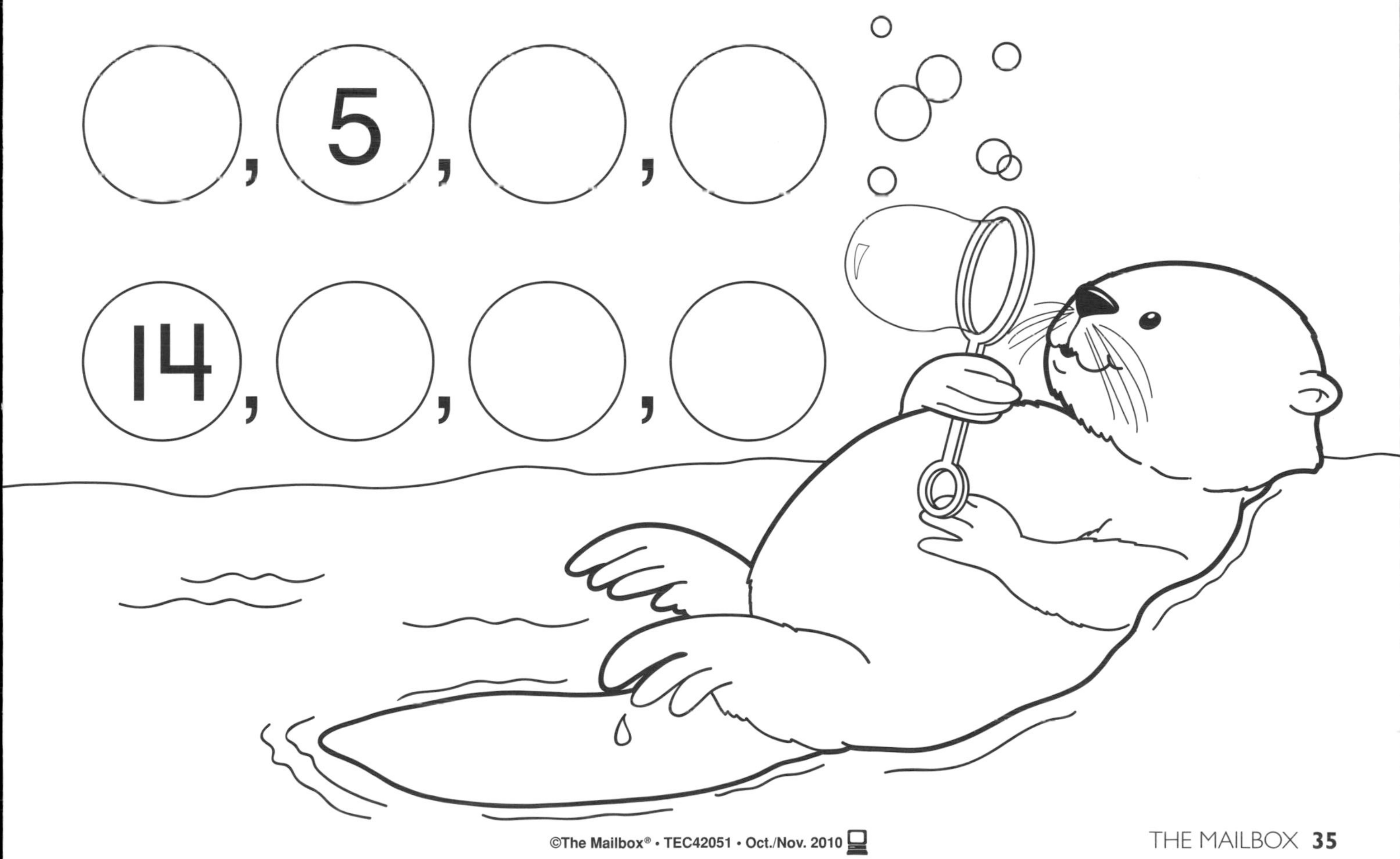

Name _____

Prizewinning Pies

Listen and do.

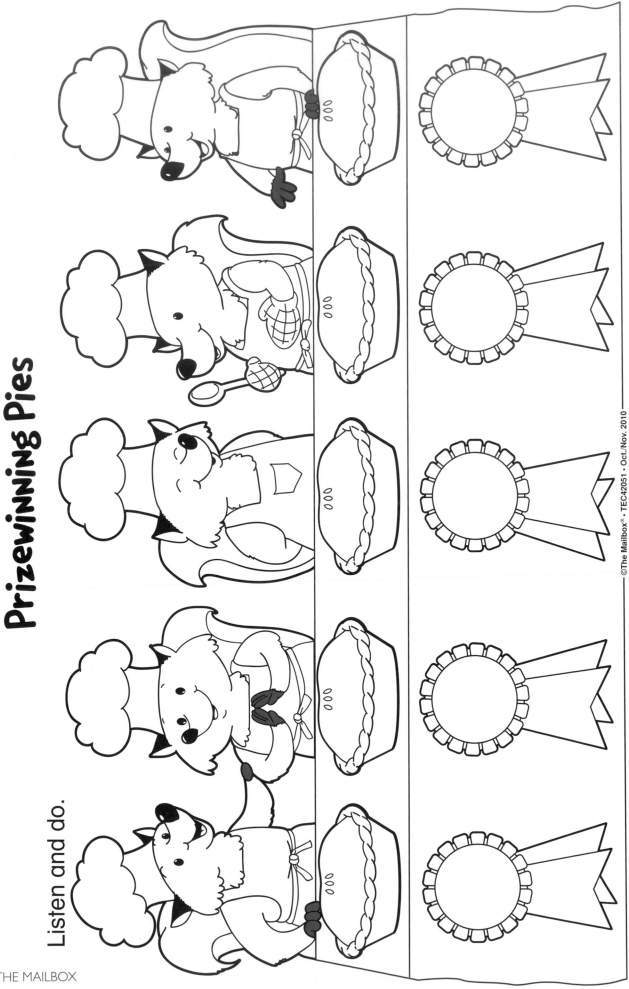

©The Mailbox® • TEC42051 • Oct./Nov. 2010

Note to the teacher: Give each student a copy of the page and make one copy for reference. On the reference copy, color-code the chef hats, pies, and prize ribbons. Refer to the reference as you give students coloring directions that incorporate ordinal numbers. For example, "Color the third pie red."

Keeping Warm

Use small  to measure each branch.
Write.

about _____ ⊂══⊃

about _____ ⊂══⊃

about _____ ⊂══⊃

about _____ ⊂══⊃

Bonus: Draw a tree with a branch that is 7 ⊂══⊃ long.

about _____ ⊂══⊃

Bye-Bye Kites!

 Count.

 Color to make a graph.

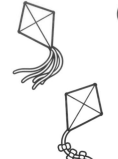
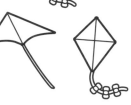

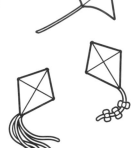

Types of Kites

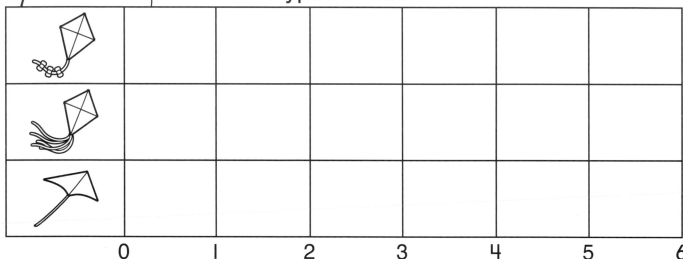

	0	1	2	3	4	5	6

 **Write how many.**

 Circle.

_____

_____

_____

Of which are there the **most?**

Of which are there the **fewest?**

 **Bonus:** How many more than are there? _____

Name _____

The Big Sale

✂ Cut.

🪣 Glue to match.

cube

cylinder

cone

○ **sphere**

Bonus: Color the sign that shows a figure that slides, rolls, and stacks.

©The Mailbox® • TEC42054 • April/May 2011

At the Bakery

Today's Special

cupcakes

Cupcakes

Add.

$1 + 6 =$ _____

$2 + 4 =$ _____

$3 + 5 =$ _____

$5 + 2 =$ _____

$9 + 1 =$ _____

$7 + 2 =$ _____

$8 + 0 =$ _____

$4 + 5 =$ _____

$2 + 8 =$ _____

Bonus: Draw a picture that shows $6 + 4$. Solve.

©The Mailbox® • TEC42054 • April/May 2011

Name_____ Addition

In the Pond

How many are in the pond?

3 🐸 + 1 🐢 = _____	2 🐸 + 1 🐻 = _____
3 🐸 + 4 🐟 = _____	4 🐟 + 2 🐸 = _____
1 🐱 + 1 🐻 = _____	1 🐢 + 2 🐟 = _____

Note to the teacher: Have each child cut out the cards from a copy of this page. Give her a sheet of blue paper (pond). Then have her place the corresponding cards on the pond to solve the addition problems.

THE MAILBOX **41**

Clock and Arrow Patterns and Dog Bone Cards
Use with "'Woof!' o' Clock" on page 33.

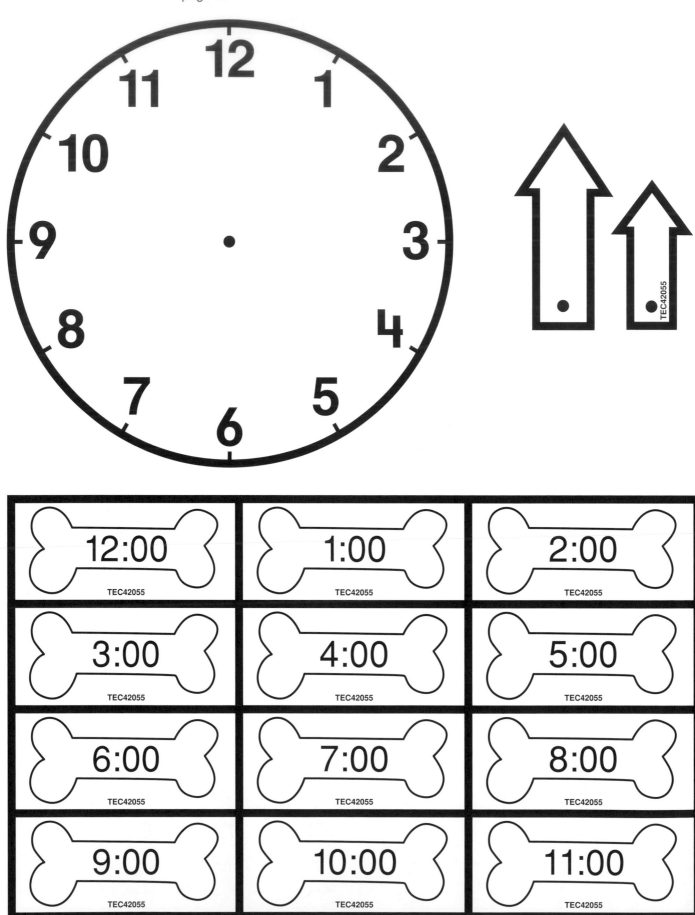

Name _____

Bubblegum Fun!

Add.
Use the counters to help you.

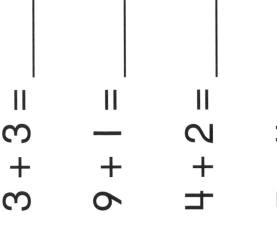

2 + 3 = ___

6 + 1 = ___

3 + 5 = ___

2 + 8 = ___

4 + 3 = ___

7 + 1 = ___

3 + 3 = ___

9 + 1 = ___

4 + 2 = ___

5 + 4 = ___

Bonus: Draw **4** green gumballs.
Draw **6** blue gumballs.
Write the addition sentence.

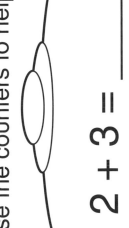

©The Mailbox® • TEC42055 • June/July 2011

Note to the teacher: Give each child ten small pom-poms (gumballs) to use as counters.

43

A Sweet Treat

 Write each number sentence.

$$5 - 2 = 3$$

$$6 - 5 = \underline{\quad}$$

___ − ___ = ___

___ − ___ = ___

___ − ___ = ___

___ − ___ = ___

___ − ___ = ___

___ − ___ = ___

___ − ___ = ___

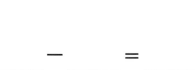

___ − ___ = ___

Bonus: Draw a picture to show 12 − 8. Write the number sentence.

BUILDING READING SKILLS

Building Reading Skills

Sing and Say!

Letter knowledge

"The Alphabet Song" is the perfect tool to foster students' mastery of each letter name! Program a different-colored paper strip for each section of letters in your version of "The Alphabet Song." Post the strips, in order, within a child's reach.

To begin, point to each letter as you sing the song, pausing and holding each note to only sing the letter that is featured. Then invite a child to use a pointer and lead youngsters in singing a fast, slow, or squeaky rendition of the alphabet song. **For an added challenge,** invite a child to point to each letter in her name or in a high-frequency word and have the class say each letter.

Jodi Gabriel
Kernersville Moravian Church Preschool
Kernersville, NC

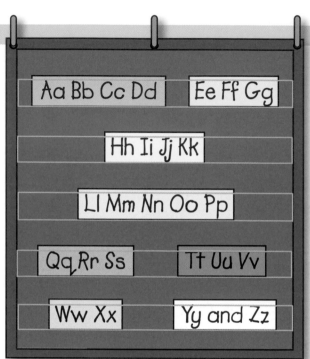

What's in the Bag?

Rhyming

In advance, put several rhyming pairs of objects in a bag. Then gather youngsters and remove two objects from the bag. Invite a child to name the items and tell whether the words rhyme. If so, put them together nearby; if not, return them to the bag. Continue to pair rhyming objects until the bag is empty. **To extend the activity,** invite youngsters to make their own mystery bags to share.

Kathi Carter
Geene County Tech Primary
Paragould, AR

Trace and Paint

Letter identification

To prepare for this hands-on activity, write each student's name in large letters on a separate sheet of construction paper. Instruct each youngster to trace her name several times using a different-colored crayon each time. Then have her lightly paint over her name for added texture.

After the paint dries, have each child use her finger to trace her name, whispering each letter as she goes. For additional practice, name individual letters in turn and have her trace each matching letter, if possible, in her name. Later, display the colorful sheets for students to practice reading each other's names.

Amy Brown, Conelway Elementary, Corry, PA

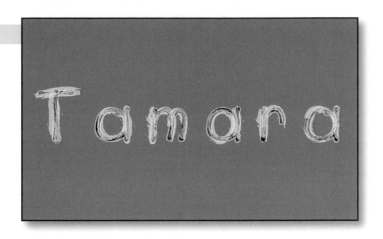

M Is for Mouse

Initial consonant **m**

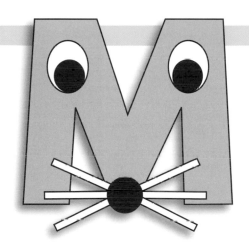

To make a mouse, give each child an *M* letter cutout. Have him cut and glue paper scraps to form a mouse's eyes, nose, and whiskers as shown. To use the mice, say, "Squeak!" and have each youngster tiptoe as quietly as a mouse to find an object or word posted in the room that begins with /m/. Then, in turn, encourage each child to share his find by pointing to it with his mouse. If desired, record students' findings on a large mouse cutout. 💻

adapted from an idea by Phyllis Prestridge
West Amory Elementary
Amory, MS

Tuned-In Time Filler

High-frequency words

Use this little ditty to encourage your kindergartners to read words. Hold up a word card or point to a word on your word wall and sing the song shown. At the end of the song, give a predetermined signal, such as a clap, and have youngsters say, whisper, or shout the featured word. **For a spelling connection,** conceal the card after the word is correctly named. Then have each child write the word on a sheet of paper before showing the card for him to check his spelling. 💻

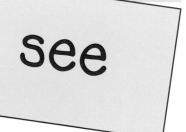

(sung to the tune of "The Muffin Man")

Oh, do you know the word you see,
The word you see, the word you see?
Oh, do you know the word you see?
Please, read it now for me.

Jodi Darter
Cabool Elementary
Cabool, MO

See page 58 for a **practice sheet** on matching uppercase and lowercase letters.

Building Reading Skills

Tall, Small, or Tail?

Letter knowledge

Looking for a fresh way to familiarize students with lowercase letters? Try this reproducible sorting activity! Give each child a copy of page 61. Guide students to relate the mouse characters to the three categories of letters. Next, instruct each child to cut out her cards. Instruct her to put the mouse cards in a column, sort the letter cards accordingly, and then share her reasoning for the placement of select letters. For reinforcement, have her store the cards in an envelope and repeat the activity later. Then instruct her to glue the mouse cards to the tops of separate papers and glue each letter card below its appropriate mouse.

Amanda Bangert
Trinity Lutheran School
Grand Island, NE

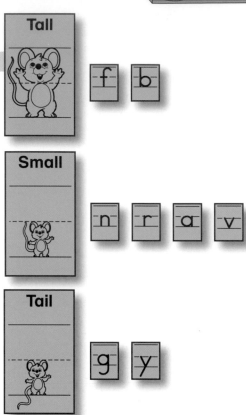

Sounds on Key

Letter-sound associations

Tune your kindergartners in to beginning sounds with this toe-tapping activity! Sing the first three lines of the song below, emphasizing the sound associated with the featured letter. Then have each student who is ready to name a word that begins with the sound raise his hand. As you sing the last line, point to three volunteers, in turn, and invite each of them to name a different word. Sing additional rounds about the same letter or feature another letter for more learning fun! 💻

> (sung to the tune of "The Mulberry Bush")
>
> Think of a word that starts with [*b*],
> Starts with [*b*]: [/*b*/, /*b*/, /*b*/].
> Who knows a word that starts with [*b*]?
> Yes, [*banana*] and [*boots*] and [*balloon*].

Beth Marquardt
St. Paul's School of Early Learning
Muskego, WI

Banana.

Boots.

Balloon.

ABC, Look at Me!

Letter knowledge

Since students are the main characters of this letter book, they'll want to read it again and again! Take a photo of each student, grouping students whose names begin with the same letter. Glue the photos to separate papers. Then title the papers and write captions as shown. For any remaining letters of the alphabet, make similar pages with photos of students performing relevant actions, such as making the quiet sign for *Q* and forming Xs with their arms to represent the letter *X*. Then bind the pages in alphabetical order between two covers.

Tammy Lutz, George E. Greene Elementary, Bad Axe, MI

A is for Ashton, Amber, and Alex.

Q is for quiet.

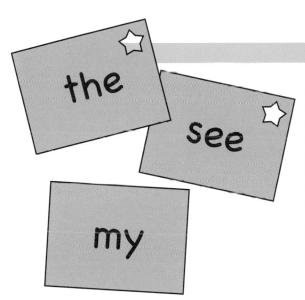

Practice and Punch

High-frequency words

Try this pride-boosting approach to using word cards! Draw a large grid on a sheet of paper and then write a different word in each grid box. Give each child a copy of the paper and have her cut out the boxes to make word cards. After she practices reading the words to herself, have her read the words to you. Use a scrapbook punch to hole-punch the card for each word she reads correctly. Then ask her to store the cards in a resealable plastic bag. For reinforcement, have her take the bag home overnight with a note explaining the holes punched. Encourage her to return the bag to school for additional practice and so she can add cards for newly learned words!

Sarah Seitz
J. Larry Newton Elementary
Fairhope, AL

Pondering Syllables

Phonological awareness

To prepare this just-ducky activity, draw three large ponds on the board or a length of bulletin board paper. Number the ponds from 1 to 3. Cut out a copy of the picture cards from page 62 and then glue the cards to separate duck cards (pattern on page 62). To begin, show students a duck card and name its picture. As students repeat the picture name, have each youngster use his hand to make one quacking motion per syllable. Ask students to identify the number of syllables. Then invite a youngster to attach the card to the corresponding pond. Continue with the remaining cards.

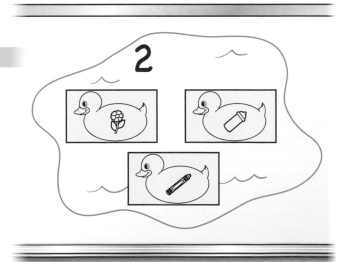

Building Reading Skills

Baker, Baker

Letter-sound associations

For this whole-group activity, display a letter-picture card for each letter you would like to review. Write the letters on separate cookie cutouts (patterns on page 67) and put the batch of cookies in a plastic jar. To begin, have a "baker" stand by the cards with a wooden spoon. Next, have youngsters pass the cookie jar while saying the chant below. At its conclusion, ask the child with the jar to remove a cookie and say the sound associated with the letter shown. Then have the baker use the spoon to point to the matching card, repeat the sound, and name a word that begins with the letter. Continue with different bakers until the jar is empty! 🖥

Baker, Baker, thanks for the batch!
Now listen to this sound and make a match!

Krista Schmied
West Boulevard Elementary
Boardman, OH

Move Those Cups!

High-frequency words

Looking for a way to heighten students' interest in reading words? Try this carnival cup–style review! For each member in your small group, tape a different word card inside an individual cup. Put the cups bottom-side up in a row. To play, each child takes a turn looking inside a cup and reading the word aloud. (Encourage her to seek help from group members as needed.) If each player is correct, the team earns a token. Then shuffle the cups for another round. Declare the students winners when the group earns five tokens.

Christy Bailey, Marion Primary School, Marion, VA

Editor's Tip:
This game can easily be adapted to review just about any kindergarten skill!

Winter Workout
Oral blending

Students pretend to drift like snowflakes while they blend these words. Think of a word and say its onset as youngsters repeat the sound(s). Next, lead students to sway lower as they repeat the rime. Then have youngsters drift to the ground as they name the word. Continue with different words as time permits. **For an added challenge,** have students blend the individual phonemes in words.

Renee Plant, Broken Arrow, OK

Setting and Characters Song
Story elements

Sing this little ditty to help your kindergartners learn the terms *setting* and *characters*. Later, lead youngsters in singing the song after reading a story aloud, stopping after each verse for students to describe the setting of the tale and then name the characters. 🖥

Patricia Hendershot
Skyvue Elementary
Graysville, OH

(sung to the tune of "The Mulberry Bush")

The setting is where the story takes place,
Story takes place, story takes place.
The setting is where the story takes place
In the books we read.

The characters are the animals and people,
Animals and people, animals and people.
The characters are the animals and people
In the books we read.

Tubs of Popcorn
Word family: -op

Students are sure to enjoy reading and responding to these tubs of words. Have each child write a different *-op* word on each of six popcorn patterns (page 67). Direct her to include one or two nonsense words. After she cuts out the patterns, have her glue them and a popcorn tub cutout to a sheet of construction paper. To review the words, invite a child to lead her classmates in reading each real and silly word on her list. **For added fun,** encourage youngsters to jump up like pieces of popping corn each time a nonsense word is announced. 🖥

Amy Ingram
Rootstown Elementary
Rootstown, OH

Building Reading Skills

Alphabet Hunt

Letter knowledge

Reading, writing, and identifying letters are a part of this whole-group activity. For each student, write a different letter on a separate card and place the cards faceup around the room. To begin, assign a different letter for each child to write. Invite a student (hunter) to find her matching letter card while you lead youngsters in saying the rhyme shown. After the last line, have the hunter show the correct letter card and her written letter. Continue as time permits. **To vary the activity,** have students hunt for final consonants or the first letter in classmates' names; or change the chant and cards so students hunt for high-frequency words. 💻

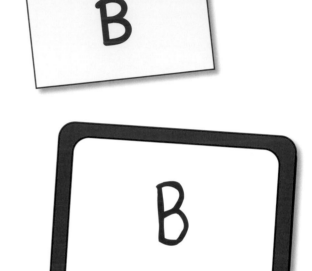

[Susie]'s going on a letter hunt!
A [/b/] hunt, a [/b/] hunt.
Yes, [Susie]'s on a letter hunt.
The letter looks like this.

Denise Dillow
FBC Christian School
Louisa, KY

Fishing for Words

High-frequency words

Students are sure to be hooked on this small-group game. Write a different word on separate fish cutouts (patterns on page 71). Tape a paper clip to each fish and drop the fish in a bucket. To make a fishing pole, tie one end of a yarn length to a wooden rod and the other end to a magnet. Then give each child a pail cutout (pattern on page 71).

To begin, ask a student to use the pole to "catch" a fish and read the word aloud. If correct, he colors a fish on his pail. Then he repeats the word, spells it for each group member to write (including himself), and returns the fish to the bucket. Players take turns fishing as time permits. Each player who colors all the fish on his pail is a winner! 💻

Kathy Price
Dupree Elementary
Jacksonville, AR

Any Place, Any Time

Phonological awareness

Reinforce phoneme manipulation with this time filler. When you have a few extra minutes or during a transition, ask a riddle such as "I'm thinking of a word that rhymes with *lip* and starts with /h/. What's the word?" Then select a youngster to respond. **For an easier version,** simplify the riddle to blend phonemes or word parts.

Jennifer Askue-Collins
The School for Small Scholars
Midlothian, VA

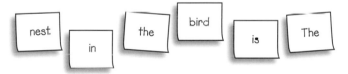

I'm thinking of a word that rhymes with *man* and starts with /k/. What's the word?

A baby cat is a kitten.

Sticky Note Sentences

Word order

Students unscramble sentences during this small-group activity. Write each word from a predetermined set of sentences on individual sticky notes. (If possible, use a different color for each sentence.) Have youngsters arrange the notes to put the words in order. Then have each child write and illustrate a sentence on story paper.

Jessie Roberts
Mount Bethel Elementary
Marietta, GA

nest   in   the   bird   is   The

The Question Box

Reading comprehension

Your kindergartners will expect a follow-up activity when they see this question mark! Label a card with a question mark. Also decorate a box with colorful question marks and put generic story-related question cards in the box. Then secretly attach the question mark card inside a book's back cover. Read the story aloud. When youngsters see the question mark, use the cards in the box to launch a review of the tale. To use the box again, simply move the question mark card to the back of a different storybook. 🖳

Jennifer Aubrey
North Dover Elementary School
Dover, DE

Building Reading Skills

Spin and Tell

Letter-sound associations

A simple spinner labeled with letters of your choice is all you need for this small-group activity. Invite a child to spin, name the letter, and make the letter's sound. If correct, have each group member give him a thumbs-up with one hand. Then have him name a word that begins with the matching letter. For this correct answer, encourage each group member to give a double thumbs-up. Continue as time permits. 🖥

Marie E. Cecchini
West Dundee, IL

Editor's Tip:
Use a paper plate or plastic lid to make a spinner base and fasten an arrow between metal washers for smoother spinning!

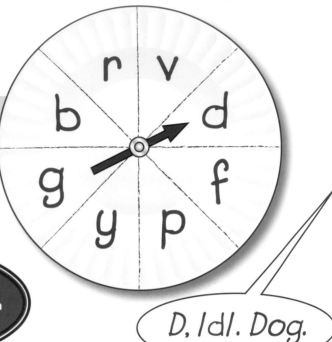

D, /d/. Dog.

Star Words

High-frequency words

Here's a fun and easy way to review words day after day! For each student, write a different high-frequency word on a star cutout (patterns on page 76). Each day, distribute the stars and choose from one of the options below. 🖥

- Have students read all the star words at their table grouping.
- Instruct each child to write her word on a sheet of paper. Then have her trace the word with a marker, a crayon, or fingerpaint.
- Have each child write a sentence that includes his star word.
- Have each child write her star word on a piece of paper and underline each vowel with a red crayon.

Thlisa Ambrose
Dade Elementary
Trenton, GA

the

what

have

Blast Off!

Number words

Students' successful reading is required to launch these rockets! Display in random order a set of cards with the number words from *one* through *ten*. Lead youngsters to read the words and put the cards in numerical order. Then give each child a paper strip and instruct her to write the words in a column, starting with *ten* at the top. When her countdown is complete, have her read the words as you check her work. If correct, respond by saying, "Blast off!" signaling her to glue her strip to a paper rectangle and to add paper or craft details to make a rocket. **For an easier version**, provide number-word cards for students to sort and glue on a paper strip. 🖥

Kimberly Fortner, Five Points Elementary, Lake City, FL

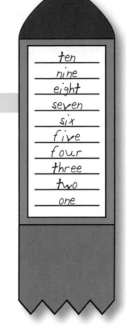

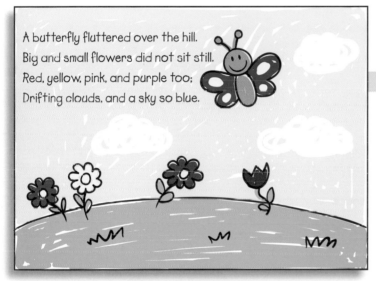

A butterfly fluttered over the hill.
Big and small flowers did not sit still.
Red, yellow, pink, and purple too;
Drifting clouds, and a sky so blue.

Picturing Poems

Comprehension

A poem is the perfect partner for developing visualization skills. Read a descriptive poem about a particular place, person, or object. Invite youngsters to share the pictures that came to mind when the words were spoken. Next, reread the poem to foster more elaborate student connections. Then have each child draw her image on a copy of the poem. **To make a personalized poetry book**, repeat the activity with several different poems and bind each student's pages between construction paper covers. 🖥

Tamara Kingsland, Oak Hill Elementary, Severna Park, MD

Flipbook Fun!

Word families

To make a flipbook, use a brad to secure four two-inch sentence-strip lengths to the top left of a four-inch length. Write a rime of your choice on the right side of the last strip. Next, have students name letters that make real words when combined with the rime; then write a different one on each of the smaller strips. Lead youngsters to read the completed flipbook before putting it at your independent reading area. As new word families are introduced, make flipbooks to create a word family flipbook collection. **For a writing extension**, have students use the flipbooks to form word family lists.

Barbara K. Johnson
Christ Our Redeemer Lutheran School
Temple Terrace, FL

Editor's Tip:
One sentence strip is long enough to form two flipbooks!

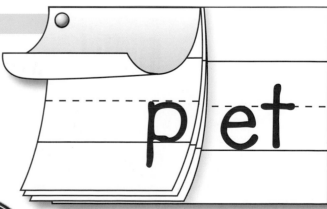

Building Reading Skills

Head, Waist, and Knees

Segmenting phonemes

Here's an activity that isolates each sound in a word and incorporates a bit of exercise too! Name a word with three phonemes. Then lead each child to slowly repeat the word, sound by sound. When he says the first sound, have him touch his head; then he touches his waist for the second sound and his knees for the final sound. If desired, have him repeat the word and actions with increased speed prior to moving on to another word. **For more advanced students,** name words that have four sounds and have youngsters touch their feet for the final sound.

Allison Pratt
Onalaska Kindergarten Center
Onalaska, WI

Chop.
/Ch/ - /o/ - /p/.

Words With Three Phonemes

hen	bug	let	cap
not	bed	man	had
with	fish	shut	chop

Beach.

Find That Bug!

Word recognition

Spark small-group members' interest in reading words with this interactive review! Display different vocabulary words or high-frequency words on individual bug cards (page 81). Then name one of the words and ask a child to use a flyswatter to swat the matching bug. If he is correct, encourage youngsters to say, "Splat!" signifying the bug was caught. If he is not correct, have youngsters whisper, "Buzz, buzz" as if the bug got away; the swatter then continues to look for the matching bug. Invite other youngsters to swat bugs as time permits. 🖥

Sparkles Brooks
Claybon Elementary
Forney, TX

A Literary Fan

High-frequency words

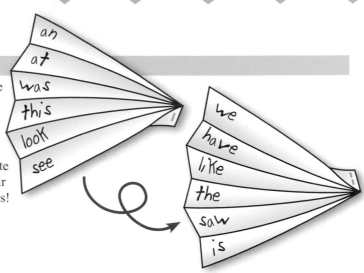

Youngsters can read words just about anywhere with these fans! Help each child accordion-fold a half-sheet of paper. Instruct her to unfold her paper and write a different word, starting at the left edge, in each section. If desired, have her write a second set of words on the back side. Then have her refold the paper and help her staple the fan at the end opposite of her words. Students are sure to read the words right at their fingertips and use the fans to cool off as the temperature rises!

Erin Roeske, Lincoln Center Elementary, South Saint Paul, MN

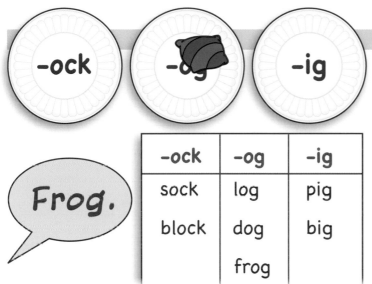

-ock	-og	-ig
sock	log	pig
block	dog	big
	frog	

Frog.

Toss and Read

Word families

Students make words with this beanbag activity. Write different rimes as column headings on chart paper and write the same rimes on individual paper plates. Then invite a child to toss a beanbag onto one of the plates. Have him read the rime and name a word that ends with it. Encourage the group to spell the word aloud as you write it in the corresponding column. Continue until each column has at least three words, forming a word family. **For a skill variation,** feature one rime on chart paper and label the plates with different onsets; have youngsters blend words to identify real and nonsense words.

Katie Zuehlke, Bendix Elementary, Annandale, MN

Predictions on Paper

Comprehension

Here's a great way for students to record personalized predictions before a read-aloud! First, read the title of a story and show the book's front cover. Then ask story-related questions coupled with specific tasks, such as the ones shown. Have each child write or draw on her paper as directed. During the read-aloud, each child is sure to be engaged as she silently compares her work to what she hears. To follow up, lead students to discuss and compare their predictions with the actual story events.

Karen Saner, Burns Elementary, Burns, KS

Do you think the story will be about a boy or a girl?
      Write *b* for *boy* or *g* for *girl*.
What do you think the new pet will be?
      Draw a picture of it.
How many main characters do you think will be in this story?
      Write the number.
Will this be a happy or sad story?
      Draw a smiley face or a sad face to match your prediction.

Name _____

Leafy Lunch

Trace.

Color to match.

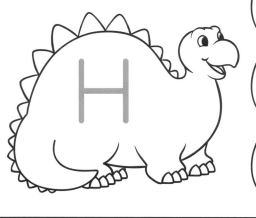 H

h

b

s

 B

d

f

b

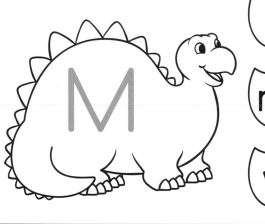 M

n

m

w

 R

p

v

r

 G

g

h

q

 T

f

l

t

Each child cuts out a copy of the cards below and sorts them on a copy of page 60. For additional practice, she puts the cards in a resealable plastic bag and takes the cards and mat home. For assessment, she completes a copy of the activity below.

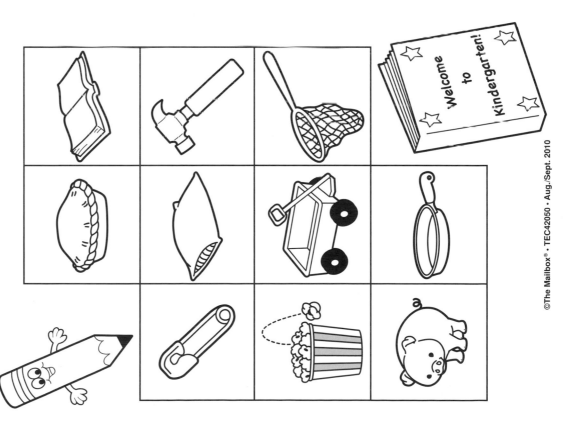

Name _____

Ready for School

Phonological Awareness
Beginning sound /p/

Color the pictures that begin like 🖊️ .

Like Pencil?

Sorting Mat

begins like ✏

does not begin like ✏

Note to the teacher: Use with the sorting activity on page 59.

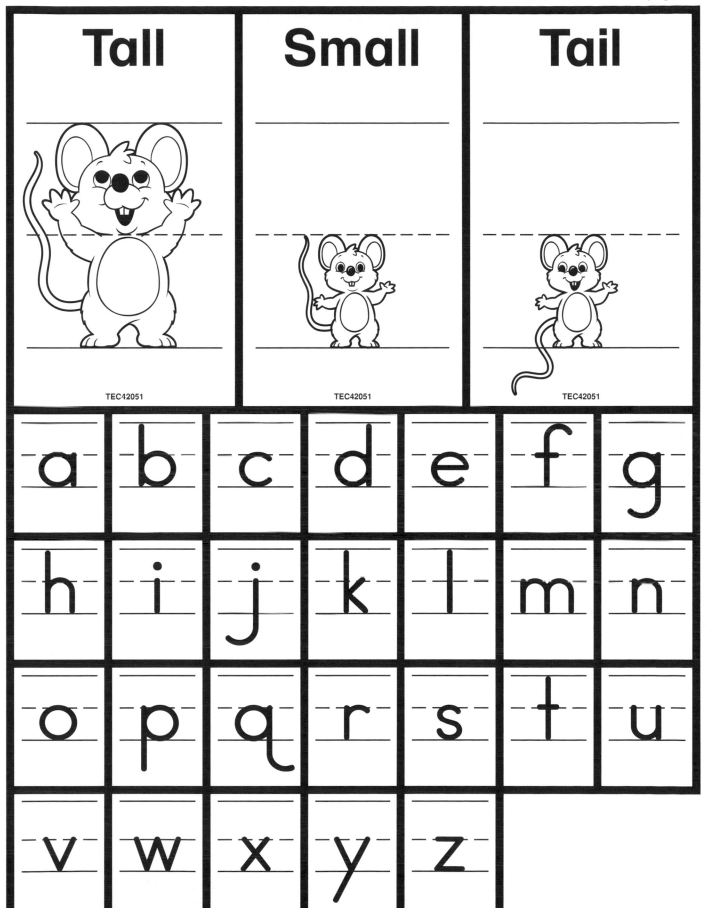

Tall	Small	Tail

TEC42051

TEC42051

TEC42051

a b c d e f g

h i j k l m n

o p q r s t u

v w x y z

Duck and Picture Cards

Use with "Pondering Syllables" on page 49.

TEC42051

Each child cuts out a copy of the cards below and sorts them on a copy of page 64. For additional practice, he puts the cards in a resealable plastic bag; then he takes the cards and mat home. For assessment, he completes a copy of the activity below.

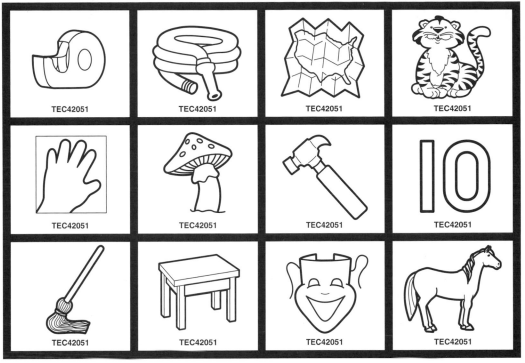

Name _____

Initial consonants
h, m, t

Caught in the Web!

🖍 Color by the code.

Color Code

begins with h as in 🏠 — red

begins with m as in 🌙 — yellow

begins with t as in 👔 — blue

Hanging Out

Sorting Mat

h as in

m as in

t as in

Note to the teacher: Use with the sorting activity on page 63.

Have each child cut apart a copy of pages 65 and 66. Then help her staple the booklet pages, in order, behind the front cover. Help students read the story and have them complete the speech bubbles.

The cow says, "**Moo.**"

1

The pig says, "**Oink.**"

3

Farm Talk

The chick says, "**Peep.**"

2

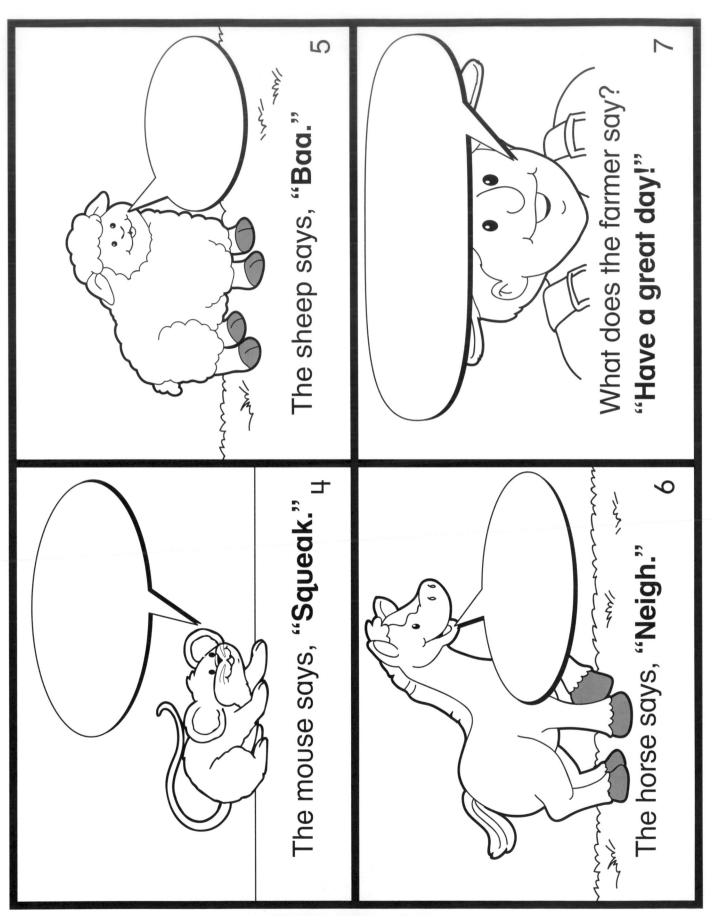

The sheep says, "**Baa.**" 5

What does the farmer say? "**Have a great day!**" 7

The mouse says, "**Squeak.**" 4

The horse says, "**Neigh.**" 6

Note to the teacher: Use with the directions on page 65.

Cookie Patterns
Use with "Baker, Baker" on page 50.

TEC42052

TEC42052

Popcorn Patterns
Use with "Tubs of Popcorn" on page 51.

TEC42052

TEC42052

Fruit Snacks

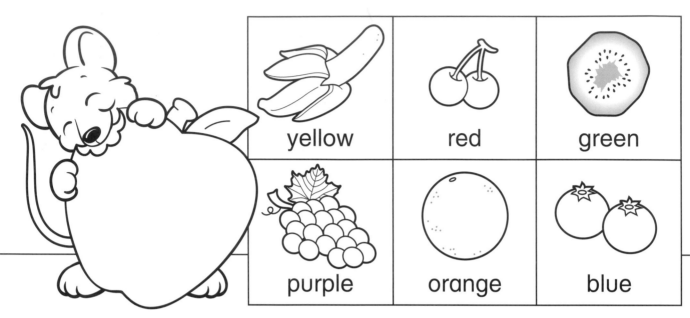

Color.

yellow	red	green
purple	orange	blue

Write.

The 🍌 is _____.

The 🥝 is _____.

The 🍊 is _____.

The 🍇 are _____.

The 🍅 are _____.

The 🍒 are _____.

Each child cuts out a copy of the cards below and sorts them on a copy of page 70. For additional practice, he puts the cards in a resealable plastic bag; then he takes the cards and mat home.

TEC42052	TEC42052	TEC42052	TEC42052
TEC42052	TEC42052	TEC42052	TEC42052
TEC42052	TEC42052	TEC42052	TEC42052
TEC42052	TEC42052	TEC42052	TEC42052

Try These Partner Activities
After the Sort!

Make a Match: Use one set of cards. Lay the cards facedown in rows. Take turns. Turn over two cards. If the pictures begin with the same sound, keep the cards and play again. If the pictures do not begin with the same sound, turn the cards back over. Play until no cards are left. The player with more cards wins.

Say a Silly Sentence: Use one set of cards. Leave the cards in the bag. Take turns. Take two cards from the bag. Name the pictures. Use the words in a silly sentence. Play until no cards are left.

TEC42052

Super Sounds!
Sorting Mat

begins like	begins like	begins like	begins like

Note to the teacher: Use with the sorting activity on page 69.

TEC42053

TEC42053

TEC42053

Sorting Activity

Each child cuts out a copy of the cards below and sorts them on a copy of page 73. For additional practice, he puts the cards in a resealable plastic bag; then he takes the cards and mat home. For assessment, he completes a copy of the activity below.

 TEC42053	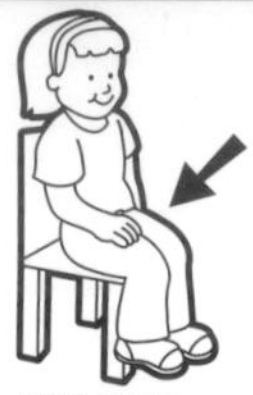 TEC42053	 TEC42053	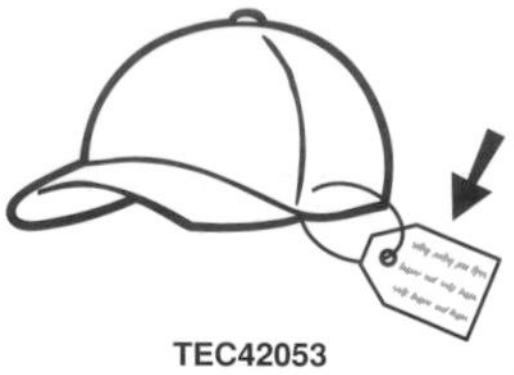 TEC42053
bag TEC42053	**cap** TEC42053	**tap** TEC42053	**rag** TEC42053
flap TEC42053	**drag** TEC42053	**flag** TEC42053	**clap** TEC42053

Name__________________

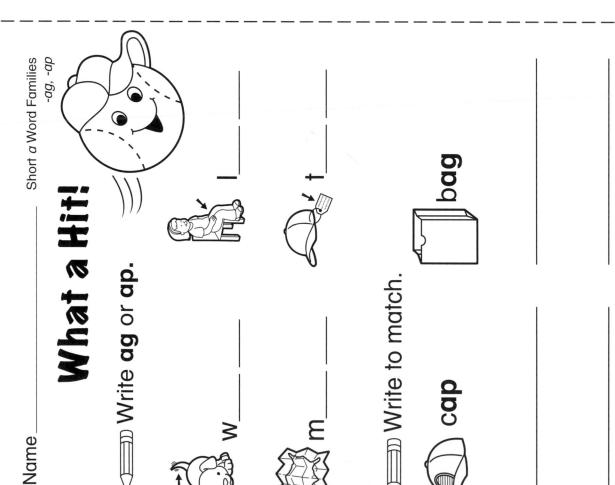

Short *a* Word Families
-ag, -ap

What a Hit!

Write **ag** or **ap**.

 w______

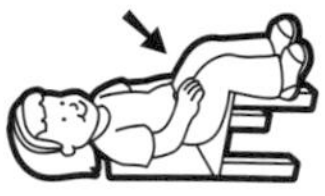 l______

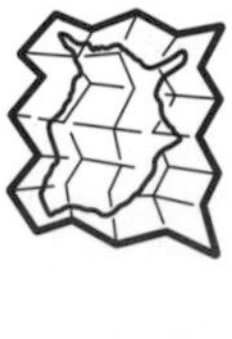 m______

 t______

Write to match.

 **cap**

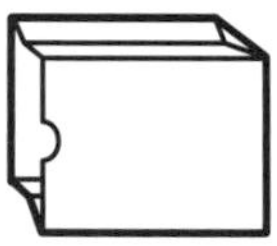 **bag**

Bonus: Use the letters **n, s, z,** and **fl** to add 4 more words to each word list.

©The Mailbox® • TEC42053 • Feb./Mar. 2011

Batting Practice

Sorting Mat

ap as in

ag as in

Note to the teacher: Use with the sorting activity on page 72.

THE MAILBOX **73**

Have each child personalize the booklet cover and add illustrations to each booklet page on a copy of pages 74 and 75. Then help her cut apart the cover and booklet pages, stack the pages in order behind the cover, and staple them together. **For additional skill reinforcement,** ask students to complete text-related tasks, such as underlining repetitive text or circling high-frequency words.

Brush, Brush, Brush!

by

©The Mailbox® • TEC42053 • Feb./Mar. 2011

Brush, brush, brush every day!

1

Rinse, rinse, rinse every day!

2

Floss, floss, floss every day!

3

Eat healthy snacks every day!

4

You will have healthy teeth that way!

5

Note to the teacher: Use with the directions on page 74.

TEC42054

TEC42054

TEC42054

TEC42054

Each child cuts out a copy of the cards below and sorts them on a copy of page 78. For additional practice, he puts the cards in a resealable plastic bag; then he takes the cards and mat home. For assessment, he completes a copy of the activity below. 🖥

TEC42054	TEC42054	TEC42054	TEC42054
TEC42054	TEC42054	TEC42054	TEC42054
TEC42054	TEC42054	TEC42054	TEC42054

- -

Name _____

Ending consonant sounds
/k/, /l/, /t/

A Silly Clown!

 Color by the code.

Color Code

ends like 🧤 —green

ends like 🐚 —yellow

ends like 🥜 —purple

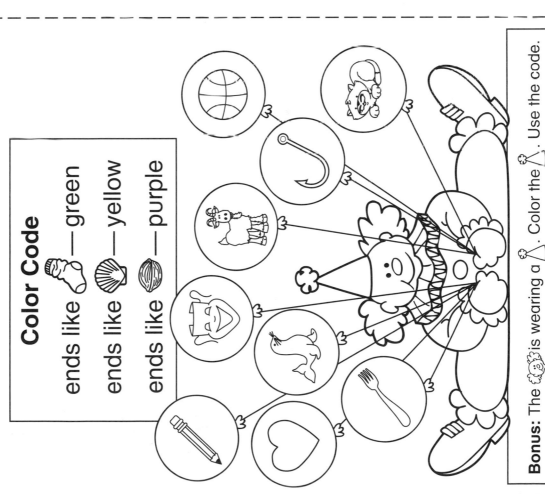

Bonus: The 🤡 is wearing a 🍦. Color the 🍦. Use the code.

©The Mailbox® • TEC42054 • April/May 2011

Under the Big Top

Sorting Mat

ends like

ends like

ends like

Note to the teacher: Use with the sorting activity on page 77.

Help each child cut apart a copy of pages 79 and 80. Then help him staple the booklet pages, in order, behind the front cover. **For additional skill reinforcement**, ask students to complete text-related tasks, such as circling high-frequency words or highlighting rhyming word sets.

1

Butterfly, butterfly, I see you.

3

You can fly down too.

Butterfly, Butterfly

Name

©The Mailbox® • TEC42054 • April/May 2011

2

You can fly up.

You can see a bee.

5

You can land on a flower.

4

Fly here to me!

7

Fly, butterfly!

6

Note to the teacher: Use with the directions on page 79.

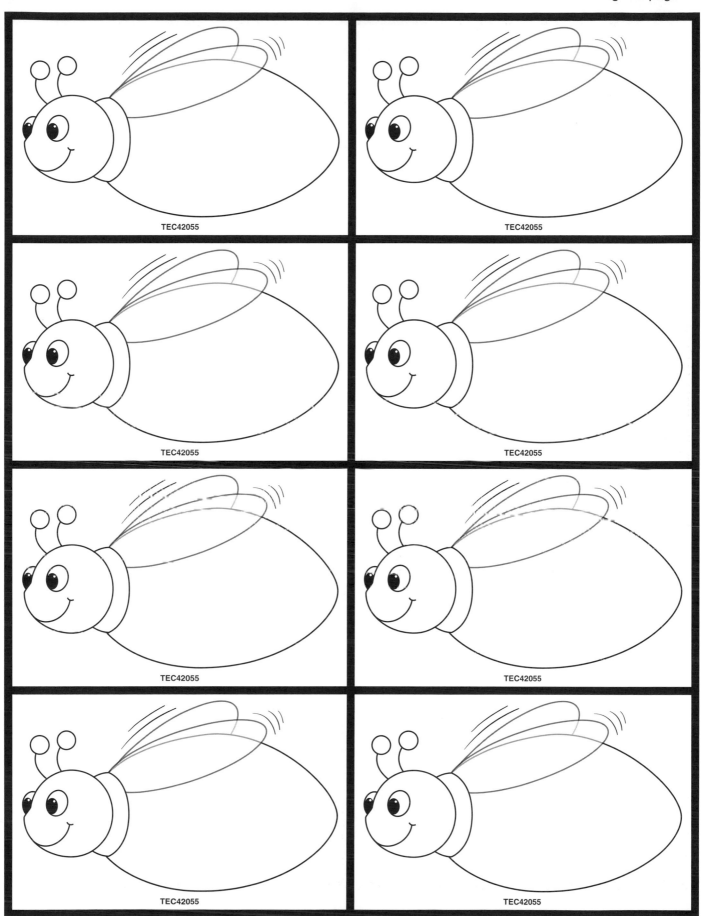

TEC42055

TEC42055

TEC42055

TEC42055

TEC42055

TEC42055

TEC42055

TEC42055

Each child cuts out a copy of the cards below and sorts them on a copy of page 83. For additional practice, he puts the cards in a resealable plastic bag; then he takes the cards and mat home. For assessment, he completes a copy of the activity below. 🖥

dot TEC42055	jog TEC42055	stop TEC42055	hot TEC42055
pop TEC42055	got TEC42055	dog TEC42055	plot TEC42055
not TEC42055	drop TEC42055	lot TEC42055	hop TEC42055
hog TEC42055	spot TEC42055	top TEC42055	frog TEC42055

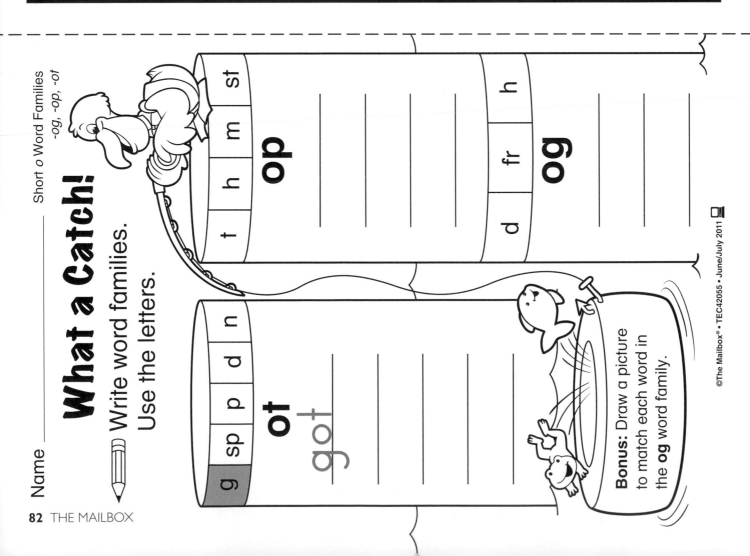

Short *o* Word Families
-og, -op, -ot

Name _____

What a Catch!

✏️ Write word families. Use the letters.

t	h	h	m	st

op

_____
_____
_____

d	fr	h

og

_____
_____
_____

g	sp	p	d	n

ot

got
_____
_____
_____

Bonus: Draw a picture to match each word in the **og** word family.

©The Mailbox® • TEC42055 • June/July 2011

Ready to Fish!

Sorting Mat

ot
as in

op
as in

og
as in

Note to the teacher: Use with the sorting activity on page 82.

Quilting Bee

✂ Cut.

Glue to match the **ŏ** or **ŭ** sound.

Ŏ

as in 🥘

Ŭ

as in ☀️

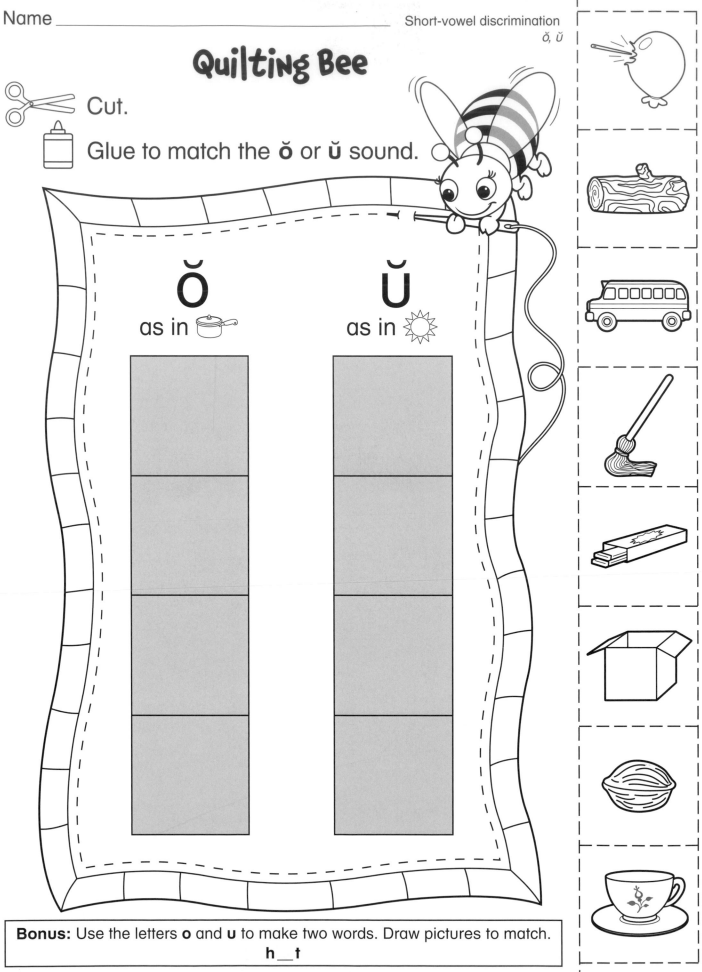

Bonus: Use the letters **o** and **u** to make two words. Draw pictures to match.

h__t

Classroom Displays

Mirror, Mirror on the Wall,

Juan   Sally   Ben   Rita   Nan   Lolita

Look Who's in Kindergarten This Fall!

Students' self-portraits are the main attraction of this back-to-school board. For each child, glue an aluminum-foil oval on a copy of the mirror pattern on page 92. Help each youngster write his name on a mirror's handle and have him cut out the pattern. Also have each child draw a likeness of his face on an oval that is slightly smaller than the foil oval (or use trimmed student photos instead). Have him glue his drawing to his mirror. Then post the mirrors on a board titled as shown. 🖥

Laurie Birt, Belinder Elementary, Prairie Village, KS

We Love to Work Together!

Juan, Camden, Gina, Laurie, Tamika, T.R., Shauna, Maxwell, Marguerite, Parker, Freida, Ms. Blair

This heart would not be complete without each member of your class, including you! Write each student's name and your own on a large paper heart and cut the names apart to make puzzle pieces. Then have each child decorate the piece that shows his name. Following a discussion of the importance of each puzzle piece, place the pieces at a table for small groups to put together. Later, display the assembled heart as a reminder of each person's value to the group.

Marilyn Blair
McRae Elementary
Keystone Heights, FL

Editor's Tip:
To add new students, ask a child to share his heart space and be the newcomer's helper for the day.

When their fish are caught on these lines, students are sure to notice job responsibilities! Make a bucket by trimming the top of a piece of tagboard and stapling each of three sides to a bulletin board. Write each child's name on a separate fish cutout and slide the fish into the bucket. Also label paper strips (fishing rods) with the names of different jobs. Attach a string to one end of each rod and then tie a paper clip to the string. To assign jobs, simply slide a fish onto each paper clip. 🖥

Jennifer A. Langdon
Fishkill, NY

Hooked on Helping!

Door Holder

Lunch Count

Suki

Line Leader

Pet Care

Matthew

Wyatt

Calendar

Teacher's Helper

Rachel

Wendy

All Aboard the Friend Ship

Looking for a way to encourage kindness? Try this! Cut a large ship from bulletin board paper and glue a trimmed photo of each youngster to the ship. Have each child decorate a sailor hat cutout (pattern on page 92) and glue it to the top of his photo. Display the ship with paper waves and the title shown. To foster friendly interactions, toot a horn or ring a bell when you observe exceptional kindness in your classroom. 🖥

BethAnn Suckstorf, Neligh-Oakdale Elementary, Neligh, NE

CLASSROOM DISPLAYS

What might you see on a coconut tree? Crafty letters, of course! After reading *Chicka Chicka Boom Boom* by Bill Martin Jr. and John Archambault, give each child a tagboard letter cutout. Instruct her to glue tissue paper squares to the letter. After the glue dries, hold each letter up for youngsters to identify; then add it to a bulletin board similar to the one shown.

Susan McGuirl and Heather Brett
Minue School
Carteret, NJ

Take a Look at Our Great Work!

This year-round display features your students' best work! Have each child draw on a skin-tone paper oval (head) a likeness of his face. If desired, provide yarn strands for hair. Help him glue semicircles (hands) to a shirt cutout and glue the head to the top of the shirt. **For a seasonal tie-in,** have him decorate a pilgrim hat cutout (patterns on page 93) and glue it to the head. Attach each craft to the top of a construction paper sheet. Then use Sticky-Tac adhesive to secure student's work to his project. 🖥

Janice Shuman, Saint Brigid School, South Boston, MA

Happy Holidays!

To create this festive tree, have each child make green fingerprints (leaves) on a paper plate. After the paint is dry, invite her to make several red thumbprints (berries) atop the leaves. Then help her attach a trimmed photograph of herself and a red paper bow to her plate to complete her wreath. Post the wreaths above a brown paper rectangle (trunk) to form a tree shape. 🖥

Stacy Wingen
Howard Elementary
Howard, SD

Editor's Tip:
Just before the holiday break, have students take the wreaths home to give as gifts.

Attach brown bulletin board paper on and above a board so it resembles a gingerbread house. Mount white border to the roof for frosting. Then use the directions shown to have youngsters decorate candy cutouts (patterns on page 94). When the cutouts are dry, mount these sweet crafts to the house along with a door cutout. If desired, use the display to inspire writing or as a graphing activity.

Candy Cane: Add a few drops of peppermint extract to red paint. Dip a cotton swab in the paint and use it to make stripes.
Gumdrop: Color the pattern. Then brush on diluted glue and sprinkle it with glitter.
Hard Candies: Color the pattern as desired.
Lollipop: Tape a circle cutout to a craft stick, cover it with plastic wrap, and tie a ribbon to secure the plastic.

Terry Schreiber, Holy Family Catholic Academy, Norwood, NJ

A Sweet Scene

Heart-shaped snowflakes offer a beautiful way to welcome Valentine's Day! Have each child write her name on a white heart cutout. Then have her hole-punch snowflake-style designs around her name. Showcase the snowflakes with a snowpal featuring a red heart and add the title shown.

Randi Austin
Stoutland R-2 Elementary
Stoutland, MO

Editor's Tip:
For different snowflake designs, use shape hole-punchers!

Feature students' recent studies with these crafty kites. Instruct each child to decorate a paper diamond (kite) with glitter, paint, or other art materials. Help him tape a length of yarn to his kite. Then have him tie three crepe paper strips to the yarn so they resemble bows. Post the kites with cloud cutouts labeled with topics your students have been learning. As new topics are introduced, post additional cloud cutouts. 🖥

Diane Bonica, Deer Creek Elementary, Tigard, OR

Oversize eggs are the perfect filler for this super-duper seasonal basket! Have each child paint or draw designs on a large oval (egg). Then help him zigzag-cut the egg into halves and secure the parts with a brad so they resemble a hatched egg. Showcase the eggs in a supersize basket cutout along with cellophane grass, a large bow, and the title shown. 🖥

Stacy Wingen and Nancy Erickson
Howard Elementary
Howard, SD

Add **student-made chicks** to the display! See page 130.

Enormous Eggs

The Very Tasty Tree

Foster students' connections to Eric Carle's *The Very Hungry Caterpillar* with these cute critters. To make one caterpillar, a youngster glues the ends of a red paper strip to make a loop (head). She repeats the process with four green strips (body). Then she cuts paper scraps to make eyes, a mouth, and antennae and glues them to the head. Next, she glues the head and the body on a large leaf cutout to form a caterpillar. Then she hole-punches the leaf so it looks as if it's been nibbled by her caterpillar. Post the completed crafts on a large tree trunk for a leafy 3-D display. 🖥

Michele Smith, Central Fine Arts Academy, Sand Springs, OK

Mirror Pattern

Use with "Mirror, Mirror on the Wall, Look Who's in Kindergarten This Fall!" on page 86.

Sailor Hat Pattern

Use with "All Aboard the Friend Ship" on page 87.

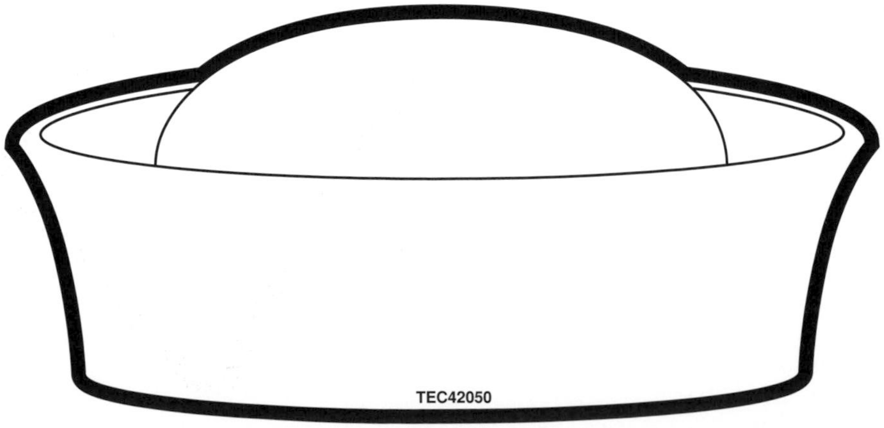

TEC42050

TEC42050

Pilgrim Hat Patterns
Use with "Take a Look at Our
Great Work!" on page 88.

TEC42051

TEC42051

Candy Patterns
Use with "A Sweet Scene" on page 89.

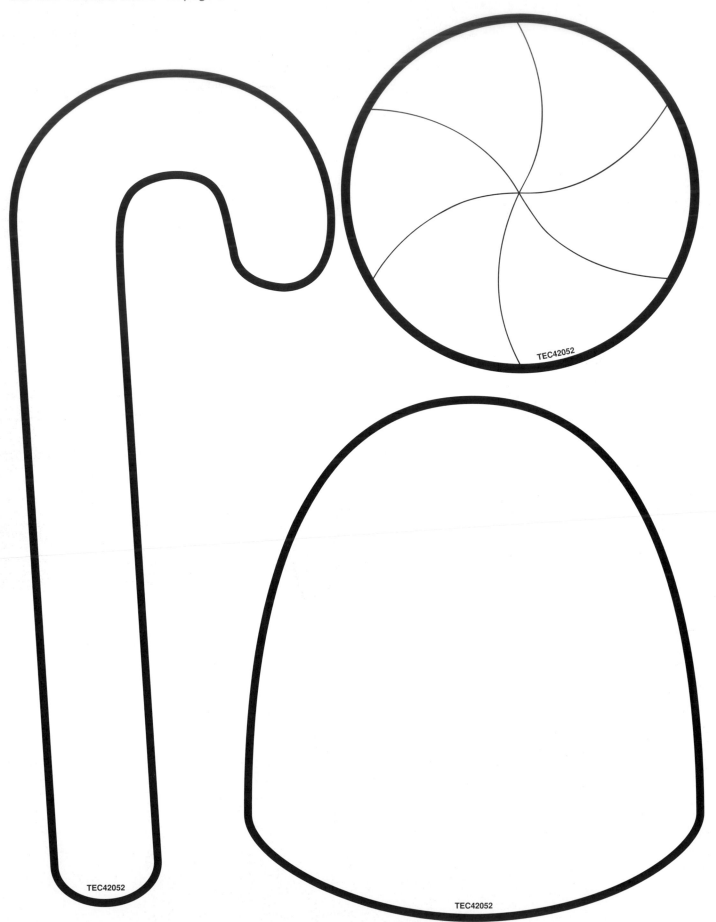

TEC42052

TEC42052

TEC42052

LEARNING CENTERS

Learning Centers

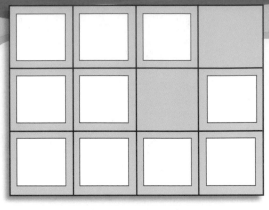

Memorable Rhymes
Literacy Center

This two-player rhyming game is sure to be a winner! Cut out a copy of the cards on page 106. If desired, mount the cards on seasonal cutouts, such as apples or acorns. Also prepare a 12-space tagboard grid. Store the cards in a bag; then set the bag and grid at a center.

Players randomly arrange the cards facedown on the grid. To take a turn, a player turns over two cards and names the pictures. If the words rhyme, he keeps the cards. If they do not, he turns the cards facedown in their grid spaces. Players alternate turns until all the cards have been paired. The player with more pairs wins! *Rhyming* 🖥️

Editor's Tip:
Use the grid to reinforce other skills, such as reading high-frequency words. Simply program two blank cards for each word you want to reinforce.

Number Caterpillars
Math Center

To make caterpillar heads, draw a face on each of several plastic lids, like the ones from liquid coffee creamers. Label the top of each head with a different number. At a center, place the heads and a collection of smaller lids or round counters. A child places the caterpillar heads in a row, leaving space between them. To make caterpillars, a child places the matching number of lids behind each head. *Making number sets*

Ellen Dischinger
Risen Christ School
Minneapolis, MN

The Box Book
Literacy Center

In advance, collect a variety of empty cereal boxes. Cut the front panel from each box and place it in a plastic sheet protector. Then put the sheet protectors in a three-ring binder. Place the binder, a set of letter cards, a wipe-off marker, and an eraser or paper towels at a center. A child takes a card and names the letter. Then he circles the letter each time it occurs in the binder. When he's finished, he erases his marks and repeats the activity using a different letter. *Identifying letters*

Kristen Darch, Skinner Road School, Vernon, CT

Learning Centers

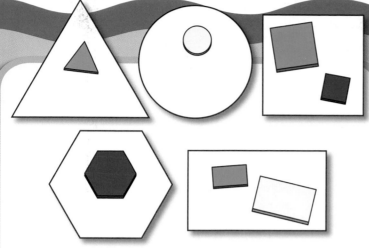

Pick a Sort
Math Center

This easy-to-prepare center can be used for four weeks with just a few simple substitutions each week. Set out a container of attribute blocks and choose a different option each week.

Sort by color: Set out a sheet of construction paper to match each color of block. A child places each block on the matching sheet of paper.

Sort by shape: Set out a large shape cutout to match each attribute-block shape. A child places each block on the matching shape.

Sort by size: Set out a large basket and a small basket. A child puts the large blocks in the large basket and the small blocks in the small basket.

Sort by thickness: Gather a thick book and a thin book of a similar size. Wrap each book with bulletin board paper and place them at the center. A child puts the thick shapes on the thick book and the thin shapes on the thin book.

Laurie Block, Cabool Elementary, Cabool, MO

Match It
Literacy Center

Prepare several sheets like the one shown, varying the letters on each sheet. Laminate the sheets or put them in plastic sheet protectors. Place the sheets at a center with a supply of wax sticks, such as Wikki Stix creative sticks, or lengths of rolled play dough. A child chooses a sheet and lays the wax sticks across the paper to match each letter pair. She repeats the activity with other sheets as time allows. **For a more challenging activity,** program the sheets for matching uppercase and lowercase letters. *Matching letters* 💻

Lila Heatherington
Prairie Valley Elementary
Callendar, IA

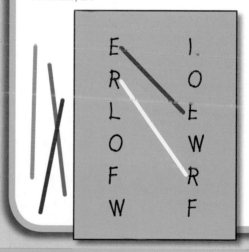

Mouse Tales
Math Center

For this matching activity, color a copy of the center mat on page 107. Color and cut out a copy of the cards on page 108. Write the matching number on the back of each card to make the activity self-checking. Store the cards in a resealable plastic bag. Place the bag and the mat at a center. A student spreads out the cards faceup. He puts a number card on the mat. Then he puts the matching book card below it. To check his work, he flips the book card and looks for the matching number. He sets those two cards aside and continues to pair the remaining cards. *Matching numbers to sets*

Catherine Broome-Kehm, Melbourne Beach, FL

Learning Centers

Crazy for Carrots
Math Center

In advance, gather a supply of orange plastic tops from empty glue bottles (carrots). Write a different number on each of several copies of the bunny mat on page 109. Put the mats and a supply of carrots at a center. A child chooses a bunny mat, reads the number, and places that number of carrots on the mat. She repeats the activity using different mats as time allows. **For an easier version,** draw a corresponding dot set on each programmed mat. A child places a carrot on each dot. *Making sets* 🖳

Jodi Darter
Cabool Elementary
Cabool, MO

Editor's Tip:
Ask your colleagues to save glue tops for you or use orange pom-poms instead.

Hook It!
Literacy Center

Cut out a copy of the cards on page 110. Glue each card on a sturdy four-inch card. Laminate the cards for durability and then punch a hole below each letter where indicated. Program the backs of the cards for self-checking. Put the cards and several pipe cleaners at a center. For each card, a child names the picture and uses a pipe cleaner to "hook" its initial consonant as shown. Then he flips the card to check his work. *Initial consonants* 🖳

adapted from an idea by Liz Mooney
Central Rayne Kindergarten
Rayne, LA

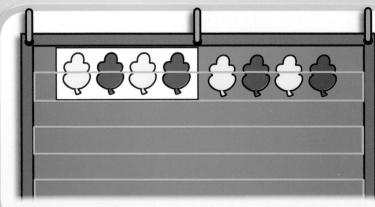

Pocket Chart Patterns
Math Center

Make several pattern strips by gluing seasonal cutouts to tagboard strips. Store the strips and a supply of cutouts for extending the patterns near your pocket chart. A child puts a strip in the pocket chart and then uses the cutouts to extend the pattern. She repeats the activity with different pattern strips. *Patterning*

Vanessa Rivera, La Luz Elementary, La Luz, NM

Learning Centers

have

On the Go
Literacy Center
On each of several vehicle cutouts (patterns on page 111) write a different high-frequency word, being sure to match the number of letters in the word to the number of windows on the vehicle. Place the vehicles at a center along with letter tiles and paper. A child takes a vehicle and reads the word. Then she places a letter on each window to spell the word. After she writes the word on her paper, she removes the letters and repeats the process with another vehicle. *High-frequency words* 🖥

Sheri Wallace, Ed White Elementary, Eldridge, IA

Trimmed Trees
Math Center
Reinforce a variety of number skills with this versatile idea. To prepare, gather colorful sticky dots (ornaments) and cut out a supply of green triangles (trees) and brown rectangles (trunks). Then choose one or more of the options below. 🖥

Matching numbers to sets: Attach a different number of ornaments to each tree. Program the trunks with numbers to match the trees. A child counts the ornaments on each tree and places the matching trunk under the tree.
Number words: Attach a different number of ornaments to each tree. Label the tree trunks with matching number words. For each tree, a child counts the ornaments and then places the matching trunk under the tree.
Counting and writing numbers: Label each trunk with a different letter and then glue each trunk to a tree. Attach a different number of ornaments to each tree. Letter a sheet of paper to correspond with the trees and make student copies. For each tree, a child counts the ornaments and writes the number next to the appropriate letter.

Kiva English
Cato-Meridian Elementary
Cato, NY

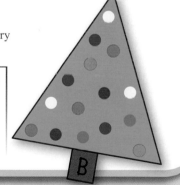

Ethan
A.
B. 15
C.
D.

Pretty Petals
Literacy Center
Watch youngsters' syllable-counting skills bloom! Cut out a copy of the petals on page 112 and place them in a small basket. Number three paper circles (flower centers) as shown and attach a paper stem to each one. Place the flowers and the petals at a center. A child quietly names the picture on a petal. Then she counts the number of syllables in the word and places the petal on the matching flower. She continues with the remaining petals. *Syllables* 🖥

adapted from an idea by Lorena Altamirano, Canoga Park, CA

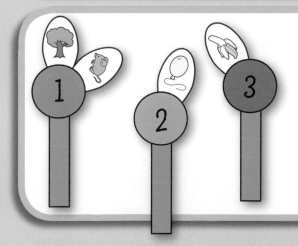

Learning Centers

Safari Ride
Math Center

A giraffe, zebra, cheetah, and lion—oh my! To prepare for this independent activity, copy onto colored paper the envelope label on page 113 and the strips and cards on page 114. Attach the label to the front of a manila clasp envelope. Cut apart the strips and cards. Write the matching pattern on the back of each strip. Then put the strips and cards in the envelope.

A student takes the cards and strips from the envelope and spreads them out faceup. Then she puts a strip on the envelope label and uses the cards to extend the pattern. She continues with each remaining strip. **For an added challenge,** have her write the letters that represent the pattern (*AB* or *ABC*) on a sheet of paper and then flip the strip to check her work. *Patterning* 🖥

Catherine Broome-Kehm, Melbourne Beach, FL

Crayon Colors
Literacy Center

Reinforce color words at each student's individual ability level. Cut out different-color crayon shapes and program a set of matching–color word cards with each word written in the corresponding color. Also create a set of color word cards with the words written in black. Assign each youngster an option below to best fit her needs. *Color words* 🖥

Extra support: Set out the crayon cutouts and the color word cards written in the corresponding colors. A child reads each card and places it on the matching crayon cutout.

Average: Set out the crayon cutouts and the color word cards written in black. A child reads each card and places it on the matching crayon cutout.

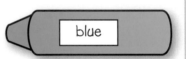

Challenge: Set out the crayon cutouts and a tub of letter manipulatives. A child chooses a crayon and places letter manipulatives on it to spell the matching color word.

Kimberly Love Hintze
Show Low, AZ

Missing Numbers
Math Center

Program a paper strip with the number sequence 1–20, replacing several numbers with blank spaces. Then write each missing number on a separate card (sized to fit the blank spaces). Place the number strip at a center and stack the cards facedown. A child takes one card at a time and places it on the appropriate space on the strip. **For extra support,** post a number line for youngsters to refer to as needed. *Number order*

1 3 4   7 8 9   11   13 14 15   18   20

Editor's Tip:
For reinforcement, have youngsters write the numbers from 1 to 20.

Learning Centers

Do-It-Yourself Dictionaries
Literacy Center

For each child, set out eight copies of the booklet page on page 115, a copy of the cards on page 115, construction paper covers, and a book ring along with a hole puncher and glue. A child cuts apart the cards and glues each one to a booklet page. Then she writes the name of the picture beside the card and writes below the card a sentence using the word. To complete the booklet, she hole-punches the pages and covers, binds them with the book ring, and adds a title to the front cover. *CVC words* 💻

Amy Lashlee
Hampton Oaks Elementary
Stafford, VA

Load the Bus
Math Center

Place at a center a yellow copy of the bus pattern on page 116, several addition problem cards, tagboard circles with faces drawn on them (passengers), and paper. A child puts an addition problem on the bus. To solve the problem, he places the corresponding number of passengers on the bus. Then he writes the problem and answer on a sheet of paper. He continues with the remaining addition problems. *Addition* 💻

Lydia Hess
Chambersburg, PA

Dino Beat
Literacy Center

These musical dinosaurs just might encourage your youngsters to clap, stomp, or tap to count syllables! Color a copy of the center mat on page 117. Color and cut out a copy of the center cards on page 118. Write the matching number on the back of each card to make the activity self–checking. Store the cards in a resealable plastic bag. Then place the bag and mat at a center. To complete the activity, a student stacks the cards faceup. She names the picture on the top card, counts the number of syllables in the word, and then places the card in the box below the matching number. After she sorts the remaining cards, she flips the cards to check her work. *Syllables*

Catherine Broome-Kehm, Melbourne Beach, FL

Tur-tle. That's 2 syllables!

Learning Centers

 -in

 -ig

 -ug

Ducks in a Row
Literacy Center

To prepare for this partner center, cut apart a yellow copy of the duck and duckling cards on page 119. Glue each duck card to the left side of a paper strip and place the remaining cards in a bag. To take a turn, a child removes a card from the bag, reads the word, and places it beside the matching duck. If he gets a "Quack!" card, he quacks like a duck, selects a word family ending, and reads each word in the row. (If there are no duckling cards on the strips, he simply quacks like a duck!) Play continues until each card has been correctly placed. *Word families* 🖥

Barbara Worobey, Deposit Elementary
Deposit, NY

A Balanced Act
Math Center

Students investigate how much gold it will take to balance the scale for this activity. Set out a balance scale, chocolate gold-wrapped coins or yellow Unifix cubes (gold), a supply of small classroom objects, and a recording sheet similar to the one shown. A child chooses an object and writes its name or draws it on her paper. She estimates how many pieces of gold it will take to equal the weight of the object and records the number in the middle column. Then she places the object on one side of the scale and places gold on the other side of the scale until it is balanced. After she counts the number of gold pieces, she writes the number in the far right column and compares it to her estimate. She repeats the process with other objects as time permits. *Measurement* 🖥

Jennifer Reidy, Halifax Elementary, Halifax, MA

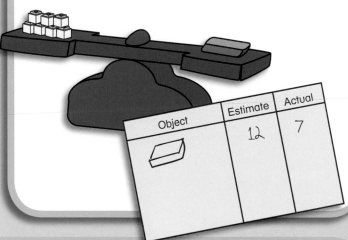

Object	Estimate	Actual
	12	7

Puddles
Literacy Center

Spark students' imaginations with these props! Put a few stuffed animals, a blue paper oval (water puddle), a brown paper oval (mud puddle), and story paper at a center. A child chooses an animal and puts it on one of the puddles. Then she draws and writes to tell about the animal's experience in the puddle. *Writing*

The elephant sat in the mud puddle. It got dirty!

Learning Centers

Build a Nest
Literacy Center

Students place eggs on these nests to spell words! Cut out a copy of the nest cards on page 120. For each nest, write the name of the picture on the back of the nest. Then write the letters for each word on individual paper ovals (eggs). Place each nest and matching egg set in a separate resealable plastic bag.

A child empties a bag, places the nest picture-side up, and names the picture. Next, he arranges the eggs to spell the word. To check his work, he flips the nest. Then he writes the word on a sheet of paper and uses it in a sentence. *Spelling*

Kim Mattioli, Big Tree Elementary
Hamburg, NY

Colorful Counting and More
Math Center

Mardi Gras–style beaded necklaces make a versatile math manipulative. Gather a supply of necklaces and choose one of the options below.

Comparing sets: Cut the necklaces into sections of varying lengths. A child takes two sections and places them side by side. Then he counts the beads in each section, writes the two numbers on a sheet of paper, and circles the larger number.

Skip-counting: Cut the necklaces into sets of two-bead, five-bead, and ten-bead sections. Put each set in a separate container. A child chooses a container and arranges the bead sections in a line. Then she touches each bead section and counts by twos, fives, or tens, according to the set she chose.

Addition: Cut the necklaces into sections of one to nine beads. Set out the bead sections and blank paper. A child chooses two sections and draws them on her paper. Then she writes an addition sentence to match the drawing.

Rae Anne Seat
Holy Spirit School
Norway, MI

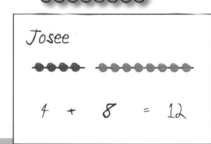

Rodeo Time
Math Center

To prepare for this independent activity, copy onto colored paper the envelope label on page 121 and the cards on page 122. Attach the label to the front of a manila clasp envelope. Cut apart the cards. Write the matching time on the back of each clock card to make the activity self-checking. Then put them in the envelope.

A student takes the cards from the envelope and spreads them out lasso-side up. Then he puts a clock card on the envelope label and places the matching time card beside it. To check his work, he flips the clock card. He continues in this manner until all the cards are paired. *Time to the hour*

Catherine Broome-Kehm, Melbourne Beach, FL

Learning Centers

How Many Frogs?
Math Center

Youngsters hop into measurement practice with this idea. Prepare six log cutouts of different lengths and number them from 1 to 6. Place at a center the logs, a supply of large green pom-poms (frogs), and student copies of the recording sheet on page 123. A child takes a log and writes on the matching row of her recording sheet an estimate of how many frogs will fit across the length of the log. Then she places frogs side by side on the log, counts the frogs that fit completely on the log, and writes the amount on her paper. She continues with each remaining log. ***Nonstandard measurement*** 💻

Katie Zeuhlke, Bendix Elementary
Annandale, MN

Word Family Search
Literacy Center

These hide-and-seek bags are sure to be a hit with your students! To make one, label a large resealable plastic bag with a word family ending and then partially fill the bag with colorful paper shreds. Hide corresponding word family cards and a few distracter cards in the bag. Prepare a different bag for each word family you would like to review. Place the bags and a supply of paper at a center.

A child takes a bag and copies the rime on a sheet of paper. Then he removes a card. If the word on the card matches the rime, he writes it on his paper. If the word does not match, he sets the card aside. He continues with each remaining card and then reads the resulting word family list. ***Word families***

Vicki Denny
All Saints Episcopal School
Lubbock, TX

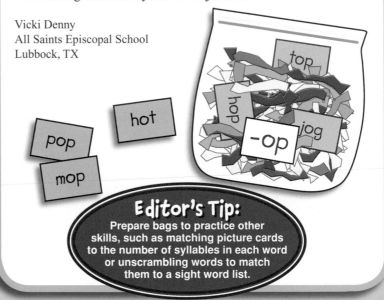

Editor's Tip:
Prepare bags to practice other skills, such as matching picture cards to the number of syllables in each word or unscrambling words to match them to a sight word list.

Block by Block
Math Center

Move your math center to your block area! Set out student copies of page 124 along with ten of each of the following block shapes: cubes, cylinders, cones, and rectangular prisms. A child uses some of the blocks to build a structure. Next, on a copy of the recording sheet, he colors the graph to match the total number of each type of block he used. Then he uses the graph to answer the questions at the bottom of his paper. ***Solid figures, graphing***

Janice Burch, Tri-Valley Elementary, Downs, IL

Learning Centers

Construction Zone
Literacy Center

Your kindergartners pretend to be construction workers as they build sentences at this center. Write "I see a" on half of a sentence strip and draw a period on a separate smaller piece of the strip. Then cut a supply of shorter sentence strip lengths in two different colors. On one color set, write a different color word on each strip; on the other set, write a different noun on each strip. Place at a center the prepared strips and a plastic toy hammer. A child reads the sentence starter and selects one strip from each color to "build" a sentence. Next, she takes the hammer and taps each word as she reads the sentence. Then she writes the sentence on her paper and draws a picture to match. **To differentiate**, see the options below. *Making sentences*

Easier: Add picture cues to the word cards.

More challenging: Write *in a* on another sentence strip length for students to build longer sentences. Also provide size-related words on a different-color set of strips.

Michelle Brown
Watervliet Elementary
Watervliet, NY

Monster Munch
Math Center

This addition puppet prop is not only cute, it serves as a self-checking tool too! To make a monster, glue a copy of the monster pattern from page 123 to a paper lunch bag. When the glue is dry, cut out the monster's mouth. Set out the monster, Unifix cubes, two number cubes, a whiteboard, and a dry-erase marker. A child rolls the number cubes and then writes on the board an addition problem using the rolled numbers. Next, she "feeds" the monster cubes to match the addition problem. After writing the sum on her board, she counts the "munched" cubes to check her answer. *Addition* 🖳

Kate Wonders
Carlisle Elementary
Carlisle, IA

Honey Bear
Literacy Center

To prepare for this independent activity, color copies of the envelope label on page 125 and the cards on page 126. Attach the label to the front of a manila clasp envelope. Cut apart the cards. To make the activity self-checking, use a code of your choice to label the back of each card. Then put the cards in the envelope.

A student takes the cards from the envelope and spreads them out honeycomb-side up. He moves the larger cards to begin three columns. Next, he sorts the word cards to match the word family endings. Then he reads each word and puts the matching picture card with it. To check his work, he flips the cards. After confirming his accuracy, he writes the word family endings and corresponding words to form three word family lists. *Short* a *word families*

Catherine Broome-Kehm, Melbourne Beach, FL

Rhyming Cards
Use with "Memorable Rhymes" on page 96.

TEC42050

TEC42050

TEC42050

TEC42050

TEC42050

TEC42050

TEC42050

TEC42050

TEC42050

TEC42050

TEC42050

TEC42050

Mouse Tales

Put a number card.
Put the matching book card.
Check.

DICTIONARY

Activity Cards

Use with "Mouse Tales" on page 97.

1	2	3	4	5	6	7	8	9	10

TEC42050

Note to the teacher: Use with "Crazy for Carrots" on page 98.

Picture Cards
Use with "Hook It!" on page 98.

p **r** **s** ● ● ●	**b** **m** **t** ● ● ●
n **l** **d** ● ● ●	**v** **c** **s** ● ● ●
m **r** **h** ● ● ●	**f** **r** **d** ● ● ●

TEC42051

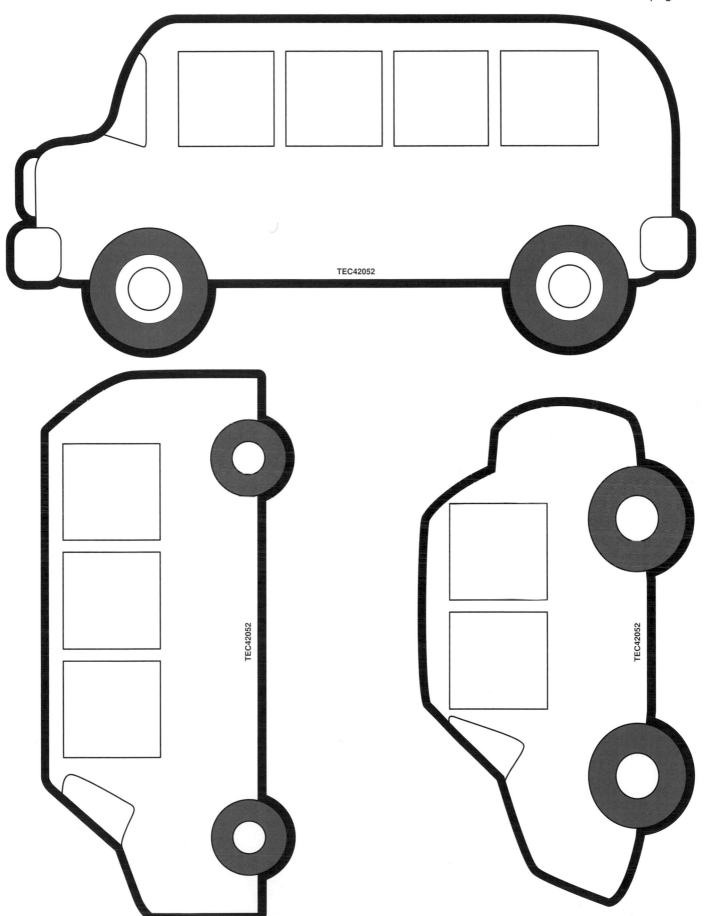

TEC42052

TEC42052

TEC42052

Petal Patterns

Use with "Pretty Petals" on page 99.

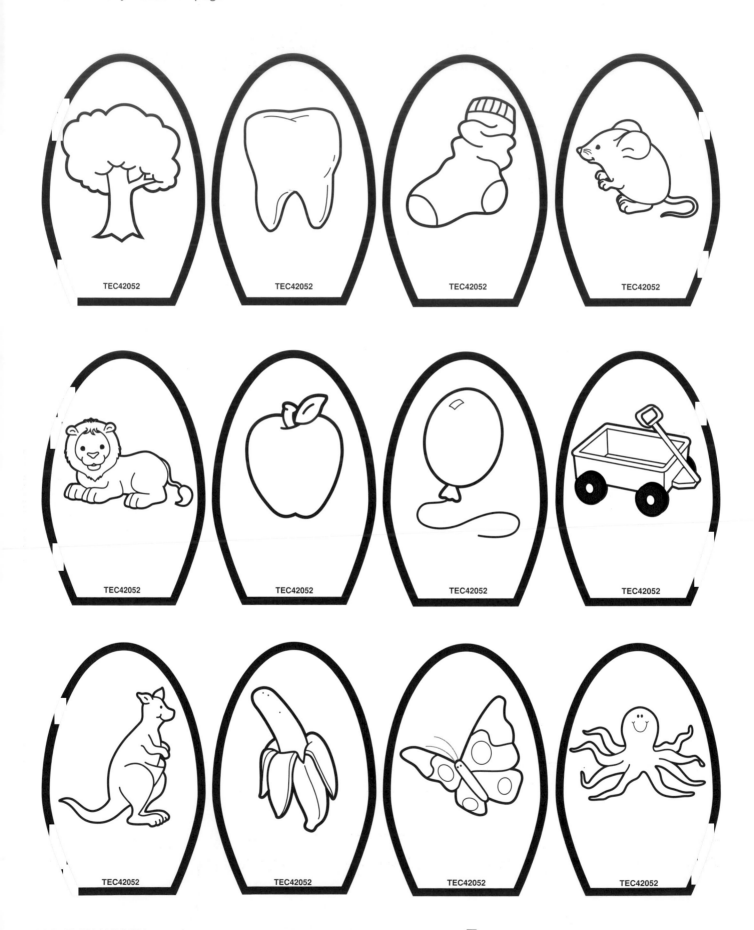

Safari Ride

Center Strips and Cards

Use with "Safari Ride" on page 100.

Bus Pattern

Use with "Load the Bus" on page 101.

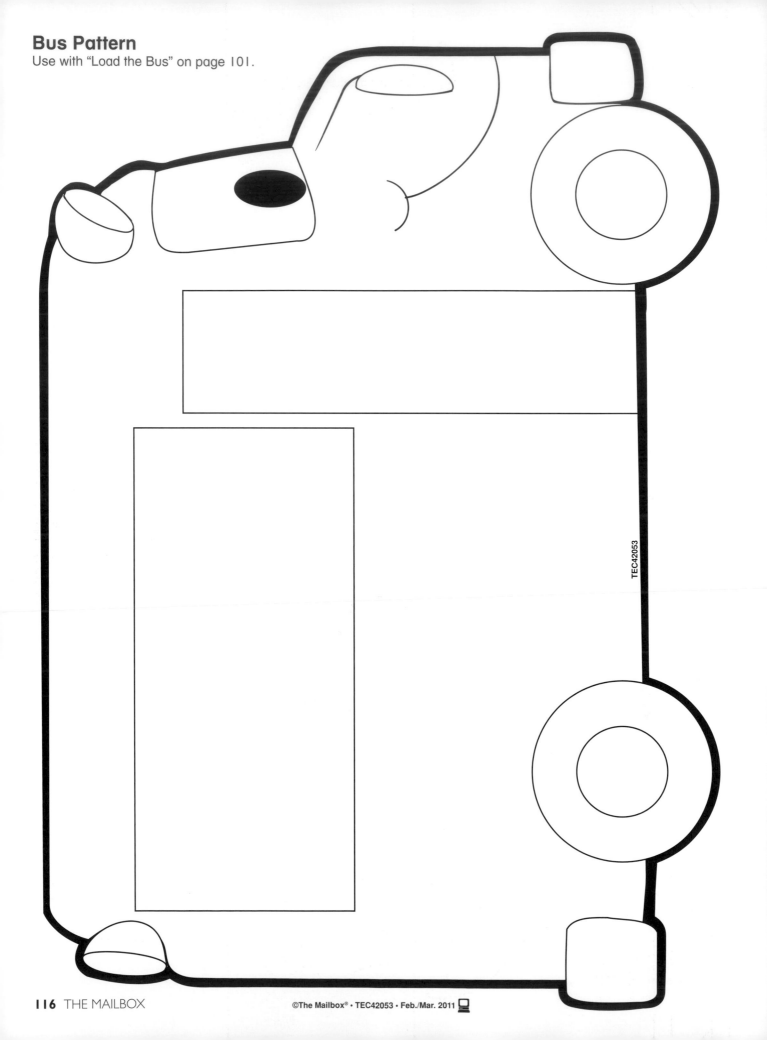

TEC42053

Dino Beat

Name each picture.
Match the number of syllables.
Check.

3

2

1

Center Cards
Use with "Dino Beat" on page 101.

Duck Cards
Use with "Ducks in a Row" on page 102.

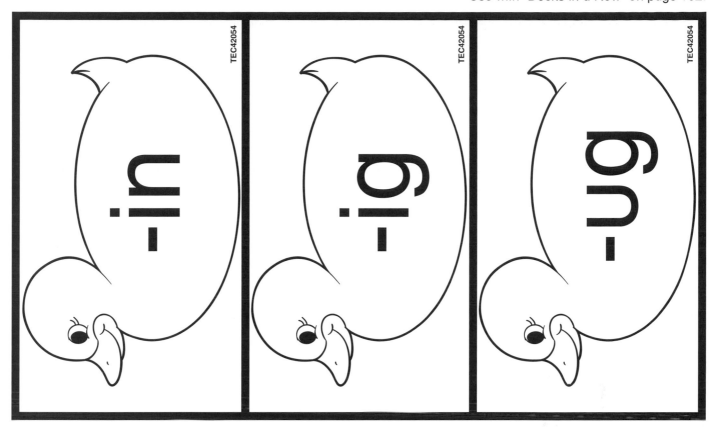

-in   TEC42054

-ig   TEC42054

-ug   TEC42054

Duckling Cards
Use with "Ducks in a Row" on page 102 and "How Many Ducks?" on page 272.

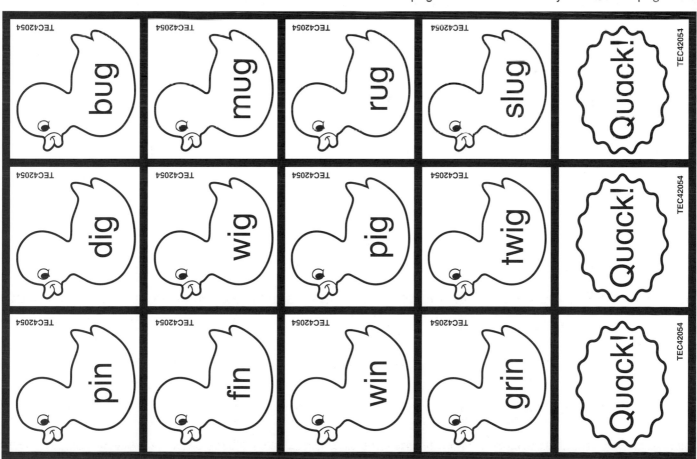

bug   TEC42054

mug   TEC42054

rug   TEC42054

slug   TEC42054

Quack!   TEC42054

dig   TEC42054

wig   TEC42054

pig   TEC42054

twig   TEC42054

Quack!   TEC42054

pin   TEC42054

fin   TEC42054

win   TEC42054

grin   TEC42054

Quack!   TEC42054

Nest Cards
Use with "Build a Nest" on page 103.

Rodeo Time

What You Do

1. Put a clock card.

2. Put the matching time card.

3. Check.

Time to the hour

Activity Cards

Use with "Rodeo Time" on page 103.

TEC42054

TEC42054

TEC42054

TEC42055

Recording sheet

Name _____

How Many Frogs?

✏️ Write your estimate.
Measure.
✏️ Write your answer.

Log	Estimate	Measure
Log		
1		
2		
3		
4		
5		
6		

Note to the teacher: Use with "How Many Frogs?" on page 104.

Block by Block

Blocks Used

	0	1	2	3	4	5	6	7	8	9	10
cube											
cylinder											
cone											
rectangular prism											

Write how many.

_____ _____ _____ _____

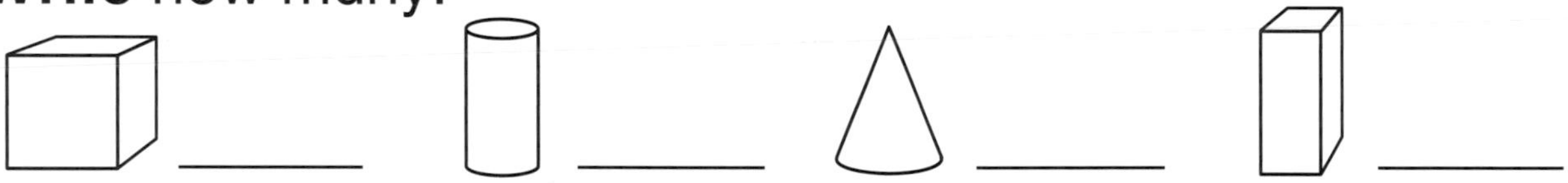

Circle.

Which has the **most**?

Which has the **fewest**?

Write a sentence about the graph.

_____

_____

Note to the teacher: Use with "Block by Block" on page 104.

Honey Bear

What you do:

1. Put the ⬡ faceup.
2. Sort the word cards. ⬭
3. Put the picture cards to match. ⬯
4. Check.
5. Write.

an

as in p**an**

TEC42055

at

as in h**at**

TEC42055

ap

as in cl**ap**

TEC42055

fan

TEC42055

bat

TEC42055

nap

TEC42055

TEC42055

TEC42055

TEC42055

can

TEC42055

mat

TEC42055

lap

TEC42055

WELCOME

TEC42055

TEC42055

TEC42055

van

TEC42055

cat

TEC42055

map

TEC42055

TEC42055

TEC42055

TEC42055

That's My Name!

What You Need

letter stamps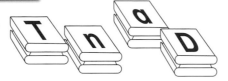

ink pad

manila paper

crayons

What You Do

① Fold.

② Stamp your name.

③ Flip.

④ Write your name.

⑤ Show.

©The Mailbox® • TEC42050 • Aug./Sept. 2010

Step-by-step center activity: Make a copy of this activity card and put it in a plastic page protector for durability. Then put the activity card and the needed materials at a center.

THE MAILBOX 127

Cupcakes and Sprinkles

What You Need

2 dice   crayons    paper

What You Do

① Draw 2.

② Toss. Draw.

③ Write.

④ Toss. Draw. Write.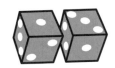

⑤ Circle the one with **more.**

   If the sets are the **same,** draw a ☺.

©The Mailbox® • TEC42051 • Oct./Nov. 2010

Step-by-step center: Make a copy of this activity card and put it in a plastic page protector for durability. Then put the activity card and the needed materials at a center.

How Many Are Left?

What You Need

stamp pad

crayons

number cube

paper strip

What You Do

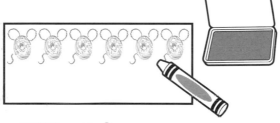
(1) Make 6.

(2) Toss.

(3) Read. Cross out.

(4) Count how many are left. Write.

(5) Flip.  Do Steps 1–4 again.

Step-by-step center: Make a copy of this activity card and put it in a plastic page protector for durability. Then put the activity card and the needed materials at a center.

Spring Chick

What You Need

 wings

 body

 beak

 feet

 legs

GLUE

What You Do

1 Trace. Cut.

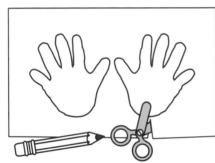

2 Glue.

3 Fold. Glue.

4 Color.

5 Flip. Tape.

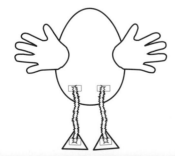

6 Flip. Bend.

©The Mailbox® • TEC42054 • April/May 2011

On-your-own art center: Make a copy of this activity card and put it in a plastic page protector for durability. Then put the activity card and the needed supplies at your art center.

Let's Do Social Studies!

Let's Do Social Studies!

Our Constitution

Constitution Day and Citizenship Day

Sing this toe-tapping ditty with youngsters to help them understand how the Constitution helps us be good citizens.

(sung to the tune of "For He's a Jolly Good Fellow")

Oh, the U.S. Constitution,
Oh, the U.S. Constitution,
Oh, the U.S. Constitution,
It lists our country's rules.
It was written in the past,
But it was made to last
So all our country's people
Would live and work together.
Oh, the U.S. Constitution,
It lists our country's rules.

Beth Marquardt
St. Paul's School of Early Learning
Muskego, WI

Who Are You?

Exploring jobs

Encourage youngsters to explore careers of interest by having a job day. Prior to job day, send a note home with each child asking his family to help him dress as a chosen worker. Invite students to accessorize their outfits by bringing safe items related to their jobs. On the special day, ask each child, in turn, to silently act out his job while his classmates guess its name. As a follow-up activity, take a photo of each child and attach it to a sheet of paper. Then have him write or dictate a sentence about his chosen job. Bind the pages between covers to make a class book.

Mackie Rhodes
Greensboro, NC

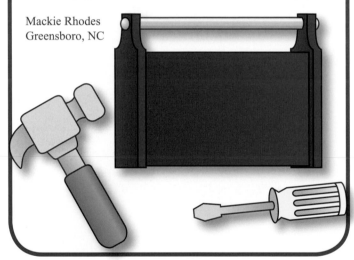

Home, Sweet Home

Knowledge of family

Have each child fold a 12" x 18" sheet of white construction paper in half and trim it, as needed, to resemble the structure— such as a house, apartment building, or mobile home—in which she lives. Invite her to decorate the outside of the paper to resemble her home. Then have the child open the paper and draw each person who lives with her and each household pet. To complete the project, help her label her drawing. Invite each youngster to share her project and tell about something she likes to do with her family.

Tracey Quezada, Presentation of Mary Academy, Hudson, NH

Let's Do Social Studies!

Celebrating Heroes

Understanding the significance of Veterans Day

Singing this catchy tune helps students understand the meaning of Veterans Day, celebrated on November 11. 🖥

(sung to the tune of "O Christmas Tree")

On Veterans Day, on Veterans Day,
We celebrate our heroes.
On Veterans Day, on Veterans Day,
We celebrate our heroes.
Soldiers who served far and near,
For their work we give a cheer!
On Veterans Day, on Veterans Day,
We celebrate our heroes.

Kathryn Wilson
Crosscreek Charter School
Louisburg, NC

All Around the Town

Using basic map skills

Here's an easy way for students to build map skills. Have each child draw different areas of town—such as a park, a school, a house, and a gas station—on a copy of a map grid like the one shown. Also have her color and cut out a bus pattern. Encourage her to "drive" the bus around the town to the different locations found on the map. 🖥

Editor's Tip:
Use tape and a length of yarn to connect each bus cutout to its map.

Then and Now

Understanding how things change over time

Use this activity after a discussion of how people lived during colonial times. In advance, title a sheet of bulletin board paper for each of the following: kitchen, bedroom, living room. Then draw and label a T chart on each paper. Give each child a half sheet of drawing paper and guide him to draw an object found today in one of the rooms. Tape each child's drawing in the "Now" column of the appropriate chart and add a label. When all the pictures are in place, revisit each chart. Draw a happy face if the object was present during colonial times and a sad face if it was not.

Living Room

Then	Now
☹	lamp
☹	TV
☹	couch
☺	computer

See page 138 for a **skill sheet** about colonial times.

Let's Do Social Studies!

Shine the Light!

Distinguishing between land and water

Invite a student to shine a light, such as from a flashlight or penlight, on a globe or map. Then lead youngsters in reciting the chant shown, snapping their fingers where indicated. After the final line, have a child answer the question by going to the globe and explaining whether the light is shining on land, water, or both. After checking her answer for accuracy, have the student with the flashlight pass it to her classmate to begin again. 🖳

Look at the map.	*(Snap, snap.)*
Look at the map.	*(Snap, snap.)*
Is the light on land or water	
On the map?	*(Snap, snap.)*

Civil Rights Song

Celebrating Martin Luther King Day

Use this little ditty to explore Martin Luther King Jr.'s life. 🖳

(sung to the tune of "The Wheels on the Bus")

Some kids said we can't play with you,
Play with you,
Play with you.
Some kids said we can't play with you.
Martin Luther King.

Continue with these lines:
Martin learned the power of words.
Dr. King wanted to change the world.
Dr. King spoke against unfair laws.
Dr. King led a bus boycott.
Dr. King said, "I have a dream."

adapted from an idea by Barbee Stueve
Wilson Arts Integration Elementary
Oklahoma City, OK

Find That State!

Locating states on a map

Quarters that display state symbols are the perfect tools for this map activity! Show a quarter and name the state and symbols featured. Then invite a child to point to the state's location on a large map. If correct, have her attach the coin to the map with Sticky-Tac adhesive. Continue until several coins mark different states on the map. **For a home-school connection,** distribute a list of the states not yet identified on your map and ask youngsters to share coins they may have in their own collections. (Be sure to label students' quarters so they can be easily returned.)

Jodi Darter
Cabool Elementary
Cabool, MO

Let's Do Social Studies!

Famous Figures

Recognizing Black History Month

Bring Black History Month to life with these kid-size figures. After sharing information about a famous Black American, have a child lie on a length of bulletin board paper; then trace his outline. Cut out the tracing and then help youngsters draw clothes and other details so it resembles the featured person. Attach a nametag to the figure. Then invite volunteers to name facts about the person. Write each fact from the person's perspective on separate paper strips. Display the figure and the facts.

Lois M. Williams
P.S. 209
New York City, NY

I was a teacher at Tuskegee Institute.

I made more than 300 products from peanuts.

I made products using pecans and sweet potatoes.

I told farmers to raise peanuts, pecans, and sweet potatoes instead of cotton.

A Ditty About Honest Abe

Recognizing Presidents' Day

Youngsters revisit facts about Abraham Lincoln as you lead them in singing this catchy tune. 🖥

(sung to the tune of "When the Saints Go Marching In")

Good Abe Lincoln,
Good Abe Lincoln
Was this land's sixteenth president.
He is known as Honest Abe.
Hip, hip, hooray for Abe Lincoln.

Good Abe Lincoln,
Good Abe Lincoln,
He promised to end slavery.
We see his face on our pennies.
Hip, hip, hooray for Abe Lincoln.

Beth Herchelroath
Oak View Elementary
Fairfax, VA

Searching for Gold

Creating and using a map

Have a colleague join you for this St. Patrick's Day activity, and the result is a map exchange that leads to hidden treasures! Each teacher puts candies wrapped in golden paper, such as Rolo candies or chocolate coins, in a pot. Then she leads her youngsters to find a hiding place in the classroom for the pot. After hiding the pot, enlist students' help to create a large map that leads the other class to the treasure. Switch maps with the other class. Invite them to follow the map to find the pot of gold as your group does the same in their classroom.

Amy DeFalco
Eagle Heights Academy
Youngstown, OH

Let's Do Social Studies!

At the Playground
Making a simple map

After reviewing map keys with students, follow up with this mapmaking idea. Brainstorm with students what might be found at a playground. Write each response on chart paper and draw a corresponding map symbol. Then instruct each child to use the symbols to create a playground map on a sheet of paper. Encourage students to share their maps with partners. 💻

Map Key

swings
slide
monkey bars
bench
climbing wall
sandbox

Wonderful Water
Conserving Earth's natural resources

After leading youngsters in singing this toe-tapping tune, have them brainstorm ways to conserve water as you list their ideas on the board. 💻

(sung to the tune of "Clementine")

Don't waste water.
Don't waste water.
It helps the animals, land, and trees.
We must protect this natural resource.
Don't waste water, if you please.

Clare Cox
Homer Davis Elementary
Tucson, AZ

Ways to Conserve Water

- Turn off water when brushing your teeth.
- Take quick showers.
- Run the dishwasher only when it is full.

Pleasing Posters
Exploring past, present, and future

Youngsters explore the passage of time by making these projects. Give each child a large sheet of construction paper labeled as shown. In the "Past" section, have him draw a baby picture of himself and write his birthdate. In the "Present" section, have him draw a current self-likeness and write a caption. In the "Future" section, help each child write a sentence about what he wants to be when he grows up and then have him illustrate it. Display the completed posters with the title "Our Past, Present, and Future Selves." **For a home-school connection**, encourage each youngster to bring from home a baby picture and birthday details, such as height and weight, to feature in the "Past" section of the poster.

Tammy Lutz
George E. Greene Elementary
Bad Axe, MI

Past	Present	Future
March 5, 2005	I love school!	I want to be a firefighter.

Let's Do Social Studies!

Step by Step
Citizenship

Increase environmental awareness with this class book. Discuss with students different ways good citizens take care of the environment, such as turning off unused lights, not running the water while brushing their teeth, and walking instead of driving in a car. Then help each youngster trace her shoe on a sheet of paper. Ask her to color the inside of the outline and write a sentence that tells how she will help the environment. Bind the completed papers between construction paper covers with a title such as "Helping Our World One Step at a Time!" **For a science connection**, introduce youngsters to the idea of leaving an environmental footprint. 💻

Nancy Foss
Wee Care Preschool
Galion, OH

All Around the School
Map skills

When your kindergartners make this map, it can be shared with your new class in the fall! To make a map, title a large sheet of bulletin board paper "Our School." Draw a few areas in the school, such as the hallways and main entrance. Give each child a piece of paper sized and labeled to represent a school location and have him draw a representative map symbol on the paper. Enlist students' help in placing and gluing the completed papers onto the map. If you need to store the map for the summer, simply roll it up until you are ready to use it next year!

Barbara Meyers
Fort Worth Country Day School
Fort Worth, TX

Make It! Use It!
Producers and consumers

Help your kindergartners understand where some of the products that they use come from with this idea. Write *Producers* and *Consumers* on individual cards. Put the cards at the top of a pocket chart to designate two columns. Then cut out a copy of the cards on page 140 and set them near the pocket chart.

To begin, explain that a producer is someone who makes a product and a consumer is someone who uses the product. Then show a card to the class and discuss the picture. Invite a child to place the card in the corresponding column of the pocket chart. After all the cards have been sorted, enlist students' help in matching each product to its user. **To extend the activity**, guide small groups of students to make posters about different producer and consumer pairs. 💻

Gerri Primak
Charlotte, NC

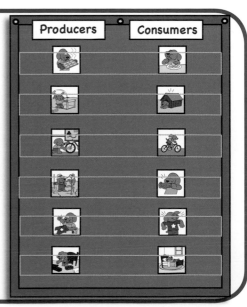

Name _____

Then or Now?

✂ Cut.

🖺 Glue to match.

Then

Now

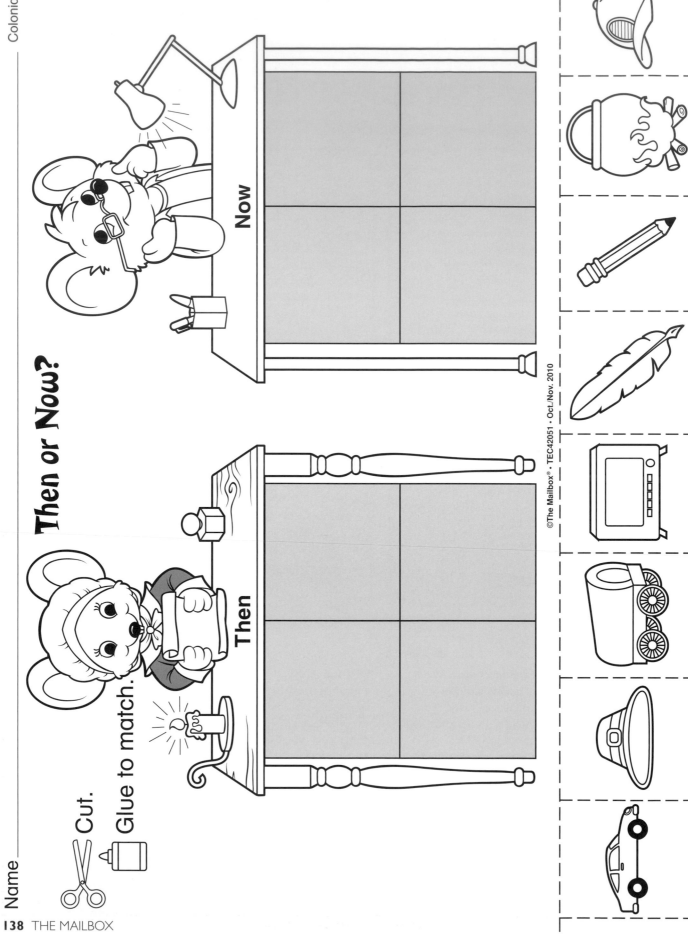

©The Mailbox® • TEC42051 • Oct./Nov. 2010

A Basic Principle

Read.

 A family can work together to wash the dog.

A family can work together to clean their home.

 A family can work together to pick up trash.

✏ **Write.** ✏ **Draw.**

I can work with my family to _____

_____ .

Producer and Consumer Cards
Use with "Make It! Use It!" on page 137.

TEC42055
TEC42055
TEC42055
TEC42055
TEC42055
TEC42055
TEC42055
TEC42055
TEC42055
TEC42055
TEC42055
TEC42055

Management Tips & Timesavers

Management Tips & Timesavers

Center Necklaces

Make lost or forgotten center cards a thing of the past! Have each child label an index card with his name and the number of centers he is expected to go to in a week. Then laminate, hole-punch, and thread each card with yarn to make a necklace. When it's center time, have each youngster wear his necklace and use a dry-erase marker to cross off the center he completes. For easy storage, collect the necklaces at the end of center time and hang them on a hook. To prepare for the next week, simply wipe the necklaces clean. *Jessica Derose, Oak Street Elementary, Bernards Township, NJ*

Brownie Points

Use this sweet idea to promote positive behavior and teamwork. Display a brownie pan in your classroom. Then cut enough brown construction paper squares (brownies) to fill the pan. Finally, laminate the brownies and attach a magnet to the back of each one. Each time the class exhibits exceptionally good behavior, add one brownie to the pan. When the pan is full, reward students with a special treat or privilege. *Amanda Treml, Assumption B. V. M. School, Pulaski, WI*

Helper of the Day

Simplify your class jobs by assigning one student each day to be your helper, doing jobs such as line leader, paper collector, and messenger. Write each student's name on a decorative cutout and laminate it. Put the cutouts in a page protector and display the page below a sign similar to the one shown. At the end of the day, move the first cutout to the back and you're ready for tomorrow. *Cathy Willetts, Calvary Christian School, Bellefontaine, OH* 🖥

Helper of the Day

McKenzie

Quick as a Wink

At the beginning of the school year, I teach parents the rhyme shown so they know which papers need immediate attention and which can wait a day or two. Then, throughout the year, I send notes home on pink or blue paper, depending on their priority. *Jodi Darter, Cabool Elementary, Cabool, MO* 🖥

> If it's **PINK**, sign and return it as quick as a wink! If it's **BLUE**, it can wait a day or two!

Exit Ticket

This dismissal tip ensures that youngsters who are not bus riders are safely picked up. Program craft sticks with the names of students who are not bus riders. At dismissal time, give each child her stick (ticket). Then stipulate that the youngster must turn the stick back in to you before she leaves. This system ensures that I make eye contact with the person picking up the child and lets me know that everyone is safely accounted for. *Mary Fowler, Butner Elementary, Fort Bragg, NC*

Management Tips & Timesavers

Start With Art!

Break the ice during parent-teacher conferences by sharing priceless works of art! Before the conference, ask each child to draw a self-portrait and place the drawing inside his portfolio. Then start the conference on a positive note by presenting parents with their child's masterpiece. *MiMi Dorn, Alliance Christian School, Portsmouth, VA*

Give Me Five!

Here's an easy way to quickly remind children to pay attention. Prepare a poster such as the one shown and hang it in a noticeable location. Then explain each of the five steps to your class. When you need your youngsters' attention, simply say, "Give me five!" and you'll have them listening in no time! *Shelley Rock, Courthouse Road Elementary, Spotsylvania, VA* 🖥

Give Me Five!

2 3 4
1 5

1. Silent voices
2. Listening ears
3. Eyes on the teacher
4. Sitting on bottom
5. Hands in lap

Take a Look

Help parents better understand the objectives on their child's report card with this simple tip. Prepare a folder for each child. As the youngster completes activities or papers that correlate with a report card objective, place them in his folder. When it's time for parent conferences, you'll have work samples ready to share. *Cherri Corning, Parkwood UpJohn Elementary, Kalamazoo, MI*

Show-and-Tell Tip

Looking for a way to make show-and-tell more manageable and efficient? Try a sign-up sheet! At the beginning of the day, ask students to write their names on the chart if they have something they wish to share. When you need a time filler, invite a child on the list to share. *Jean Harrison, Tampa, FL* 🖥

Morning Work Made Easy

Here's a simple way to provide early birds with morning work. Copy a variety of skill sheets on cardstock and laminate them. When a child arrives in the morning, have her select a sheet and complete it using a wipe-off marker. After checking for accuracy, simply wipe the sheet clean so it's ready to use another day. *Kerri Davis, Suncoast Elementary, Spring Hill, FL*

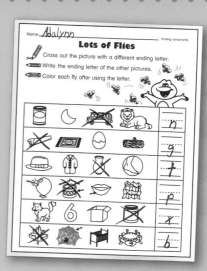

Management Tips & Timesavers

Crayon Holders

For sturdy crayon holders, use rectangular plastic soap containers. Each container holds a 42-pack of crayons perfectly. What a simple way to keep crayons contained! *Erin Gates, Juniata Elementary School, Altoona, PA*

Skill Sticks

These simple props are terrific time fillers! Write skill-related tasks on separate jumbo craft sticks. Place the sticks in a basket. When a child finishes an activity early, invite him to choose a stick and complete the task named. *Katharine Petitt, Lutheran Home Child Care, Wauwatosa, WI*

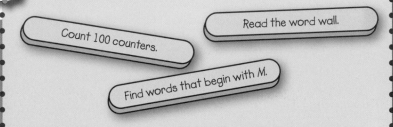

Count 100 counters.

Read the word wall.

Find words that begin with M.

Lions and Lambs

Theme Folders

This simple folder system makes it easy to organize ideas! Place several slash pocket folders in a binder and label each folder with a sticky note stating the unit theme. As you gather ideas, place them for safekeeping in the appropriate folder. Then, when it's time to create your unit, simply pull out the ideas! *Vanessa Rivera, La Luz Elementary, La Luz, NM*

Been There, Done That!

To keep track of the youngsters who have visited the computer area, hang a red and a green ribbon from the ceiling (or attach them to a wall). Clip a personalized spring-style clothespin for each child to the green ribbon. After each student has visited the area, he moves his clothespin to the red ribbon and then notifies a child whose clip is on the green ribbon that it's her turn. Simple! *Sherrie Poirrier, Holly Springs Elementary, Canton, GA*

Sweethearts!

Here's a way to encourage random acts of kindness and decorate your room for Valentine's Day! Set out a supply of heart cutouts for easy access. When you see a student (or students) exhibiting kindness, share the observation. Then write the child's name on a heart and post it on a display. For extra encouragement, reward the class with a special treat or privilege when each child has been recognized at least one time.

Jake

Willis

Debbie

Management Tips & Timesavers

Ready Roots

This transition tip requires youngsters to grow like little plants! Encourage students to pretend to be roots, squatting or lying on the floor and being very still and quiet. Point out youngsters who are being exceptional roots and have those youngsters slowly "grow" into trees. Then have the trees quietly move to the next activity. Continue until all the students have transitioned. *Sosha Kowalczyk-Harper, Waterloo Middle School, Waterloo, WI*

Classroom Visitors

When students need to focus on the task at hand, keep your classroom distraction-free with this friendly message. Simply post a sign on your door with the text shown. Then, when visitors are welcome to come in, simply remove the sign and open your door. *Tracy Ashfield, Buford Presbyterian Weekday School, Sugar Hill, GA* 🖥

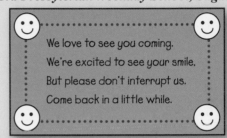

We love to see you coming.
We're excited to see your smile.
But please don't interrupt us.
Come back in a little while.

A Pet Fish

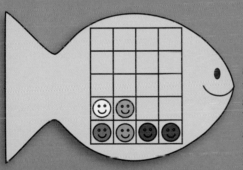

This incentive chart is sure to make a splash with your youngsters! Display a chart similar to the one shown. Whenever a teacher, parent, or staff member compliments your class, attach a sticker to the chart. When the bottom row is filled, place a fishbowl in your room with great fanfare. For the next row, place aquarium gravel in the bowl. Continue in the same way, providing fish food for the next row, then water for the row after that; and, finally, a fish for the last row of stickers! *Kali Offreda, Locke Hill Elementary, San Antonio, TX* 🖥

Book Recordings

To help with lesson planning, label books and their accompanying cassette tapes (or CDs) with the length of the recording. Store the books and tapes in separate resealable plastic bags. Then, to select a story that will fit in the time allotted, simply look at the labels. *Marla Cobb, Barhitte Elementary, Burton, MI*

Not Just for Laundry!

To avoid bent and dog-eared big books, simply store them in a rectangular laundry basket. Laundry baskets come in a variety of attractive colors, and the big books fit in them upright without bending. *Christy Bailey, Marion Primary School, Marion, VA*

Planting a Rainbow by Lois Ehlert

Management Tips & Timesavers

Free-Time Cart

Stock a cart with a variety of activities, such as rhyming picture cards, alphabet tracing cards, simple picture books, and lacing cards. When youngsters finish their work before their classmates, they go to the free-time cart to choose a bonus activity. To keep interest level high, replace the items on the cart every few weeks. *Lindsey Hall, W.E. Cundiff Elementary, Vinton, VA*

Time-Filler Fun!

Label slips of paper with quick activities and place the slips in a sand bucket or other seasonal object. When you need a time filler, invite a child to take a strip. Then read the strip out loud and have youngsters follow the directions! *Tracy Shaner, Eastside Christian School, Marietta, GA* 💻

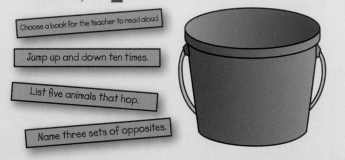

Choose a book for the teacher to read aloud.

Jump up and down ten times.

List five animals that hop.

Name three sets of opposites.

Valuable Treasure

Renew interest in your reward incentives program with this simple idea! Label plastic coins for special privileges, such as extra computer time or being first to choose a center. Then mix the coins in with existing prizes. The new coins are sure to be a treasured favorite. *April Langford, Crockett Early Childhood, Crockett, TX*

Long-Lasting Die-Cuts!

Here's a timesaving tip for creating laminated die-cuts! Laminate construction paper and cut the paper into strips. Then die-cut the needed shapes or letters from the prelaminated strips. They come out absolutely perfect! *Leslie Wright, Aviara Oaks Elementary, Carlsbad, CA*

A Bug and a Wish

Display a bug cutout and a wishing well cutout to remind youngsters of this problem-solving strategy! Explain to students that, when a classmate is bothering them, they need to use the following response: "It *bugs* me when you [state the problem], and I *wish* that you would [state how to resolve the problem]." What an easy way to promote positive problem solving! *Marcia Hull, Wauseon Primary School, Wauseon, OH* 💻

OUR READERS WRITE

Our Readers Write

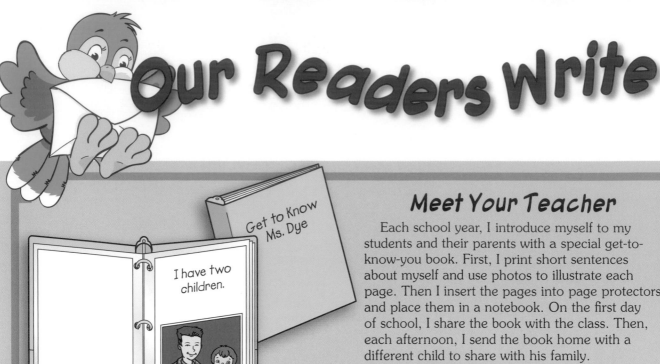

Meet Your Teacher

Each school year, I introduce myself to my students and their parents with a special get-to-know-you book. First, I print short sentences about myself and use photos to illustrate each page. Then I insert the pages into page protectors and place them in a notebook. On the first day of school, I share the book with the class. Then, each afternoon, I send the book home with a different child to share with his family.

Christy Dye, Peek's Chapel Elementary
Conyers, GA

From the Heart

For a simple National Grandparents Day gift, I have my students create this handmade project. I give each child a paper programmed with the text shown and an outline of a heart. I have each youngster make red thumbprints along the heart outline and then stamp his handprint in its center. Finally, I help the child glue his work to a larger sheet of red paper.

Phyllis Prestridge
West Amory Elementary
Amory, MS

My Name Is...

Looking for a quick and easy nametag system for the first days of school? Try this! For each student, I program a strip of stick-on labels; on each label, I write the student's name, my name, and our room number. On the first day of school, I give each parent her child's labels and ask that she put one on her child each morning before school. (I also keep extra labels on hand, just in case.) It's so nice when the youngsters walk through the door ready to begin the day.

Mary Fowler
Butner Elementary
Fort Bragg, NC

On a Personal Note

To create a special thank-you note, I take a digital photo of my class holding letter cards that spell *thank you*. Then I print several copies on cardstock and keep them in a file. Whenever we need to send a note of thanks, I add a special message, have the children sign the card, and send it on its way!

Cathy Willetts
Calvary Christian School
Bellefontaine, OH

GRANDPARENTS

hold our hands for a short while and our hearts forever.

Love,
Alston

Our Readers Write

Transporting Masterpieces

To help my students get their monthly artwork home, I use paper grocery bags with handles. I collect a class supply of bags and glue a note to the front of each one as shown. When I take down artwork at the end of each month, I simply put each child's work in his bag and send it home. 💻

Leslie Wright
Aviara Oaks Elementary
Carlsbad, CA

Carter's
End-of-the-Month Bag
Please empty this bag and send it back to school with your child so we can reuse it next month. Thank you!

Happy Birthday!

So I'm always prepared for students' birthdays, I make birthday goody bags at the beginning of the year. First, I decorate a paper lunch bag for each child plus a few extra bags for students who may join our class later in the year. Then I fill each bag with inexpensive items, such as small toys, pencils, and stickers. I store the bags in my closet so they are readily available on each student's birthday.

Amy Cole, Daphne Elementary, Daphne, AL

Thumbs-Up!

To help my kindergartners remember to use the proper scissor grip, I tell them to do a thumbs-up job. Each child puts his thumb up, grasps the scissors, and gives me a thumbs-up. If a child turns his hand upside-down or sideways, I simply say, "Thumbs up!"

Caitlin Johnson, T. C. Hamlin School, Randolph, ME

Shoe Sheriff

Shoe Sheriff

Shoe-tying used to take up a large chunk of my day. Now, if a child can tie his shoes, I appoint him the shoe sheriff and give him a special badge. Whenever other students need their shoes tied, they ask the shoe sheriff for help instead of me. As the year continues and I have more shoe-tying experts, I rotate sheriffs. This system saves me time and motivates each youngster to learn to tie his shoes so he can be the new sheriff in town. 💻

Elizabeth Kickert
T. C. Cherry Elementary
Bowling Green, KY

Picture-Perfect Assessment

Organizing materials for assessment was a challenge until I started using 4" x 6" photo albums. I label each album with a different skill and fill it with assessment tools, such as letter or number cards. When I assess a student, I just grab the album for that skill and flip through the pages to find what I need.

Jennifer Selvek
Piney Grove Elementary
Charlotte, NC

Counting to 20

The Great Pumpkin Night

After a field trip to the pumpkin patch, I hold a family math night for my students and their parents. I set up different centers around the classroom and prepare a booklet to guide everyone through the centers. Families weigh pumpkins, discover if they float or sink, graph their sizes, and measure their circumferences. Finally, they carve the pumpkins, count the seeds, and weigh the pumpkins again. I also have a contest for guessing how many candy corn pieces are in a jar. I wrap up the event with cookies and apple cider. It's a fun evening for the whole family!

Katie Lawver, St. Mary's School, Storm Lake, IA

Old Game, New Fun!

I make musical chairs a fun review game in which all students learn and participate the entire time. In advance, I program seasonal cutouts with letters of the alphabet, numbers, or high-frequency words. Then I have students form a circle with their chairs, and I place a cutout underneath each seat. When the music starts, students walk around the chairs, and then they sit when the music stops. I call on one youngster to read his cutout. If he responds correctly, I give him a sticker. We continue playing until each student has been called at least once.

Alisa M. Stevens, Old Town Elementary
Winston-Salem, NC

Every Minute Counts!

When my youngsters are working on art projects or lessons that require glue, I look for any opportunity to squeeze in some math and literacy practice. For example, if youngsters are making an apple tree, I might ask them to draw circles or other shapes to attach the green bushy tops to the trees. To attach apples, I might ask them to form the letter a on the back of each apple. With just a little glue, I can make every moment a learning experience.

Janie Gillen, Plaza School, Baldwin, NY

Say It With Shoestrings

For a fun way to practice letter, number, and shape formation, I have my youngsters use shoelaces on their desks or the floor. They're quiet, unique, and inexpensive manipulatives!

Suzanne Ward, Caledonia Centennial Public School
Caledonia, Ontario, Canada

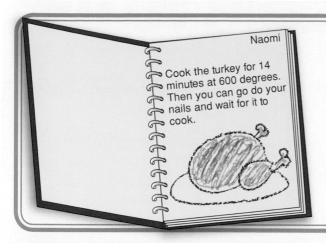

Naomi

Cook the turkey for 14 minutes at 600 degrees. Then you can go do your nails and wait for it to cook.

One-of-a-Kind Recipes

Looking for that perfect Thanksgiving gift for parents? I ask each child how she would prepare the Thanksgiving turkey and trimmings and record her response. Then I type and print each recipe and have the child illustrate her Thanksgiving meal. I copy the pages and bind the recipes into books for children to give their parents for Thanksgiving. I receive rave reviews from parents every year!

Laura Petro, Mountview Road School, Morris Plains, NJ

Five, Four, Three, Two, One!

When my students need to put booklet pages in order, I have them pretend their books are rockets about to blast off into space. I ask youngsters to start with the last page and count backward, adding pages on top of the stack until they reach the cover. It's a great way to help students order their own pages and get a little extra counting practice.

Jodi Darter, Cabool Elementary, Cabool, MO

Cleanup Time!

Since paint cleanup can be a chore, I came up with a quick and easy way for students to help out. I fill a dishpan with soapy water and ask students to place their brushes in the "brush bath" after they finish painting. I also call our drying rack the "parking garage" and have students park their wet paintings so they can dry.

Georgene Bemis, Myrtle Elementary, Pittsburgh, PA

Fire Safety Words — Wesley

hydrant — hydrant
fire — fire
truck — truck
hat — hat
firefighter — firefighter

Fun With Foam

I use self-adhesive foam shapes to motivate my students to practice their writing skills. I type words and glue strips of writing lines on blank paper as shown. Then I make student copies of the sheet. Students write each word and attach the corresponding shape beside it.

Anita Swanson, Bethany Christian School
Fort Lauderdale, FL

It's Magnetic!

I have a magnet center in my classroom that includes a wide variety of activities. I cut out and laminate pictures from magazines and attach magnets to the backs. Then I have students use the pictures for story-telling. I also create magnetic puzzles by cutting and laminating pictures from calendars or cereal boxes and then attaching magnets to the backs. Finally, I place a supply of magnetic letters and numbers for students to spell words or practice counting. These activities can be completed on a cookie sheet or the side of a file cabinet or metal desk.

Marcia Snarski, St. Paul's Childhood Center, St. Paul, MN

Our Readers Write

Winter Is Here!

To celebrate the changing of the seasons, I have my students create winter scenes. I give each child a sheet of construction paper, a rectangle, a triangle, a tree cutout without leaves, and glue. I ask each youngster to use the materials to create a winter scene. Then I have him brush on a layer of diluted glue and sprinkle white confetti over it. Finally, I post students' scenes with the title "Fall Is Gone. Winter Is Here!" 🖥

Sima Zucker, Beth Jacob Beth Miriam School, Bronx, NY

The Sounds of Christmas

My kindergartners love making up movements to go with this holiday variation of "The Wheels on the Bus." 🖥

The [children in their beds] go [/z/], [/z/], [/z/], [/z/], [/z/], [/z/], [/z/], [/z/], [/z/].
The [children in their beds] go [/z/], [/z/], [/z/],
All through the night.

For verses 2–6, replace the underlined text with the following:
bells on the sleigh; ting-a-ling
elves on the sleigh; hee, hee, hee
reins on the sleigh; clap, clap, clap
gifts on the sleigh; rustle, rustle, rustle
reindeer on the sleigh; up and down

Verse 7:
The Santa on the sleigh goes, "Ho-ho-ho, ho-ho-ho, ho-ho-ho!"
The Santa on the sleigh goes, "Ho-ho-ho,"
And says, "Merry Christmas!"

Lori McGuire, Arlington Elementary, Arlington, OR

Made Just For You!

I found a clever way for my youngsters to safely transport home the holiday ornaments that they make. I have each child slip her project inside an empty tissue box. I help her cover the box with white paper. Then the youngster uses arts-and-crafts materials to decorate it so it resembles a snowpal. (Tip: Fabric works great for a scarf and a washing detergent cap makes a perfect hat!)

Nichole Buwalda
Randolph Elementary
Randolph, WI

Soap Saver

Little hands on a soap dispenser can use a lot of soap! To avoid this problem, I twist a rubber band around the neck of my pump soap dispenser. The rubber band allows students to get just enough soap to wash their hands while keeping them from using too much. It's that simple!

Amy Rodriguez, Public School 212, Brooklyn, NY

Skin-Deep Differences

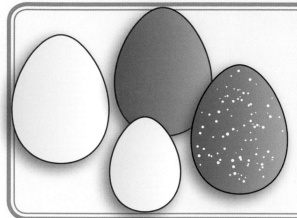

In honor of Martin Luther King Jr.'s birthday, I bring in a variety of fresh eggs (large, small, white, different shades of brown, and even speckled). I ask students to name the differences they see. Then I break each egg into a bowl and ask youngsters whether they can identify individual eggs. When they can't tell one yolk from another, we talk about how eggs are just like people; each person has his own shell but everyone is very similar on the inside.

Candace Horch, Maywood Hills Elementary, Bothell, WA

Show Me 100!

To celebrate the 100th day of school, I ask each youngster to bring in 100 similar items. Then I challenge her to form the number 100 with her pieces. It's a great problem-solving activity because students have to manipulate their formed numbers to accommodate all the items.

Betty Alvarez
School of Little Scholars
Duarte, CA

Weather Report

I post the newspaper's weather forecast to review math skills. Each day my students read the numerals and compare them. They also use the numerals to name one more or one less. As students progress throughout the year, I challenge them with harder tasks.

Susan Braverman
Council Rock Primary
Rochester, NY

Magnetic Alphabet

Instead of placing an alphabet display above my board, I cut apart its letters and attach a magnet to each one. I place the letters in alphabetical order on my whiteboard. Then I have students use the letters to make words. What a great way to maximize use of an alphabet display!

Tammy Wood, Lobelville Elementary, Lobelville, TN

Resource Rings

For a quick and easy way to provide students with important information, I make resource rings. I laminate card sets, such as letters, cardinal numbers, ordinal numbers, shapes, sight words, or students' names. Then I hole-punch the cards and place each set on a metal ring. Finally, I hang the rings on a clearly labeled wall for my youngsters to use independently.

Tracy Morain
Reedy Creek Elementary
Cary, NC

Resource Rings

circle

Our Readers Write

Kind Deeds

I use this take-home journal activity to encourage students to demonstrate and write about kindness. To make a kindness journal, I decorate the cover of a spiral-bound notebook. Each day, I send the journal home with a different student. With the help of her family, the child writes about and illustrates a kind act she has done. The following day she shares her entry with her classmates.

Amanda Hoffman
W. W. Robinson Elementary
Woodstock, VA

Frame It!

These simple word frames are the perfect tool to help kindergartners find words in text. To make one, I use a craft punch to punch an oval shape in the lower right corner of a tagboard card. Then I add a catchy label like the one shown and laminate the frames for durability. My students enjoy using these frames so much that I keep a supply on hand to give out as rewards. 💻

Joy Barnes
Hellen Caro Elementary
Pensacola, FL

Time to find a word.

Make a Mark

Here's a simple rhyme I use to teach students how to make tally marks.

Making tallies is easy to do.
Make four marks and slide the fifth one through.

Doria Owen
William Paca/Old Post Road Elementary
Abingdon, MD

Colorful Writing

I use a ring of color words to reinforce color recognition, spelling, word recognition, and handwriting. I write a different color word on each of several sentence strips. Then I laminate the strips, hole-punch the top left corner of each strip, and bind them with a book ring. To use the strips, a child writes each word with the corresponding-color wipe-off marker. Throughout the year, I make different word rings to review high-frequency words and theme-related words. 💻

Vanessa Rivera, La Luz Elementary, La Luz, NM

Our Readers Write

Kindness Blooms

Let Kindness Bloom

I use this display to encourage kind behaviors in school and at home. To prepare, I post a title and flowers without petals. I keep a supply of petal cutouts near the display and send a few home with each student. When a child exhibits a kind act at school, I write about it on a petal and attach it to the display. When a child is kind at home, an adult writes on a petal about the act and returns it to school. Then I invite the child to add the petal to the display.

Kate Wonders
Carlisle Elementary
Carlisle, IA

Quick Laminating

When I don't have time to laminate game cards or gameboards before I need them, here's what I do! I place each card in a separate resealable plastic bag and seal the bag. Then students can use the cards, and I don't worry about the cards becoming damaged.

Sheila Ransom
Marquette Elementary School
Marquette Heights, IL

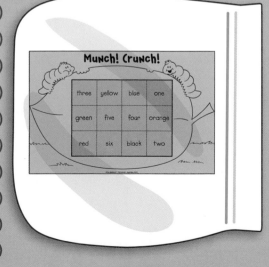

How to Play

Keep directions for store-bought games at your fingertips with this simple idea. I label a folder "How to Play." When I purchase a game for use in my classroom, I place the instruction sheet or manual in the folder. No more lost directions!

Amy Ryan, Grace Lutheran School, Saint Petersburg, FL

Think and Write

For this time filler, I give each pair of youngsters a whiteboard and a marker. The partners decide who will be the thinker and who will be the writer. Then I name a CVC or spelling word. The thinker repeats the word and then spells it. The writer records the spelling on the board. After each pair has finished, we check the spelling as a group. Then the partners switch roles to repeat the activity.

Big.

big

Susan Cortright
Pittsford Area Schools
Pittsford, MI

Our Readers Write

Super Sticker Surprise

I've found a great use for sticker sheets that have only a few stickers left. I cut around each sticker and place the cutout stickers in a gift bag. Each Friday, we have Super Sticker Surprise Friday. I invite each child who has demonstrated positive behavior during the week to take a sticker from the bag. Youngsters always look forward to receiving their surprise stickers!

Heidi Mather
Saranac Central School
Saranac, NY

Puzzle Book

My students enjoy my reusable puzzle center, and I get to save paper! I gather copies of dot-to-dots, mazes, simple crosswords, and hidden-picture puzzles. Next, I slide the sheets back-to-back into plastic sheet protectors. Then I place the prepared pages in a three-ring binder. I set out the binder along with dry-erase markers and paper towels for erasing. Students simply complete a puzzle and then wipe it clean!

Annie Fitch
Echo Mountain Elementary
Phoenix, AZ

Story Celebrations

In my classroom, we love to throw parties in honor of favorite classroom books! One of my favorite parties is for *If You Give a Pig a Pancake* by Laura Numeroff. We play variations of familiar games, such as Pin the Tail on the Pig and Pig, Pig, Wolf. For a fun craft, we make pig-ear headbands to wear while celebrating. For a snack, we have pancakes and syrup. We celebrate different books throughout the year; the possibilities are endless!

Deborah Ryan, Milwaukie, OR

A Personal Thank You

Volunteers always cherish this class-photo card. For each student's family member who volunteers in our classroom, I make a personalized thank-you sign. I give the corresponding students the signs to hold and take a class photo. Then I glue a copy of the photo to the front of a construction paper card for each volunteer and have all my students sign the cards. 🖥

Diane Bonica
Deer Creek Elementary
Tigard, OR

PARTNER GAMES
LITERACY AND MATH

Fancy Feathers

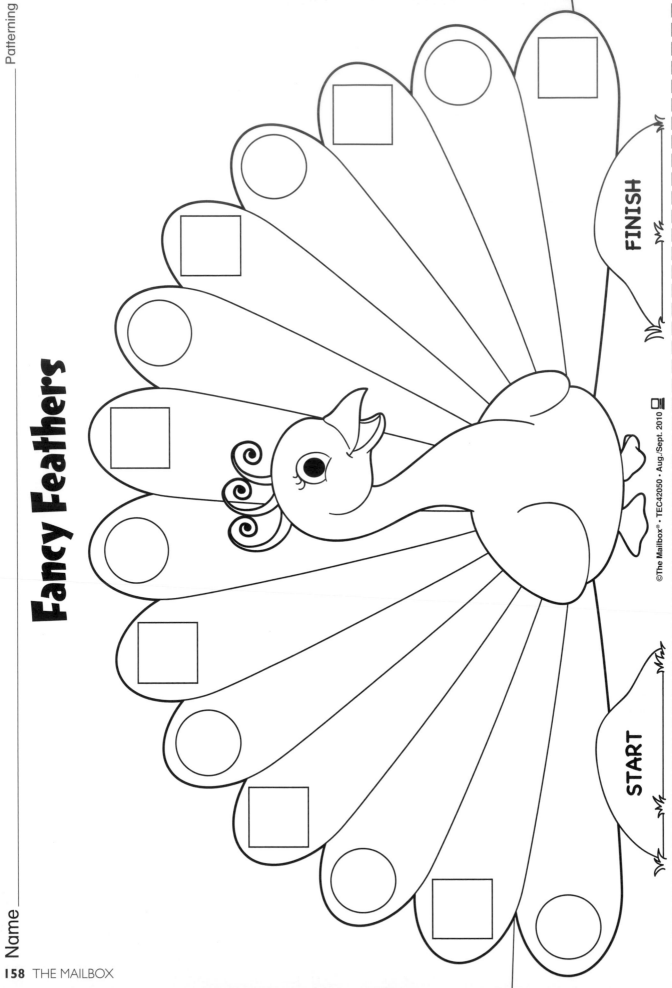

FINISH

START

Partner Game Use with the directions on page 160.

Name _____

Letter identification

Mouthwatering Meatballs

Spinner letters: g · B · m · R · N · s · h · T

Meatball strips:
B · h · s · R · N · B · m · T · h · g

©The Mailbox® • TEC42050 • Aug./Sept. 2010

Partner Game Use with the directions on page 160.

THE MAILBOX 159

Fancy Feathers

Skill: Patterning

How to play:

1. Play with a partner. Begin at START.

2. Before play begins, color the first 2 shapes on your gameboard. Use both crayons.

3. When it is your turn, flip the counter.

4. If the counter lands on the next color in your pattern, color the next shape. If it does not, your turn is over.

5. Play until you reach FINISH.

What You Need

2 gameboards
2-sided counter
2 crayons
  (colors to match counter)

Mouthwatering Meatballs

Skill: Letter identification

How to play:

1. Play with a partner. When it is your turn, spin the spinner.

2. Name the letter. Look for a matching meatball. If there is one, color it.

3. Play until both players color all their meatballs.

What You Need

2 gameboards
paper clip
pencil
brown crayon

TIP

When Lynn Downing of Pandora-Gilboa School in Pandora, Ohio, introduces a new game, she has all her students play it together for a week. By day three, her class is playing the game independently, which increases playing time and skill review!

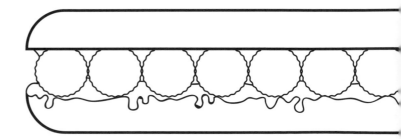

Note to the teacher: Use with "Fancy Feathers" on page 158 and "Mouthwatering Meatballs" on page 159.

A Cat Nap

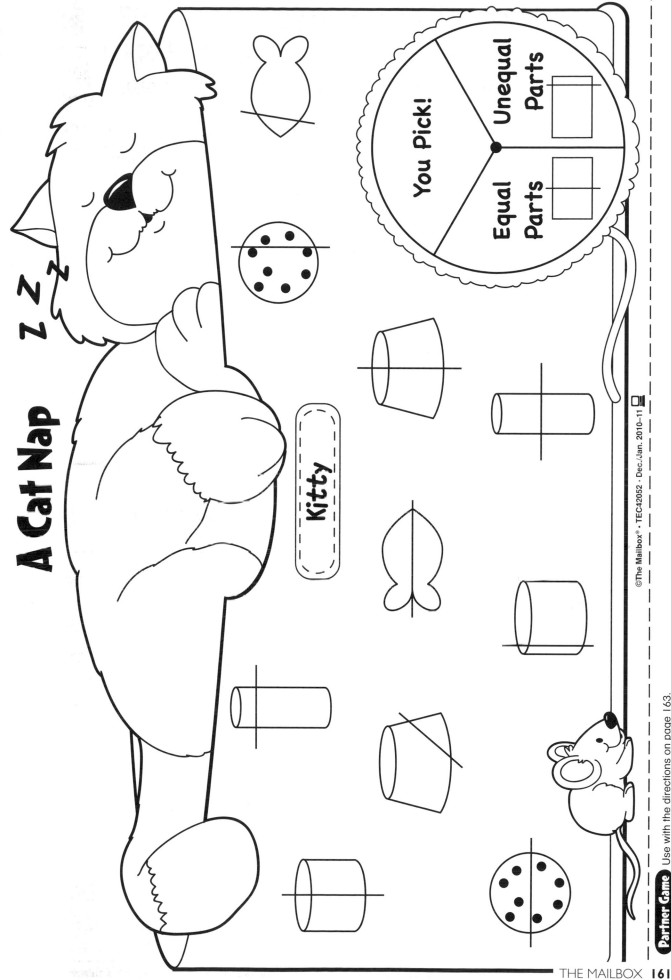

Kitty

You Pick!

Equal Parts

Unequal Parts

©The Mailbox® • TEC42052 • Dec./Jan. 2010–11

Partner Game Use with the directions on page 163.

Ending sounds

Bumper Car Buddies

©The Mailbox® • TEC42052 • Dec./Jan. 2010–11

Partner Game Use with the directions on page 163.

A Cat Nap

Skill: Equal and unequal parts

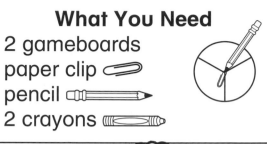

What You Need
2 gameboards
paper clip
pencil
2 crayons

How to play:

1. Play with a partner. When it is your turn, spin the spinner.

2. Find and color a matching shape. If all the matching shapes are colored, your turn is over. If you spin "You Pick!" pick a shape, tell how the shape is divided, and then color it.

3. The first player to color all the shapes wins.

©The Mailbox® • TEC42052 • Dec./Jan. 2010–11

Bumper Car Buddies

Skill: Ending sounds

What You Need
2 gameboards
2 game markers
die
crayons

How to play:

1. Play with a partner. Put your game marker in a curve on the gameboard.

2. When it is your turn, roll the die and move your marker. Name the object and the driver whose name has the same ending sound *(octopus, lion,* or *crab)*. Then color one space on the driver's flag.

3. The first player to color all the spaces on one flag wins. (You may need to go around the board more than once.)

©The Mailbox® • TEC42052 • Dec./Jan. 2010–11

Note to the teacher: Use with the gameboards on pages 161 and 162.

Name _____

Yummy!

▪ ▪ ▪ ▪ ▪ 2 + 3 = ___	▪ ▪ 5 + 1 = ___	▪ ▪ ▪ ▪ ▪ ▪ 4 + 4 = ___
▪ ▪ ▪ ▪ ▪ 1 + 8 = ___	▪ 3 + 0 = ___	▪ ▪ ▪ ▪ ▪ ▪ ▪ ▪ 2 + 7 = ___
▪ ▪ ▪ ▪ ▪ ▪ 4 + 6 = ___		▪ ▪ ▪ ▪ ▪ ▪ 3 + 4 = ___
▪ ▪ ▪ ▪ ▪ ▪ 3 + 6 = ___	▪ ▪ ▪ ▪ ▪ ▪ 5 + 5 = ___	▪ ▪ ▪ ▪ 2 + 2 = ___
		▪ ▪ ▪ ▪ ▪ ▪ 1 + 7 = ___

5   8   6   7   10   9   3   4

©The Mailbox® • TEC42053 • Feb./Mar. 2011

Partner Game Use with the directions on page 166.

Players: _____

_____ and

Blastoff!

like

you

are

we

went

am

all

and

this

Apollo Pup

up

me

did

not

see

to

on

the

yes

can

not

©The Mailbox® • TEC42053 • Feb./Mar. 2011

Partner Game   Use with the directions on page 166.

Yummy!

Skill: Addition to ten

How to play:

1. Play with a partner. Put your game marker on a game space.

2. When it is your turn, roll the die and move your marker.

3. Read the problem and say the sum. Write the sum and then color the fish with that number if it is not already colored. If the sum is already written, your turn is over.

4. Play until one player colors all his or her fish or time is up. The player who colors more fish wins.

What You Need

2 gameboards
2 game markers
die
pencil
crayons

Fab Fish Food

©The Mailbox® • TEC42053 • Feb./Mar. 2011

Blastoff!

Skill: High-frequency words

How to play:

1. Play with a partner. Pick a crayon.

2. When it is your turn, toss the counter. Read aloud that number of words.

3. After you read a word, color its star.

4. Play until every star is colored or time is up. The player who colors more stars wins.

What You Need

gameboard
labeled counter
2 crayons (different colors)

©The Mailbox® • TEC42053 • Feb./Mar. 2011

Note to the teacher: Use with the gameboards on pages 164 and 165.

Name _____

Saving for Cheese!

©The Mailbox® • TEC42054 • April/May 2011

Partner Game Use with the directions on page 169.

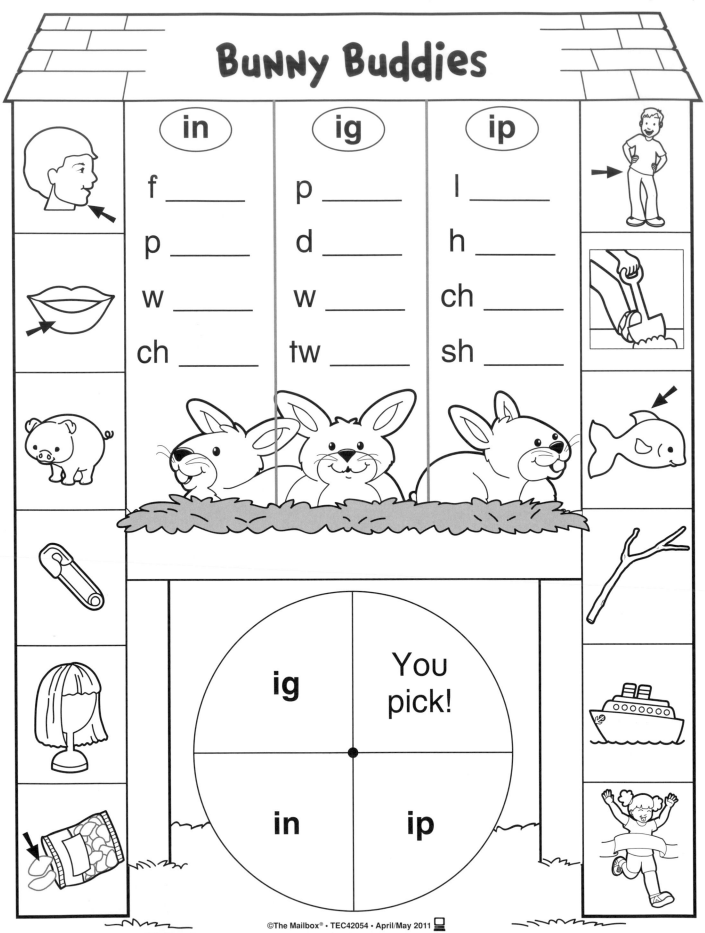

Name _____

Word families -ig, -in, -ip

Bunny Buddies

in	ig	ip
f ____	p ____	l ____
p ____	d ____	h ____
w ____	w ____	ch ____
ch ____	tw ____	sh ____

ig

You pick!

in

ip

©The Mailbox® • TEC42054 • April/May 2011

Partner Game Use with the directions on page 169.

Saving for Cheese!

Skill: Counting coins

How to play:

1. Play with a partner. When it is your turn, toss the counter.

2. Draw an X on the matching number of coins.

3. Write the matching money amount on a line. Trace the ¢. Then color the coins.

4. Play until both players have a money amount on every line.

5. The player who colored more coins wins.

What You Need

2 gameboards
labeled counter ②⤳③
crayon

Bunny Buddies

Skill: Word families *-ig, -in, -ip*

How to play:

1. Play with a partner. When it is your turn, spin the spinner.

2. Use the word ending to make a word on the bunny hutch. (Choose an ending for "You pick!") Then read the word and color the matching picture.

3. The first player to color each word family picture wins.

What You Need

2 gameboards
pencil
paper clip
crayon

Note to the teacher: Use with the gameboards on pages 167 and 168.

Players: _____ and _____

Time for a Ride!

2:00	8:00	12:00	9:00
4:00	5:00	6:00	10:00
1:00	3:00	7:00	11:00

©The Mailbox® • TEC42055 • June/July 2011

Partner Game Use with the directions on page 172.

ABC Grooming

A · B · C · D · E · F · G · H · I · J · K · L · M · N · O · P · Q · R · S · T · U · V · W · X · Y · Z ·

START	S	C	T	B	M
	K	Y	N	I	J
		G	W	H	
	R	E			
	P	D	V	L	Q	O	U	F FINISH

Before ↓ After ↑

Bow Wow

©The Mailbox® • TEC42055 • June/July 2011

Partner Game Use with the directions on page 172.

Time for a Ride!

Skill: Time to the hour

How to play:

1. Play with a partner. Put your game marker on a "You pick!" space. Pick a crayon.

2. When it is your turn, roll the die and move your marker.

3. If you land on a clock, read it and color the matching time on the boat. If the time is colored, your turn is over. If you land on "You pick!," move your marker to any clock, read it, and color the matching time.

4. Play until each time on the boat is colored or time is up. The player who colors more times wins. If each player colors six times, the game ends in a tie.

What You Need
gameboard
2 game markers
die
2 crayons (different colors)

ABC Grooming

Skill: Alphabetical order

How to play:

1. Play with a partner. Put your game marker on START.

2. When it is your turn, roll the die and move your marker.

3. Spin the spinner and say the letter that comes before or after the letter on which you landed.

4. The first player to reach FINISH wins.

What You Need
gameboard
2 game markers
die
paper clip
pencil

Note to the teacher: Use with the gameboards on pages 170 and 171.

SIMPLE SCIENCE

SIMPLE SCIENCE

Flip and Sing
Five senses

Getting ready:
- Write the song on paper strips, as shown, and display them in a pocket chart.
- Gather several objects that are easily associated with the senses.

Activity: Lead youngsters in singing the song shown. If desired, have students perform actions for each of the five senses, such as wiggling their fingers in the air for the sense of touch. Then show an object. Point to each of the sense cards and discuss how each one applies to the object. If it does not apply, flip the card facedown. Then have youngsters sing the song, humming the parts that correspond to facedown cards. Continue with different objects as time permits.

(sung to the tune of "Row, Row, Row Your Boat")

> We use five senses
> Every single day:
> Hearing, seeing, smelling, tasting,
> And touching. Hip, hooray!

Christina George, Santo Elementary, Santo, TX

Splendid Shades
Mixing colors

Getting ready:
- Set out several ice cube trays partially filled with water in each section.
- Put an eyedropper and a bottle of food coloring by each tray.
- Have paper towels available for easy cleanup.

Activity: Gather a small group of youngsters and have each child sit by an ice cube tray. Help her squeeze several drops of food coloring into one section of her tray. Then have her use the eyedropper to transfer some of the tinted water into a different section of the tray and notice the shade of the color. Write her observations on chart paper. Encourage each student to repeat the process to make darker and lighter shades of tinted water. After youngsters have had several minutes to explore, read their observations aloud and add any new observations to the chart.

Janice Sutherland
Louisiana Schnell Elementary
Placerville, CA

Observations
The color I moved is not as dark.
The more color drops I use, the darker the color gets.
I moved a light color into a water section and I didn't see the color change, but I know it's there!

SIMPLE SCIENCE

I Wonder Why!
Experimenting with sinking and floating

Getting ready:
- Partially fill a bowl with water.
- Obtain several pieces of aluminum foil.
- Have paper towels available for easy cleanup.

Activity: Gather a small group of students and ask them to predict whether aluminum foil will sink or float. Then demonstrate the activities below.
- Crumple a piece of foil into a medium-size ball and drop it in the bowl.
- Push a flat piece of foil to the bottom of the bowl and release it.
- Lay a flat piece of foil on the water.
- Fold a piece of foil and push it to the bottom of the bowl.

Lead youngsters to realize that air, such as the air trapped in the foil ball, and *surface tension* (what holds water together and makes the surface act as if it has skin) affect whether an object sinks or floats.

Marie E. Cecchini
West Dundee, IL

It floats!

It sinks!

Flow or No Flow?
Solids and liquids

Getting ready:
- Obtain a pitcher of water and a bowl with several ice cubes.
- Set out clear containers of various shapes and sizes.

Activity: To activate prior knowledge, ask students to share what happens to the shape of water when it is poured from one container to another. Then pour water into different containers so youngsters can observe how water flows as a liquid and takes the shape of its container. Next, ask youngsters to predict what will happen when the ice cubes are moved to a different container. As the ice cubes continue to melt, encourage further exploration for students to determine that liquid water will flow, but as a solid it maintains its shape.

Heather E. Graley
Grace Christian School
Blacklick, OH

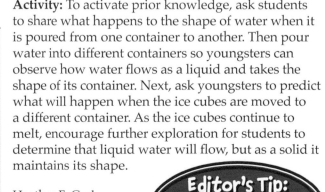

Editor's Tip:
Add food coloring to the water for a better view of water movement.

SIMPLE SCIENCE

Healthy Snacks
Nutrition

Getting ready:
• Gather a class supply of grocery store circulars.
• Set out a class supply of paper, scissors, crayons, and glue sticks.

Activity: Lead students in discussing the qualities of healthy snacks. Then guide each child to fold a sheet of paper in half, draw details so it resembles a refrigerator, and write "My Healthy Snacks" on the front. Give her a grocery circular and have her cut out several healthy snack choices. Instruct her to glue each cutout to the inside of her refrigerator booklet. Use the completed projects to review nutrition and then send the refrigerators home for students to share with their families.

Nellie Eyerman
Valley Brook Country Day School
Long Valley, NJ

Brush Away Stains
Dental health

Getting ready:
• Gather two hard-boiled eggs with white shells, a toothbrush, and toothpaste.
• Set out a container of water and a container of dark-color soda.

Activity: Show students the eggs and lead them to conclude that the eggs are white, just like their teeth. Then place one egg in each container. Ask youngsters to predict what will happen when the eggs sit in the liquids for several hours. The next day, have students watch as you remove the eggs from the containers. *(The egg from the soda will be brown, and the egg from the water will be white.)* Lead youngsters to make connections between their teeth and the discoloration of the egg. Then squeeze toothpaste on the toothbrush and invite youngsters, in turn, to gently brush the tinted egg to remove the brown stains. If desired, have youngsters draw and write about their observations.

Jami Brown
Severn, MD

SIMPLE SCIENCE

Drip, Drop, Splash!
Investigating rain

Getting ready (per small group):
• Partially fill a small cup with water for each child.
• Put an eyedropper and two cotton balls by each cup.
• Have paper towels available for easy cleanup.

Activity: Have each child sit by a cup of water. Direct him to pick up a cotton ball and feel the lightness and fluffiness of the object. Next, have the child hold the cotton ball "cloud" above his cup and use the eyedropper to transfer water from the cup (evaporation) onto the cotton ball (condensation). After several squirts, have him pick up the other cotton ball to compare the changed weight and texture of the cotton ball holding the water. Then encourage him to continue squirting water onto the wet cotton ball until it is saturated and "rains" water back into the cup (precipitation)! Conclude by recording students' observations of how the experiment mimicked the water cycle.

Mary Ryan
Ridge Lawn Elementary
Chicago Ridge, IL

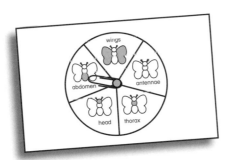

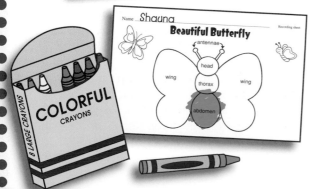

Spin, Say, and Color
Identifying parts of a butterfly

Getting ready:
• Attach a brad and a paper clip to a copy of the butterfly spinner on page 179.
• Copy the recording sheet on page 179 for each student.

Activity: Gather a small group of youngsters and give each child a recording sheet. Name each butterfly part and have each student point to the matching part on her paper. Then invite a child to spin the spinner and name the body part. If correct, direct her to color the corresponding body part on her paper; if the part is already colored, her turn is over. Youngsters continue to take turns until one child colors her entire butterfly. 💻

Diane L. Flohr
Orchard Trails Elementary
Kent City, MI

SIMPLE SCIENCE

Use Some Force!
Experimenting with force of motion

Getting ready:
- Make a copy of page 180 for each student.
- Set out four bins, each with one of the following: crayons and drawing paper, Unifix cubes, soft balls, stuffed animals.

Activity: Gather the class in a circle and place a pencil in the center of the circle. Ask youngsters whether the pencil can move on its own. Then ask a child to move the pencil. Describe what she does by explaining that if she picked up the pencil, it was a pull; if she rolled the pencil, it was a push. Lead youngsters to understand that pushing and pulling are forces that can move an object. Then guide groups of students to explore pushing and pulling by using objects in each of the four bins. To conclude, reconvene as a group to discuss students' experiences and then have each child complete a copy of the practice page.

Jennifer Reidy, Halifax Elementary, Halifax, MA

Shape Strength
Making and testing predictions

Getting ready:
- Fold and tape a half sheet of paper to make each of the following: a cube, a cylinder, and a triangular prism.
- Fold and tape a full sheet of paper to make a triangular prism.
- Gather a matching set of lightweight books, such as a storybook set from your reading series.
- On the board, draw a three-column chart with each shape as a separate heading.
- Obtain a class supply of sticky notes.

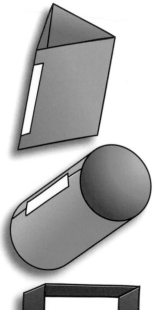

Activity: Show students the large triangular prism. Then stack books, one at a time, on an open surface. Guide them to observe how the shape collapses under the added weight. *(The triangular prism buckles at the folds until it finally collapses.)* Next, ask each child to predict which of the three remaining figures will hold the most books before collapsing. To show his prediction, have him write his name on a sticky note and place it in the corresponding column on the chart. To continue, use the books to test each of the figures and record the results. *(The cylinder holds the most books because there are no folds and the weight is evenly distributed.)* Then guide youngsters to compare their predictions to the results. **To extend the activity,** provide experiences with large and small sets of figures to confirm the cylinder has the greatest shape strength!

Jane Wulf, Gainesville, FL

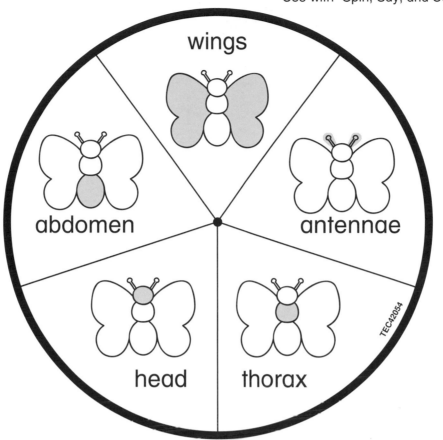

wings

abdomen

antennae

head

thorax

TEC42054

Name_____

Beautiful Butterfly

antennae

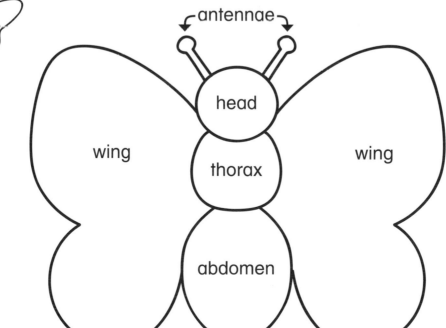

head

wing

thorax

wing

abdomen

Move It!

 Circle **push** or **pull**.

push   pull

push   pull

push   pull

push   pull

✏️ Write to tell about something you **pushed**.

_____

_____

✏️ Write to tell about something you **pulled**.

_____

_____

Note to the teacher: Use with "Use Some Force!" on page 178.

'TIS THE SEASON

'Tis the Season

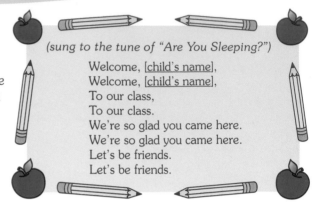

A Welcoming Song

Greet each student with this catchy tune that also reinforces name recognition. Write each child's name on a separate card and store the cards in a bag. To begin, draw a card and display it for the class. Encourage the child whose name is displayed to stand as you lead the class in singing the song shown. Continue until the group has sung to each student. 🖳

Deborah Hembrook
Lowell School
Waukesha, WI

Editor's Tip: This song is great for welcoming students who join the class later in the year!

(sung to the tune of "Are You Sleeping?")

Welcome, [child's name],
Welcome, [child's name],
To our class,
To our class.
We're so glad you came here.
We're so glad you came here.
Let's be friends.
Let's be friends.

Little worm, little worm,
Look and see.
Pick your apple
From the tree.

Apples Aplenty

Youngsters wiggle into letter knowledge practice with this versatile idea. Label a supply of apple cutouts (pattern on page 188) with different uppercase letters. Then, for each apple, label a worm cutout (pattern on page 188) with the matching lowercase letter. Choose one of the options below. 🖳

Center activity: Set out the apples and the matching worms. A child names the letters on each apple. Then she places each worm on its matching apple.

Group activity: Place a large tree cutout on the floor. Put a few apples on the tree and place the matching worms near the tree trunk. Invite a child to take a worm and name the letter. Then lead youngsters in the chant shown as the child picks the matching apple from the tree.

Beth Kickert, T. C. Cherry Elementary, Bowling Green, KY

Along the Stem

This sunny center provides practice with making number sets. Number ten sunflower cutouts (patterns on page 188) from 1 to 10. Then tape a green pipe cleaner stem to each flower and put the sunflowers in a plastic vase. Place the vase and ten leaf cutouts at a center. A child takes a sunflower, reads the number, and puts the matching number of leaves along the stem. She checks her work by recounting the leaves; then she removes the leaves and takes another flower. 🖳

Marie E. Cecchini, West Dundee, IL

'Tis the Season

Spiffy Spiders

Each verse of this fun-to-sing song teaches students a spider fact. Introduce the song one verse at a time and challenge students to find the spider fact. 🖥

Deborah Davenport-Gibbone
Saint Andrew School
Drexel Hill, PA

(sung to the tune of "The Farmer in the Dell")

I wish I were a spider.
I think it would be fun.
I could use my eight long legs
To help me when I run.

I wish I were a spider.
I'd hang out in a tree.
I could use my many eyes
To see all I could see.

I wish I were a spider.
I think it would be neat.
I could weave a sticky web
And catch a bite to eat.

I wish I were a spider.
I'd dangle from a thread.
I could swing back and forth
And drop on someone's head! Eek!

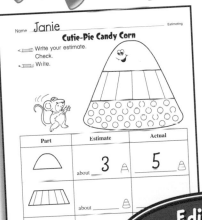

Candy Corn Estimation

Youngsters sweeten their math skills at this seasonal center! Put student copies of page 190 at a center along with a supply of candy corn manipulatives. A child estimates the number of candy corn pieces needed to cover the top section of the pictured candy corn. She writes the number on her paper, uses the manipulatives to check her work, and records her findings. She continues in this manner with each remaining section.

Sara Porter, Indian Trail Elementary, Canal Winchester, OH

Editor's Tip:
Foam candy corn manipulatives are an inexpensive alternative to real candy corn pieces.

Thankful Thoughts

During the month of November, grow a tree of thankful thoughts! Post a cutout of a leafless tree and prepare a supply of colorful leaf cutouts. Then, throughout the month, students prepare leaves for the tree by writing, dictating, and/or illustrating their thankful thoughts. Invite each author to share his thankful thoughts with the class before adding each of his leaves to the tree. 🖥

Kimberly Jones, Corydon, KY

See pages 191 and 192 for seasonal **practice pages.**

I am thankful for my family.
Sam

'Tis the Season

Snowballs for Snowpal

This idea can be used over and over to help youngsters practice estimating. Post within students' reach a large snowpal labeled as shown. Place several cotton balls (snowballs) in a clear plastic jar.

To begin, show students the size of one snowball, and then show them the jar. Ask each child to write on a sticky note his name and an estimate of how many snowballs are in the jar. Then lead the group in counting the snowballs. Have each student compare his estimate to the actual number and then place his sticky note in the correct section of the snowpal. Discuss the comparisons. Repeat this activity on subsequent days, using a different number of snowballs each time.

Jodi Darter, Cabool Elementary, Cabool, MO

Winter Is...

Here's a cool idea that encourages students to write captions. Ask each child to bring to school a winter-related item, such as mittens, a plastic mug for hot chocolate, a scarf, or a paper snowflake. Take a photo of each child holding her item. Have her glue the photo to a sheet of paper. Then direct her to use the word wall and other environmental print to write a caption telling how her item relates to winter. Display the projects with the title "Winter Is Wonderful!"

Betty Silkunas, Lower Gwynedd Elementary, Ambler, PA

I drink hot chocolate in the winter.

Tasty Gingerbread Man

Try this yummy graphing activity to inspire students' interest in math! Make a tally chart on the board and give each child a gingerbread man cookie. Ask each child to take only one bite of his cookie. Next, have each student, in turn, show his cookie as you tally the results. Then instruct students to use the tally chart to complete a copy of the graph on page 193. After leading the group in a discussion of the results, invite each youngster to finish eating his cookie. 💻

Katie McCutcheon
Ben Franklin Elementary
Indiana, PA

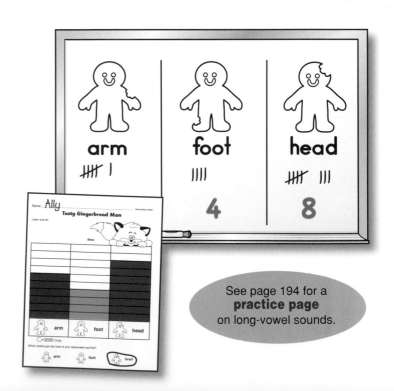

See page 194 for a **practice page** on long-vowel sounds.

'Tis the Season

Looking for Shadows

Lead youngsters in performing this action poem about the furry weather predictor, the groundhog. 💻

Fuzzy little groundhog, asleep underground,
Come on up and look around.
If you see your shadow, there could be
Six more weeks of winter for you and me!

Crouch down and pretend to sleep.
Jump up and look around.
Point behind yourself.
Point to a friend and then to yourself.

Fuzzy little groundhog, asleep underground,
Come on up and look around.
If you don't see your shadow, hip hip hooray!
Winter is almost over, and spring is on the way!

Crouch down and pretend to sleep.
Jump up and look around.
Point behind yourself.
Cheer silently.

Beth Marquardt, St. Paul's School of Early Learning, Muskego, WI

Lion or Lamb?

Students flip a springtime card to create this wild and woolly graph. Make a class supply and two more of the lion and lamb cards on page 197. Cut out two copies of the cards; glue a lion and a lamb back-to-back to make a flipcard and use the second pair to label a graph like the one shown. Show students the flipcard and encourage each child to predict which animal will land faceup more often when the card is flipped. On his copy of the cards, have the child color one animal to show his prediction. Next, direct him to cut out and glue his cards to a sheet of paper. Then have youngsters take turns flipping the flipcard. For each flip, color the corresponding space on the class graph and instruct each child to make an X by the matching animal on his paper. After each child has had a turn, lead a discussion to compare students' predictions to the graph. 💻

Treasured Words

This seasonal pot is perfect for storing word family words. Give each youngster a copy of the pot of gold pattern on page 197 and five yellow paper circles (coins). Instruct her to write a word family ending on the pot; then have her write a different word on each coin to form a word family. After checking for accuracy, have her put the words in a trimmed lunch bag and glue the bag to the back of her pot. **For an added challenge,** have the child feature more than one word family to make a word family word sort. 💻

Elaine Curtiss
Thoreau Park Elementary
Parma, OH

See page 198 for a **practice page** on counting pennies.

'Tis the Season

April Showers Bring May Flowers

Turn an inexpensive shower curtain into a spring skill builder. Use a permanent marker to draw several large raindrop outlines on the shower curtain and then choose from one of the options below. 🖥

Addition: In each raindrop, write an addition problem. Then write each answer on a separate flower cutout (pattern on page 239). A child solves each problem and places the flower with the matching sum on the raindrop.

Initial consonants: Write a different consonant in each raindrop. For each consonant, cut out a small picture of an object whose name begins with the letter. Then glue the pictures on separate flower cutouts made using the pattern on page 239. A child matches beginning sounds to initial consonants by placing each flower on its corresponding raindrop.

Kate Wonders, Carlisle Elementary, Carlisle, IA

Fantastic Froggies

Hop into spring with these cute frog planters! For each child, punch a hole near the rim of a green container, such as a plastic drinking cup. Next, help him scoop a mixture of potting soil and grass seeds into the container. Help him tape a large paper eye to each of two green pipe cleaner halves and "plant" the eyes in the soil mixture. Then have the child twist a red pipe cleaner through the hole so it looks like a tongue. If desired, provide paper scraps for him to cut out a fly and glue it to the tongue. Invite each child to keep his frog planter in a sunny place and water it daily. **To extend the activity**, have students keep a daily journal to show the growth of the grass.

Angela Morris, Jefferson Elementary, North Platte, NE

Twist and Read

Use plastic eggs to review word families at this seasonal center! Label each right half of several eggs with a different rime. Along the edge of each left half, write beginning letters or blends that make words when combined with the rime. Place the eggs in a basket. A child takes an egg and twists it to read each word. Then he writes the words on a sheet of paper.

Debbie Heide, Lake Linden Hubbell Elementary, Lake Linden, MN

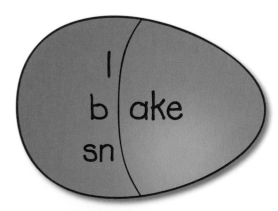

'Tis the Season

Sunny Words

This bright center highlights students' word blending skills. Program a class supply of yellow paper circles (suns) with a rime and write on cards different onsets, most of which form real words when coupled with the rime. Set out the programmed materials, orange paper strips (rays), and writing paper. A child places a card in front of the rime and reads the word. If it is a real word, she writes the word on a ray and glues it to the sun. After adding several rays to the sun, she writes sentences using the words.

Jennifer Reidy, Halifax Elementary, Halifax, MA

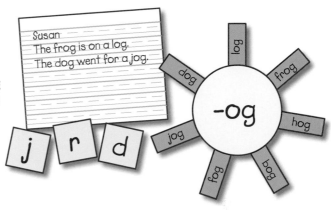

At the Beach

Build descriptive writing skills with this beach-themed graphic organizer. On the board, draw and label a sand castle–shaped graphic organizer similar to the one shown. Ask youngsters to imagine that they are at the beach and invite them to name things that they might taste, smell, touch, see, and hear. Write each phrase under the appropriate heading. Then have each child refer to the graphic organizer to write a descriptive sentence about the beach. Encourage each child to illustrate his writing before sharing it with his classmates. 🖥

Marie E. Cecchini
West Dundee, IL

Shell Search

Since summer's on the mind, play this seashell-inspired Lotto game with students! To prepare, label each of 30 shell cards (patterns on page 200) with a different number from 1 to 30. Set out a plastic pail and scatter the cards facedown around the pail. Give each child a copy of the gameboard on page 200 and a supply of game markers. Instruct her to write a different number from 1 to 30 on each shell on her gameboard. Encourage her to cross out each number in the number line as it is used.

To play, invite a youngster to take a shell card, read the number aloud, and then place the card in the pail. Direct each child with the matching number on her board to cover it. Play continues until a child covers all the numbers on her board and announces, "Summer seashells!" 🖥

adapted from an idea by Jennifer Reidy

Apple and Worm Patterns
Use with "Apples Aplenty" on page 182.

TEC42050

TEC42050

Sunflower Patterns
Use with "Along the Stem" on page 182.

TEC42050

TEC42050

The Pick of the Crop

  Count the on each .

 Write each number.

Color the  with **more.**

Cutie-Pie Candy Corn

✏️ Write your estimate.
   Check.
✏️ Write.

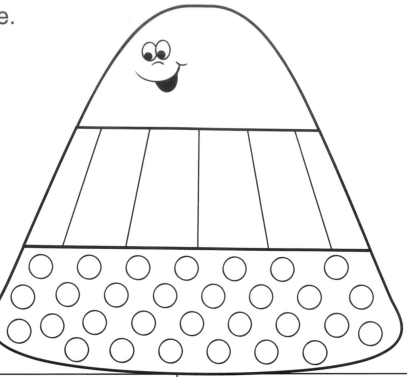

Part	Estimate	Actual
⌒ (half dome)	about _____ 🍬	_____ 🍬
▱ (trapezoid)	about _____ 🍬	_____ 🍬
▱ (dotted base)	about _____ 🍬	_____ 🍬

Note to the teacher: Use with "Candy Corn Estimation" on page 183.

Name

That's Nutty!

Count.   Write.

Color the   that has more.

3

Lots of Leaves

Write the lowercase letter.

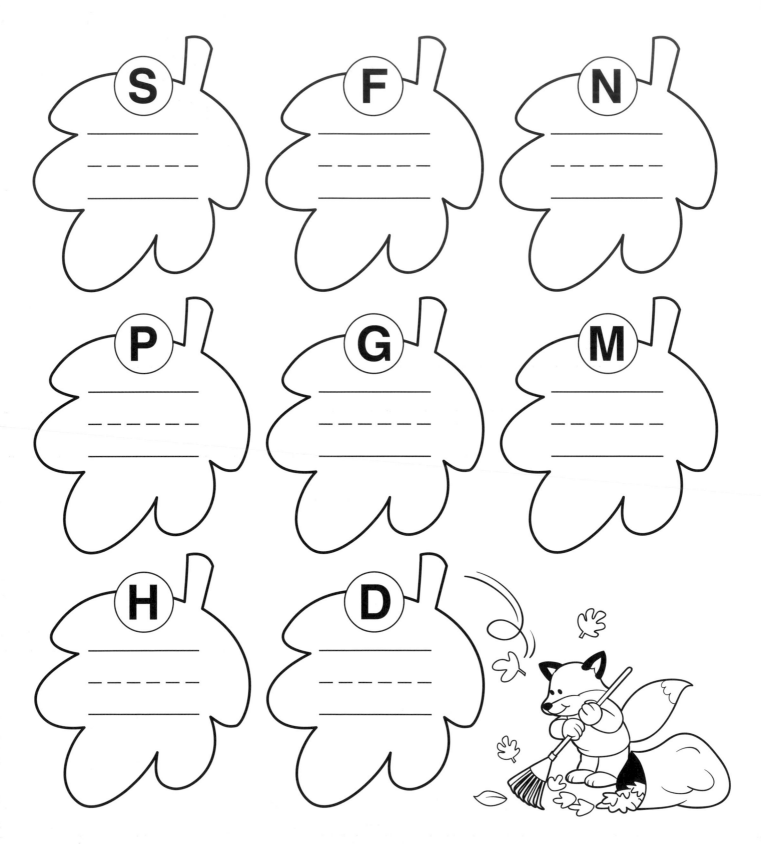

Tasty Gingerbread Man

Listen and do.

Bites

arm	**foot**	**head**

✏️ **Circle.**

Which cookie part did most of your classmates eat first?

 arm   **foot**   **head**

Note to the teacher: Use with "Tasty Gingerbread Man" on page 184.

THE MAILBOX **193**

Name _____

Fishing for Snacks

Color to match the vowel sounds.

ō as in

ā as in

Bonus: Which words have the same vowel sound as in ? Draw a picture that has those two items in it.

Have each child cut apart a copy of pages 195 and 196. Then help him staple the booklet pages, in order, behind the front cover. **For additional skill reinforcement,** ask students to complete text-related tasks, such as underlining the number words, circling the color words with matching-color crayons, and coloring the pictures to match the text.

Candy Counting

Name _____

©The Mailbox® • TEC42052 • Dec./Jan. 2010–11

I like candy.
Yes, I do.

1

One is green.
Two are blue.

2

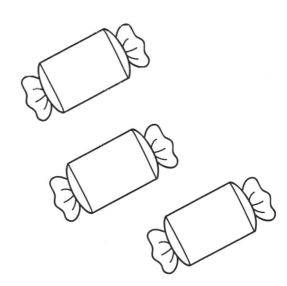

Three are yellow.

3

Four are red.

4

Five are orange
on my head.

5

Six are pink
on my tummy.

6

I like candy.
Yum, yum, yummy!

7

Note to the teacher: Use with the directions on page 195.

Lion and Lamb Cards
Use with "Lion or Lamb?" on page 185.

TEC42053

Pot of Gold Pattern
Use with "Treasured Words" on page 185.

I'm as lucky as can be.
I can read this word family!

TEC42053

Pick One!

Read.

Color pennies to match.

5¢ 	**8¢** 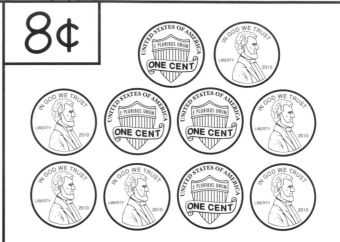
9¢ 	**6¢** 
10¢ 	**7¢** 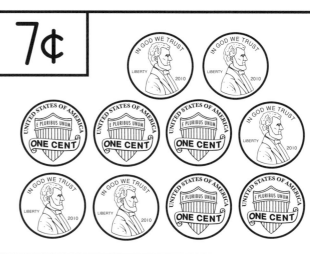

Bonus: Mouse wants a card that costs 12¢. Draw the pennies he needs. Use this symbol. 1¢

Just Lounging

Read each sentence.

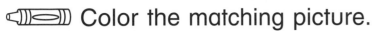 Color the matching picture.

I see a hat.

I like apples.

I see a tree.

I see a van.

I like to read books.

I see a dog.

I like to eat pizza.

I see a car.

 Bonus: Read. Draw a picture to match. **I see a big cat.**

Shell Cards and Gameboard

Use with "Shell Search" on page 187.

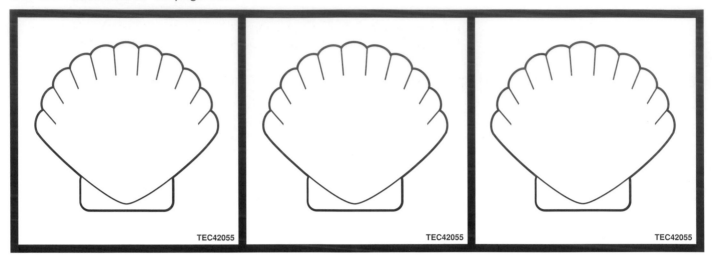

TEC42055   TEC42055   TEC42055

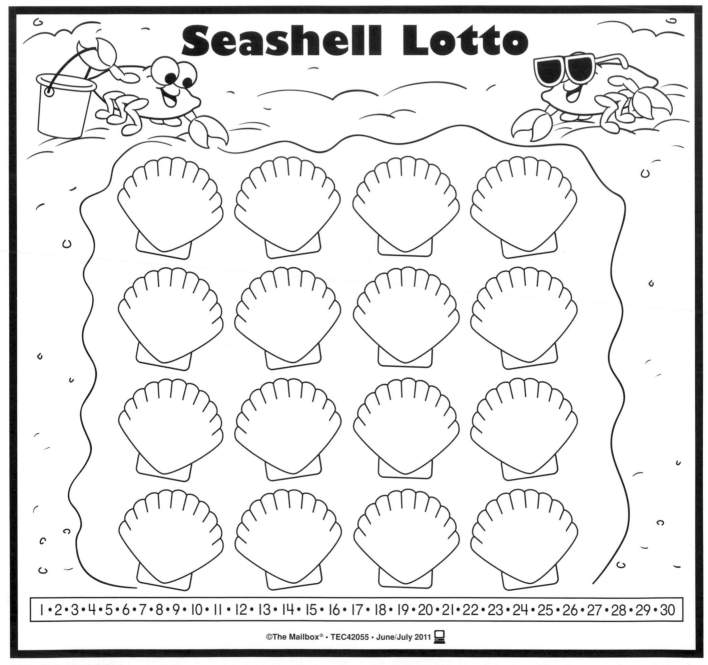

Seashell Lotto

1•2•3•4•5•6•7•8•9•10•11•12•13•14•15•16•17•18•19•20•21•22•23•24•25•26•27•28•29•30

Have each child cut apart a copy of pages 201 and 202. Then help her staple the booklet pages, in order, behind the front cover. **For additional skill reinforcement,** ask students to complete text-related tasks, such as circling high-frequency words, highlighting the punctuation on each page, or comparing the word *we* on pages 6 and 7 to review capitalization.

1

Let's have a picnic.

3

We can pack sandwiches.

Picnic Day

Name _____

©The Mailbox® • TEC42055 • June/July 2011

2

What can we pack?

5

We can pack fruit.

7

Then we can eat!

4

We can pack drinks.

JUICE

6

We can pack cheese.

Note to the teacher: Use with the directions on page 201.

A Whole Lot of Apples!

©The Mailbox® • TEC42050 • Aug./Sept. 2010

Lotto game: numbers to 12 or environmental print Cut out a copy of one set of cards from page 204 to make caller's cards.
Give each child a copy of this page and a copy of the appropriate game cards. Instruct her to cut out the cards and glue each card to a
randomly chosen board space. Then have students play the game like traditional lotto. (To call a space for the math game, call a number
or use a phrase such as "comes before" or "comes after" to describe a number.)

Game Cards

Use with "A Whole Lot of Apples!" on page 203.

number cards

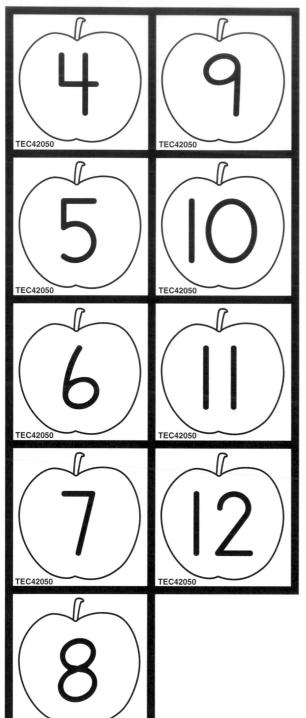

environmental print cards

Editor's Tip:
When time allows for multiple lotto games, try these fun variations! **Four Corners Lotto:** the winner is the first player to cover each corner of his gameboard. **Top Row Lotto:** the winner is the first player to cover the top row of his gameboard.

Name _____

Wow, What a Nut!

©The Mailbox® • TEC42051 • Oct./Nov. 2010

Lotto game: writing numbers to 20 or beginning sounds Cut out a copy of one set of cards from page 206 to make caller's cards. Give each child a copy of this page and a copy of the appropriate game cards. (For the math game, each child traces the numbers.) Students cut out the game cards and glue each card to a randomly chosen board space. Then they play the game like traditional lotto. (To call a space for the literacy game, say beginning sounds only.)

Game Cards

Use with "Wow, What a Nut!" on page 205.

number cards

9 TEC42051	15 TEC42051
10 TEC42051	16 TEC42051
11 TEC42051	17 TEC42051
12 TEC42051	18 TEC42051
13 TEC42051	19 TEC42051
14 TEC42051	20 TEC42051

beginning sound picture cards

Kittens in a Mitten

Lotto game: surfaces of solid figures or high-frequency words Cut out a copy of one set of cards from page 208 to make caller's cards. Give each child a copy of this page and a copy of the appropriate game cards. Instruct him to cut out the cards and glue each card to any board space. Then have students play the game like traditional lotto. (For the surfaces of solid figures cards, call the surface shape and then give a description of the item, such as, for a die, "a shape with square surfaces labeled with dots.")

Game Cards

Use with "Kittens in a Mitten" on page 207.

surfaces of solid figures

TEC42052

high-frequency words

and	the
TEC42052	TEC42052
like	here
TEC42052	TEC42052
see	go
TEC42052	TEC42052
my	on
TEC42052	TEC42052
we	this
TEC42052	TEC42052
look	up
TEC42052	TEC42052

Five in a row wins!

Frame Game

Literacy or math

Free

Lotto Frame game: final consonants or symmetry Cut out a copy of one set of cards from page 210 to make caller's cards. Give each child a copy of this page and a copy of the appropriate game cards. (For the literacy game, each child circles the final consonant of each pictured item.) Students cut out the cards and glue each one to an empty board space. Then they play the game like traditional lotto. (To call a space for the literacy game, name the object; then name both consonants. A student gives a thumbs-up for the correct consonant and a thumbs-down for the incorrect one. To call a space for the math game, name the shape and whether it has equal or unequal parts.)

Game Cards

Use with "Frame Game" on page 209.

final consonant cards

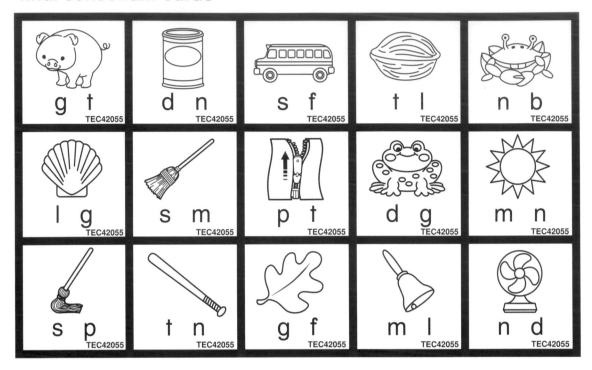

equal and unequal parts cards

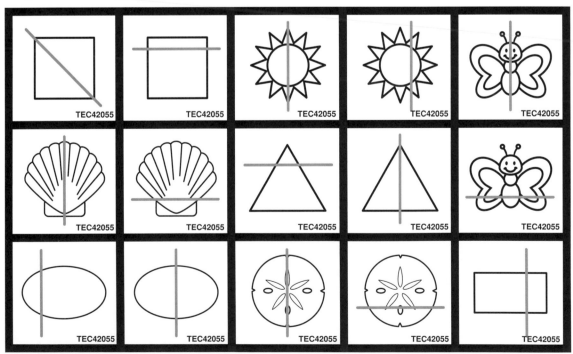

WRITING

A Colorful Leaf

Listen for directions.

Color Code

🍂—yellow 🍂—red 🍂—orange 🍂—brown

_____

- -

My leaf is _____

_____

- -

_____ .

Note to the teacher: Give each child a copy of this page. Guide students to color the leaves in the color code. Next, ask each student to draw a large leaf (or leaf character) and to color it using one or more of the colors in the code. Then have her write, or dictate for you to write, a sentence that describes her leaf. For a literature connection, see *Leaf Man* on page 248.

Fall word bank

Fall Fun!

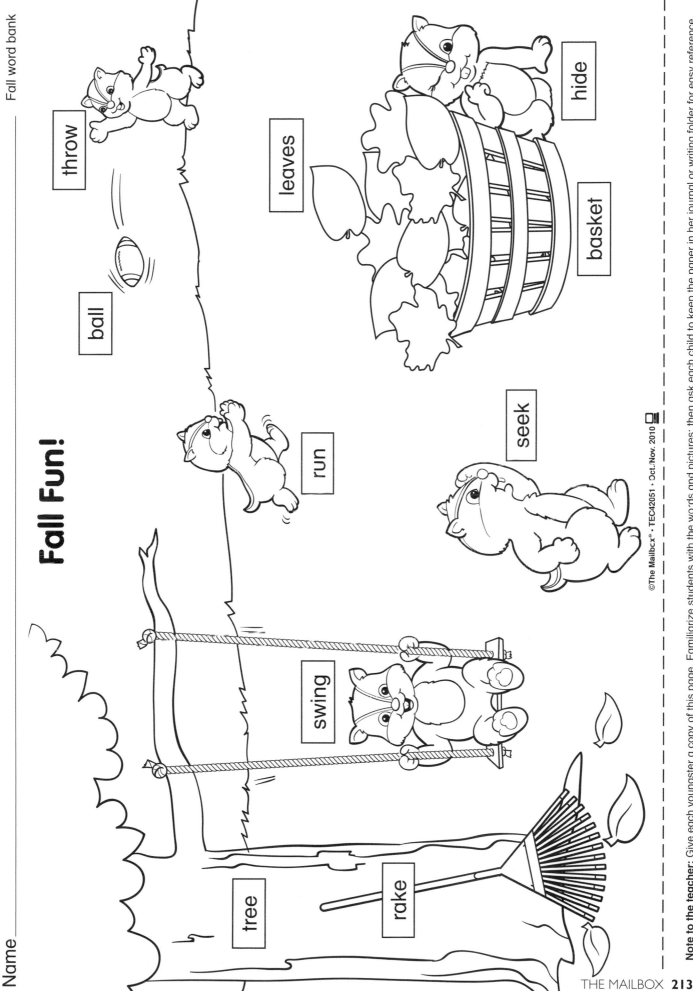

throw

ball

leaves

hide

basket

run

seek

swing

tree

rake

©The Mailbox® • TEC42051 • Oct./Nov. 2010

Note to the teacher: Give each youngster a copy of this page. Familiarize students with the words and pictures; then ask each child to keep the paper in her journal or writing folder for easy reference.

Name _____

Pick a Prompt

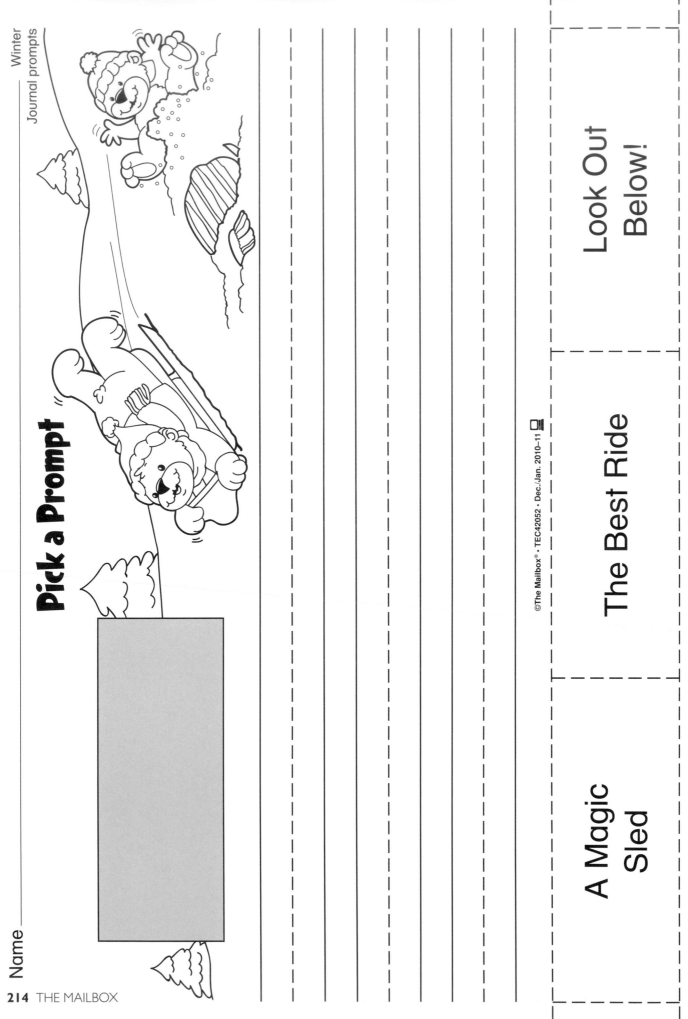

©The Mailbox® • TEC42052 • Dec./Jan. 2010–11 💻

A Magic Sled	The Best Ride
	Look Out Below!

Note to the teacher: Give each child a copy of this page. Read the prompts aloud. Then have each student cut out the prompts, glue one prompt to his paper, and respond to it.

Name _____ Word bank

Holiday Words

 candle

 stocking

 candy cane

card

 gingerbread house

jingle bell

 present

 tree

 wreath

Name _____

Valentine's Day Deliveries

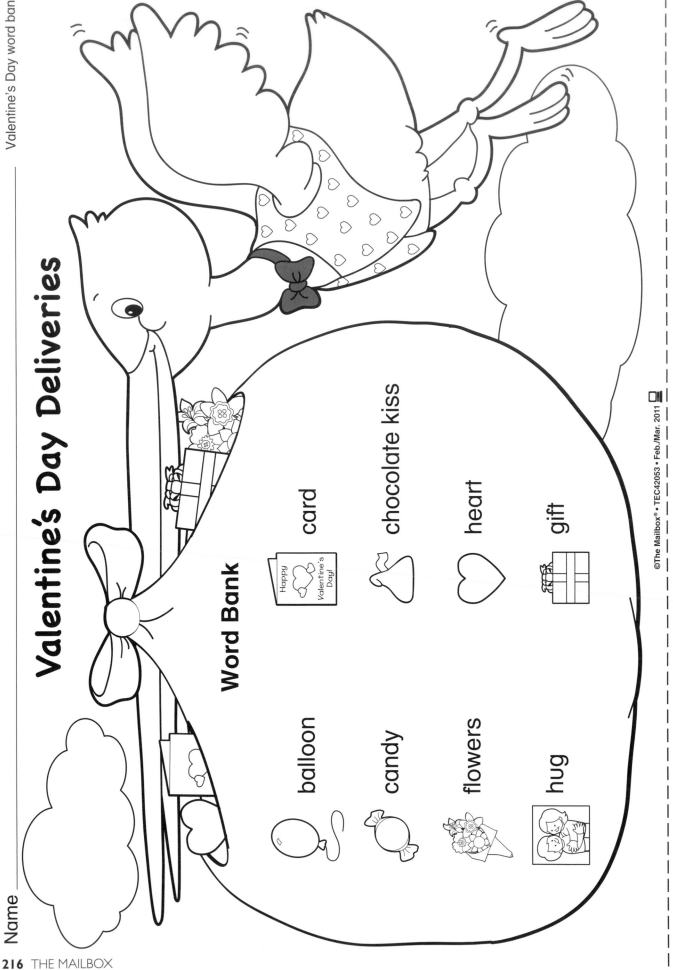

Word Bank

card

chocolate kiss

heart

gift

balloon

candy

flowers

hug

Note to the teacher: Give each child a copy of this page. Read the words aloud and invite him to color the paper as desired. Then ask him to keep the paper in his journal or writing folder for easy reference.

Friends Are Fun!

Prompt: Think about a time you had loads of fun with a friend.

What did you do?

Plan

Where were you?

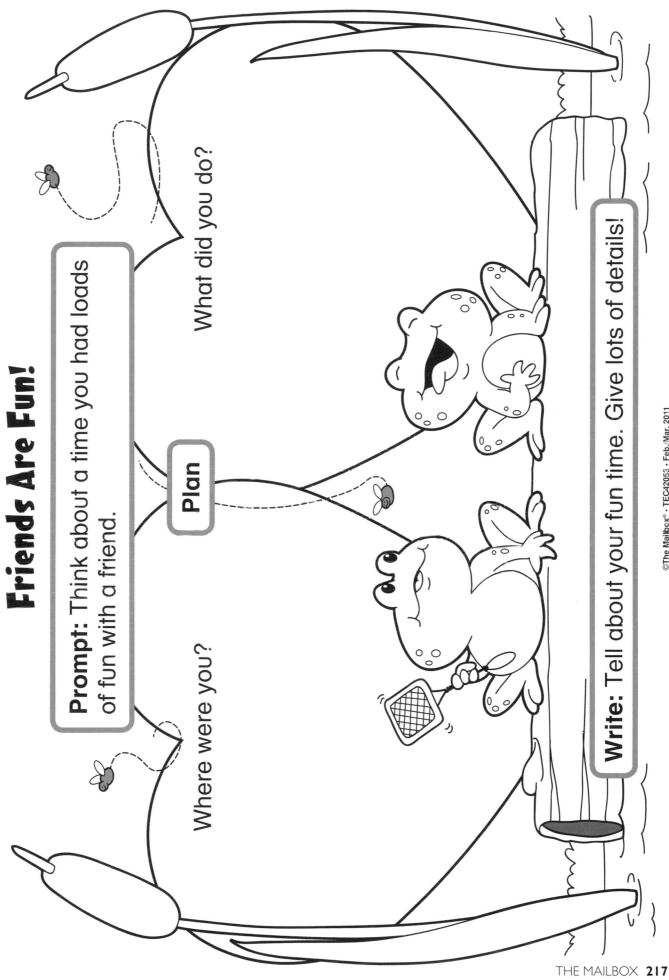

Write: Tell about your fun time. Give lots of details!

Name _____

Pick a Prompt

©The Mailbox® • TEC42053 • Feb./Mar. 2011

The Happy
Leprechaun

Gold for
Everyone!

On St. Patrick's Day,
I like to...

Note to the teacher: Give each child a copy of this page. Read the prompts aloud. Then have each student cut out the prompts, glue one prompt to her paper, and respond to it.

A Fast Flier!

Think: Pretend you can fly as fast as a dragonfly.

Draw. Where will you go? What will you do?

Write.

_____

- -

_____

- -

_____

- -

_____

- -

_____

Note to the teacher: For extra writing inspiration, explain that a dragonfly is a very skillful flier. It can fly almost 38 miles an hour, and it can make quick, dramatic turns in midair!

Pick a Prompt

Name

©The Mailbox® • TEC42054 • April/May 2011

The Egg That Rolled Away

A Special Little Chick

The Eggs Are Hatching!

Note to the teacher: Give each child a copy of this page. Read the prompts aloud. Then have each student cut out the prompts, glue one prompt to her paper, and respond to it.

Let's Eat!

Think:
What yummy foods do you eat during the summer?

Draw.

Write: Tell what you like best about each food.

Name _____

Pick a Prompt

©The Mailbox® · TEC42055 · June/July 2011

A Perfect
Summer Day

When it gets
very hot,...

Slip and Slide!

Note to the teacher: Give each child a copy of this page. Read the prompts aloud. Then have each student cut out the prompts, glue one prompt to her paper, and respond to it.

LITERACY UNITS

Letter-Perfect Introductions

From singing a song to making books, the ideas in this collection can be used with any letter!

Sing-Along
Letter-sound associations

Be sure to include this song when you introduce each letter of the alphabet! 🖥

(sung to the tune of "Clementine")

Sounds and letters,
Sounds and letters,
Let's sing the sound of letter [P].
[/p/, /p/, /p/, /p/, /p/, /p/, /p/, /p/]!
That's the sound of letter [P].

adapted from an idea by Jennifer Truckly
Gockley Elementary
Whitehall, PA

B is the mystery letter!

Mystery Bag
Initial letter sounds

Looking for a home-school connection? Try this secret letter activity! Conceal a letter card in a bag and include a note with a due date asking family members to help their child put objects in the bag that begin with the letter's sound. (Be sure to mention in the note the importance of the child's keeping the letter a mystery to her classmates.) Then send the closed bag home with a student.

When the bag is returned, invite the child to name each of her objects (except the letter card) as she removes it from the bag. Then have her ask, "Who can name the mystery letter?" When her classmate names the correct letter, she holds up the letter card. For each new letter introduction, you are sure to have plenty of volunteers willing to prepare the mystery bag! 🖥

Denise Evans
Hodge Elementary
Denton, TX

Editor's Tip:
Take a photo of each letter collection and compile the photos into a class book.

Animated ABCs
Letter knowledge

Your kindergartners are sure to look forward to surprise visitors from Alphabet Land! In advance, enlist the help of upper-grade students, parents, or volunteers. Ask each helper to represent a different letter of the alphabet on a predetermined date. Encourage helpers to be creative; for example, a guest may dress up as a football player, display *"Ff"* on his shirt, and serve fish crackers as a snack! Each time you introduce a new letter, warmly welcome the guest from Alphabet Land and enjoy the letter-related memories that are sure to be made.

Jeanne Pinkman
Cathedral of the Risen Christ Elementary
Lincoln, NE

Cute Quilts
Letter-sound associations, recognizing letters

The student-made art on this visual display is sure to attract attention. Write the matching uppercase and lowercase letter you would like to feature on individual paper squares. After announcing the letter and the associated sound, have each youngster draw on a paper square a picture of something or someone whose name begins with the letter. Help him label his drawing and instruct him to underline the featured letter. Then tape the papers on a large piece of fabric or paper, as shown, and display the resulting quilt.

Stacey Helders-Pevan
Prince of Peace School
Milwaukee, WI

Alphabet Books
Letter knowledge

These class books can be easily reassembled to make personalized reading booklets later in the year! Help each youngster complete a page similar to the one shown when you introduce each letter of the alphabet. (Be sure each youngster writes his name on his paper.) Slip each completed page in a page protector and put the pages in a binder. Attach the matching letter cutout on the binder's front cover and put the book in your student reading area. After each of 26 binders are complete, remove the student pages, re-sort them by name, and bind each stack, in order, between construction paper covers. Then encourage each youngster to read his resulting booklet to family members, teachers, and friends. 🖥

Jamie Goehring, Hermes Elementary, La Grange, TX

Beginning Letter Bears

What happens when *A* is paired with Astronaut Bear and *M* is paired with Magician Bear? Students make memorable letter-sound connections!

idea by Terri Strong, Santa Paula, CA

A Booklet of Bears

Give students' beginning sound skills a boost with this booklet project. Have students contribute pages to a class booklet or make booklets of their own using the directions below. Alphabetize the completed pages, place a cover on top, and then bind the project as desired. 🖥

To make a booklet page:
1. Cut out a brown construction paper copy of the bear pattern on page 228.
2. Glue the cutout on a sheet of construction paper.
3. Label the top right corner with a letter.
4. Choose a job that begins with the corresponding letter's sound.
5. Use paper scraps and craft supplies to decorate the bear to match its job.

Beginning Letter Bears

By Brandon

Possible Bear Jobs

actor, astronaut	jeweler, judge	sailor, singer
baker, ballerina	key maker, king	teacher, tennis player
carpenter, conductor	librarian, lifeguard	umpire, usher
dentist, doctor	magician, mail carrier	violinist, veterinarian
electrician, engineer	newscaster, nurse	waiter, waitress
farmer, firefighter	oceanographer, office worker	X-ray technician
goalie, guitarist	poet, police officer	yard worker, yarn maker
hairstylist, housekeeper	queen, quilter	zookeeper, zoologist
inventor, investigator	racecar driver, reporter	

See page 16 for a different booklet option.

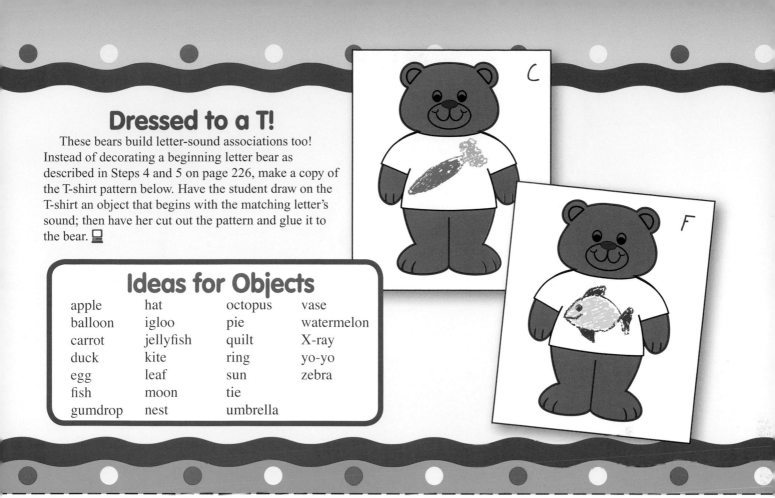

Dressed to a T!

These bears build letter-sound associations too! Instead of decorating a beginning letter bear as described in Steps 4 and 5 on page 226, make a copy of the T-shirt pattern below. Have the student draw on the T-shirt an object that begins with the matching letter's sound; then have her cut out the pattern and glue it to the bear. 💻

Ideas for Objects

apple	hat	octopus	vase
balloon	igloo	pie	watermelon
carrot	jellyfish	quilt	X-ray
duck	kite	ring	yo-yo
egg	leaf	sun	zebra
fish	moon	tie	
gumdrop	nest	umbrella	

T-shirt Pattern
Use with "Dressed to a T!" on this page.

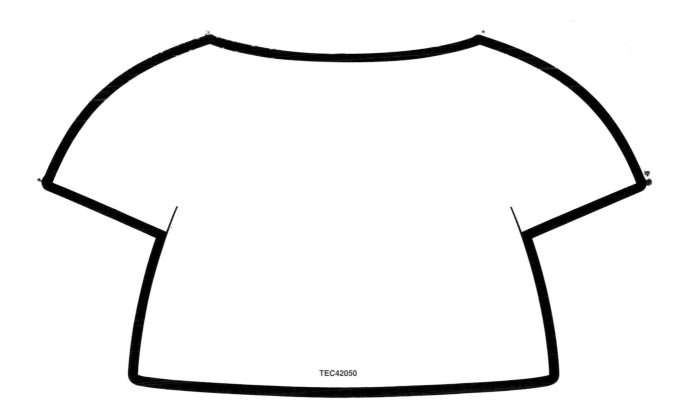

TEC42050

TEC42050

Making the Most of Morning Messages!

Cock-a-doodle-doo! Start the morning
with these fresh and creative ideas!

Skill Alert

Morning messages are jam-packed
with opportunities for skill reinforcement. Keep the skills shown in mind as
you craft and share morning messages.

Skills

Left-to-right progression
Letter formation
Word spacing
Letter-sound associations
Capitalizing names
Spelling
Recognizing letters, words,
   and sentences
Punctuation
Sight words

Happy Tuesday!
A visitor is coming
to see you this
afternoon.

Critter Tales

When a cuddly critter leaves the morning message, students' interest
is sure to soar! Designate an animal toy to be the message writer. Tell
students that the critter writes its message each morning before they
arrive. Possible message topics include special activities and events,
student birthdays, and school secrets that only the critter knows!

Barbara Ozminkowski, Mary Helen Guest Elementary, Walled Lake, MI

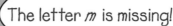

The letter *m* is missing!

Take a Close Look!

Use magnetic letters to spell sight words and other familiar words in the
message. Occasionally misspell a word by scrambling the letters or omitting a
letter. Invite volunteers to make the corrections.

Debbie Patrick, Park Forest Elementary, State College, PA

What's Your Answer?

Encourage writing skills by including a question in the morning
message. To save paper, have each child write or draw his answer on an
individual whiteboard. Invite students to share their responses during
calendar time or later in the day.

Debbie Patrick

Read and Respond

Morning messages are great for building comprehension skills and making connections! Conclude a message with a yes-or-no question. Then draw and label three columns like those shown. Each child writes her name in one column. Later in the day, reread the message. Invite volunteers to share their answers with their classmates. For a fun alternative, have students write their names on individual sticky notes and ask them to post the notes on a graph.

Nicole Hoke
Liberty Elementary
Margate, FL

Today we will read books about pumpkins. Have you ever picked a pumpkin in a pumpkin patch?

Yes ☺	No ☹	Not sure ?
Lilly	Izzy	Eli
James		
Kendra		

Try and Check

Here's a fun way to reinforce spelling strategies with your morning message. For each child, make a booklet like the one shown by stapling several pages between construction paper covers. Each day include a spelling mistake in the morning message. First, have a volunteer identify and underline the mistake; then have each child try to correct the misspelling in his booklet. After you correct the morning message, have each child check his work. If his correction matches yours, he draws a smiley face in the "Check" column. If not, he copies the correct spelling of the word in the "Check" column. 💻

Estelle Sharpe, A. R. Knight School, Cherry Hill, NJ

Try	Check
dog	☺
sop	stop

Color-Coded Words

Tuck some word family practice into your morning message! When a grade-appropriate rime is included in your message, bring it to your students' attention. To do this, write the word family ending in a second color. During your discussion of the morning message, circle the word and invite students to name words that rhyme with the circled word. List these words nearby, color-coding the rimes. Help students notice how the rime is spelled.

Susan Walker
Blowing Rock, NC

bug
mug
hug
jug

Name _____

Heading Home

Color by the code.

-**at** as in 🎩 —yellow

-**ug** as in —blue

-**op** as in 🧹 —red

sat	pat	pop	hug
bug	hat	dug	mug
hop	rat	mop	jug
mat	cat	tug	top
fat			
bat			

Bonus: The yellow path takes the bears home. Read the words on that path. Write the words.

At Home With Word Families

This "bear-y" special collection of ideas is just right for any word family.

Porridge, Please!

Sorting words

Youngsters pretend to be bears serving porridge at this nifty center. To prepare, write a different word family ending on each handle of three plastic spoons. Put each spoon in a different bowl. Then write words from the corresponding word families on separate tagboard cards. Place the cards and a large spoon in a pot (porridge).

A student scoops each word from the pot and puts it in the matching bowl. When the pot is empty, she reads the words in each bowl. **For a writing connection,** draw a bowl outline on each of three sheets of paper (placemats) and have her record each word family list on a different placemat.

Kathy Ginn
Miami Trace Elementary
Washington Court House, OH

Who Is Reading These Words?

Reading words

Rereading lists of word families is sure to be popular when students get to use different bear voices! Lead youngsters in singing the song shown, using the specified singing voices for each of the first three lines. Then invite a child to use her favorite bear voice to read a designated word family list. Continue singing and reading various word family lists as time allows.

(sung to the tune of "He's Got the Whole World in His Hands")

If you read the words like Papa, read like this!   *(Sing with a papa bear voice.)*
If you read the words like Mama, read like this!   *(Sing with a mama bear voice.)*
If you read the words like Baby, read like this!   *(Sing with a baby bear voice.)*
Who'd like to read a word list now?

adapted from an idea by Kathy Ginn

Someone Is Making Words on My Bed!

Blending words

To prepare this center, label a lunch bag with the name of a word family. Write the corresponding rime on a 5" x 7" rectangle (blanket); then on 3" x 5" cards (pillows), write different onsets that form real words when coupled with the rime. Store the blanket and pillows inside the bag.

A child empties the bag and then folds it flat to use as the bed. Next, she puts a pillow and the blanket on the bed to form a word. She blends the onset with the rime, reads the word, and writes it on a sheet of paper. She continues to swap pillows, read, and write until she lists each word to form a family. 🖥

Katie Zuehlke
Bendix Elementary
Annandale, MN

All in the Family

Writing words

The result of this whole-group activity is a handy reference of word family bears! Write a rime on a large bear cutout and post it in a child-friendly location. Then name an onset and the featured rime for youngsters to write, blend, and read silently. On your signal, have students announce the word. As you write the word on the bear, have each child check his spelling. Repeat the activity with different rimes to create a family of bears. 🖥

Kathy Ginn, Miami Trace Elementary, Washington Court House, OH

Bears in Chairs

Making and reading words

For this whole group game, label three chairs with a different word family ending and position the chairs in front of the class. Have each child draw a bear on a sticky note; then ask her to write a letter (or a blend) on the bear.

To play, stand behind a chair and ask, "Who has been sitting in the [-*ip*] chair?" Then invite a student to form a word by attaching his bear to the chair. Have the child read the word aloud and direct her classmates to each give a thumbs-up or thumbs-down to tell whether it is a real word. If it is a real word, write it on the board. Continue with different bears and chairs to make three word family lists on the board. 🖥

Who has been sitting in the [-ip] chair?

See page 231 for a practice page.

Taking Off With **Writing**

Your kindergartners' writing skills are sure to soar with these kid-pleasing ideas!

Sentence With a String
Connecting pictures and words

Use seasonal or theme-related cutouts to jump-start students' thinking! Give each child a cutout and a sheet of paper. Have her draw a picture associated with the cutout. Then have her turn the paper over and write a sentence that connects the cutout to her drawing. To complete the project, hole-punch the cutout and her paper; then tie the cutout below the paper using a foot-long length of string. Encourage each child to take a turn demonstrating how her cutout relates to the picture as she reads her sentence aloud. 🖥

Melanie Pallotta, Petersham Center
Petersham, MA

The car goes over the bridge.

Characters

crocodiles

Setting

house

Problem

Tall Tales
Story elements

This group writing experience prompts youngsters to create the beginning, middle, and end of a story. Cut apart a copy of the cards on page 236. Glue each large card to an individual envelope (or container). Put each strip in its matching envelope. To begin, have a student remove one strip from each envelope. Lead students to craft an interesting story that includes the selected characters and setting (beginning), the problem (middle), and a solution (end). Record the story on chart paper with help from students. Then return the strips to the envelopes for future use. 🖥

Alicia K. Shaffer
Mechanicsburg, PA

Editor's Tip:
Use different-color markers to distinguish the **beginning, middle,** and **end** of the story.

Cloudy Skies
Responding to a prompt

Cotton-ball clouds are a fun way to encourage writing. Have each child pull apart several cotton balls and glue them into a shape on a sheet of paper. Then help him copy and complete the sentence "My cloud looks like…" **To emphasize capitalization and punctuation,** have him use glue to trace the first letter and the period to create a 3-D effect when it dries. 🖥

Alicia K. Shaffer, Mechanicsburg, PA

My cloud looks like a big tree.

I can fly my kite on a windy day. My kite is pink and yellow. It is fun!

Picture Perfect
Main idea and details

Looking for a way to keep youngsters on task when writing? Try this! Give each child a sticker (or a simple cutout) to serve as the main idea. Have her put the sticker on a sheet of paper. Then have her draw details related to the sticker's topic. When finished, encourage her to write about the completed scene. The sticker not only serves as the main idea but also guides her drawing and writing to stay on topic.

Kiva English, Cato-Meridian Elementary, Cato, NY

End That Sentence!
Editing punctuation

Students will be reminded to add end marks to their sentences when a punctuation checker is around! Attach ribbons to a marker and give it to a child designated as the punctuation checker. During predetermined times of the day, such as morning message and writer's workshop, instruct him to look for the appropriate punctuation and edit as needed. After he performs his task, invite him to make a smiley face by the writing to show he has checked the work. In a short time, students are sure to remember to add end marks!

Alicia K. Shaffer

Story Element Cards

Use with "Tall Tales" on page 234.

Characters	**Setting**	**Problem**
TEC42053	TEC42053	TEC42053

● frogs	● crocodiles
TEC42053	TEC42053
● monkeys	● dogs
TEC42053	TEC42053
● teachers	● children
TEC42053	TEC42053
■ forest	■ pond
TEC42053	TEC42053
■ classroom	■ playground
TEC42053	TEC42053
■ airport	■ house
TEC42053	TEC42053
▲ The characters are lost.	▲ A character gets in a hot-air balloon, and the balloon takes off.
TEC42053	TEC42053
▲ A character falls into a hidden cave.	▲ The characters smell something burning.
TEC42053	TEC42053
▲ A character hears someone yell for help.	▲ The characters see a spacecraft land a few feet away.
TEC42053	TEC42053

Spotting
High-Frequency Words

This springtime collection of ideas can be used with any high-frequency word list.

Ladybugs in a Line

Introducing words

These little ladybugs call attention to the first letter in a word. Write letters on individual ladybug cards (see page 239) and post them in alphabetical order. Write different high-frequency words on individual flower cutouts (pattern on page 239). To begin, show a flower to the group and read the word aloud. Have students repeat and spell the word. Then invite a child to "fly" to the flower and put it by the ladybug with the matching first letter. Continue with each remaining flower. **For an independent follow-up**, put the flowers and matching letter ladybugs (provide multiple copies of a letter as needed) at a center for youngsters to read, spell, and write each high-frequency word. 💻

Jennifer Frankle, M.C. Riley Early Childhood Center, Bluffton, SC

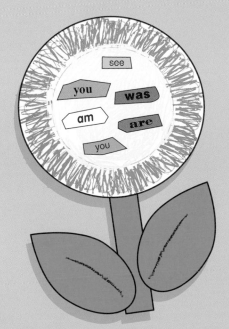

Garden of Words

Matching words

What do flower blossoms and reading words have in common? Check it out with these student-made flowers! Have each child color a paper plate to resemble a flower blossom with a large center. Review with youngsters a list of high-frequency words. Then instruct each youngster to refer to the list and cut out matching words from magazines and catalogs. Have her glue each word to the flower blossom. When finished, display the completed crafts with stem and leaf details to feature a flower garden worthy of reading.

Lisa Callis
Mary Munford Elementary
Richmond, VA

Lucky Ladybugs!

Recognizing words

Students hunt for words during this small-group game. On a sheet of paper, write different high-frequency words in separate circles and make a copy for each student. Write the matching words on individual cards. To begin, read a word card and have the first player find the matching word on his paper. If he is correct, show the word card to the group as the first player draws ladybug details around the word. If the player is not correct, his turn is over and the next player seeks the same word on her paper. Continue reading words, reusing the cards as needed. The first player to turn all her circles into ladybugs exclaims, "Lucky ladybugs!" 🖥

Marie E. Cecchini
West Dundee, IL

Three Flowers in a Row!

Reading words

To prepare this partner center, tape string on the floor to make a large tic-tac-toe grid. Then tape a different high-frequency word card in each space. Set out two different-color sets of five flowers (pattern on page 239). To play, a child reads a word to claim a space on the board. Partners continue to read words, playing the game as traditional tic-tac-toe, until one player gets three in a row or the game ends in a tie. 🖥

Jennifer Frankle, M.C. Riley Early Childhood Center, Bluffton, SC

Flower Fun

Reading words

For this group game, post a paper circle (flower center) for each team. On individual paper ovals (petals), write different two-, three-, and four-letter words. Then cover the 1, 5, and 6 on a number cube with 2, 3, and 4. To take a turn, the first team has a player roll the die, find a word with the same number of letters, and read it aloud. If she is correct, she puts the petal by her team's flower. Play continues until one team has earned a predetermined number of petals. 🖥

Jennifer Frankle

Flower Pattern

Use with "April Showers Bring May Flowers" on page 186, "Ladybugs in a Line" on page 237, and "Three Flowers in a Row!" on page 238.

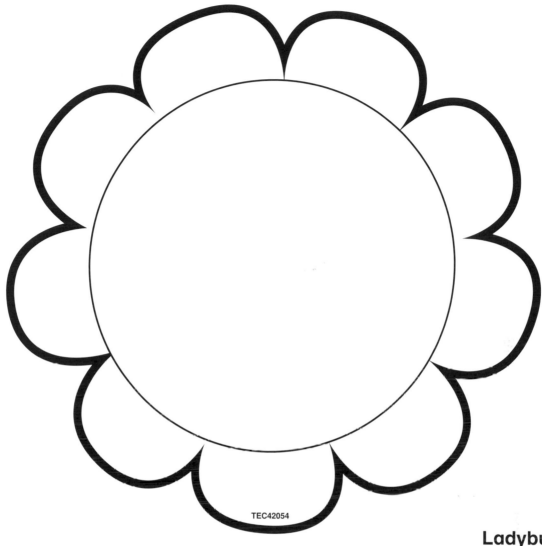

TEC42054

Ladybug Cards

Use with "Ladybugs in a Line" on page 237.

TEC42054

TEC42054

Name _____

Mixed-Up Tulips

Unscramble the letters.
Write the word.
Color the matching 🐞.

reeh

evah

eefl

kiel

aws

het

uyo

ese

have

feel

like

here

you

the

was

see

Bonus: Write the words in **ABC** order.

Letter Fun for Everyone!

Students are sure to have a grand time reviewing letter knowledge with these big top ideas!

A "Letter-Ring" Circus

Sorting objects by **beginning letters** is the highlight of this circus center. For each letter you would like to feature, loop a length of yarn to form a circle (circus ring). Then put a letter card in each ring. Set out objects (or pictures of objects) whose names begin with the featured letters. A youngster sorts the objects in their matching rings. Then she chooses one ring, writes its letter on a sheet of paper, and draws pictures of its objects. If desired, set up a different "letter-ring" circus for students to sort objects by **ending letters**.

Andrea Singleton
Waynesville Elementary
Waynesville OH

Clowning Around

Here's a **letter-sound association** activity that is sure to be a hit! Seat students in a circle and spread out letter cards facedown in the center of the circle. To begin, a child (clown) walks, skips, or takes baby steps around the circle as you lead the group in singing the song shown. When the last word is sung, the clown stops and gently taps the nearest child. That child takes a card, names the letter, and makes the sound associated with the letter. Next, encourage youngsters to name words that include the letter. Then have students switch places for another round. 🖥

(sung to the tune of "The Mulberry Bush")

The circus clown goes round and round,
Round and round, round and round.
The circus clown goes round and round
Until we say, "Stop!"

adapted from an idea by Jennifer Frankle
M. C. Riley Early Childhood Center
Bluffton, SC

Roll the Hoop!

Your little performers match **uppercase and lowercase letters** for this partner center. Write an uppercase letter on a piece of masking tape and tape it on a plastic hoop. Continue with several more uppercase letters. Then write the matching lowercase letters on individual cards. Place the cards in a pocket chart and put the hoop nearby. Partners take turns rolling the hoop to each other. When a child catches the hoop, he names the letter closest to his thumb and points to the matching lowercase letter. Then he rolls the hoop to his partner for her to take a turn. **For a more advanced version,** label the cards with words that begin with the letters on the hoop. The child who catches the hoop finds and reads a word that begins with the letter closest to his thumb.

adapted from an idea by Jennifer Frankle
M. C. Riley Early Childhood Center
Bluffton, SC

Editor's Tip:
For a seated version of the activity, replace the hoop with a ball.

Jazzy Jugglers!

For this class act, students review **letter formation** each time a beanbag drops! Invite a child to juggle two beanbags (or toss and catch one beanbag). As she juggles, lead the group in singing letters of the alphabet until one beanbag falls to the floor. Then, on a sheet of writing paper, each youngster uses her best handwriting to write the last letter sung. If the juggler can juggle all the way to *Z,* have the group say, "Jazzy juggler!" and no letter is written for that round. Continue singing, beginning with the last letter students wrote on their papers. **To extend the activity to include letter-sound associations,** instruct each child to draw an object next to each letter whose name begins with the letter.

Jennifer Frankle

A, B, C, D, ...

At the Big Top

Review a **variety of letter skills** with this listen-and-do activity. Give each child a copy of page 243. Then have her use crayons and a pencil to complete the page as you read the directions aloud.

Jennifer Frankle

See page 244 for a **practice page** on final consonants.

Name _____

The Circus Tent

Listen and do.

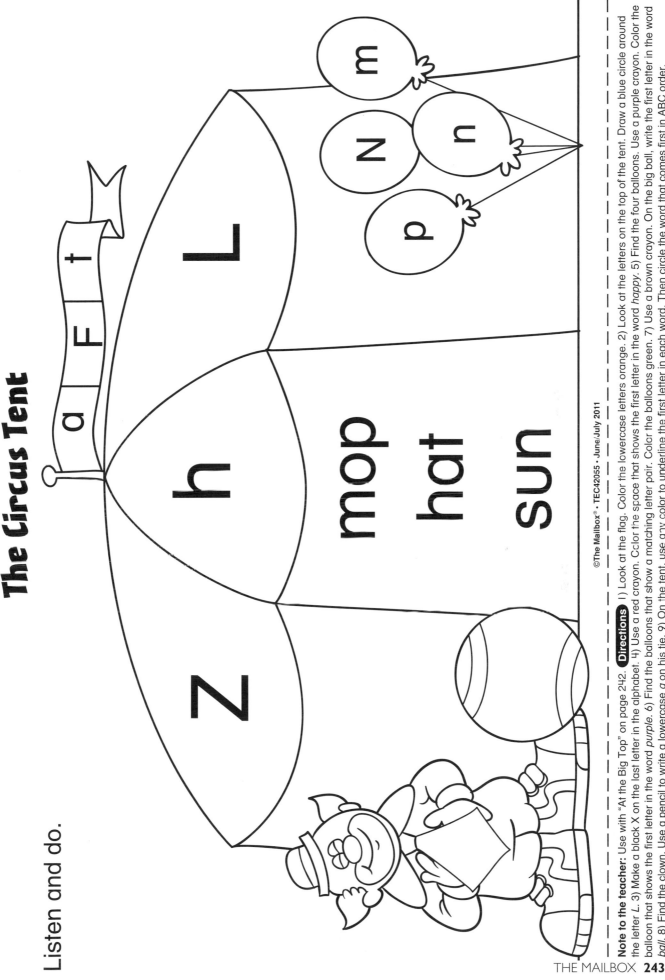

Note to the teacher: Use with "At the Big Top" on page 242. **Directions** 1) Look at the flag. Color the lowercase letters orange. 2) Look at the letters on the top of the tent. Draw a blue circle around the letter *L*. 3) Make a black X on the last letter in the alphabet. 4) Use a red crayon. Color the space that shows the first letter in the word *happy*. 5) Find the four balloons. Use a purple crayon. Color the balloon that shows the first letter in the word *purple*. 6) Find the balloons that show a matching letter pair. Color the balloons green. 7) Use a brown crayon. On the big ball, write the first letter in the word *ball*. 8) Find the clown. Use a pencil to write a lowercase *a* on his tie. 9) On the tent, use any color to underline the first letter in each word. Then circle the word that comes first in ABC order.

Plenty of Popcorn!

✏️ Write the ending letter for each word.

🖍️ Color the matching letter on a 🍿.

Bonus: Circle the word that has the same beginning and ending sound.

peanut ___

balloo ___

jum ___

elephan ___

clow ___

ba ___

ten ___

gu ___

foo ___

cra ___

   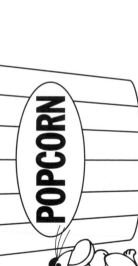 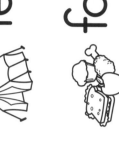

POPCORN

m n t n
t b g s d p

LITERATURE UNITS

If You Take a Mouse to School

Written by Laura Numeroff
Illustrated by Felicia Bond

"If you take a mouse to school, he'll ask you for your lunchbox." Thus begins an energetic romp that takes a mouse and his boy companion through a fun-filled school day. At the end of the day, the mouse realizes that he's left the lunchbox behind. That's when this adorable tale comes full circle in a supremely satisfying conclusion.

Mouse's School Day
Making predictions

Before a read-aloud of this engaging story, show students the book cover. Then ask youngsters what they believe Mouse will do when he is at school. Write students' ideas on a sheet of chart paper, making connections between Mouse's possible school activities and activities that your kindergartners experience. Next, read the story aloud and encourage students to revisit their predictions.

Kathy Ginn, Miami Trace Elementary, Washington Court House, OH

> Mouse will...
> eat lunch
> play with blocks
> read a book
> play outside
> make friends
> draw
> listen to things

Cookie Questions
Comprehension

Mouse stuffs several cookies into the boy's lunchbox so he will have a snack at school. So it's only fitting that these thoughtful story questions are provided on cookie cutouts! Cut apart a copy of the cards on page 247 and place them in a lunchbox. Seat students in a circle and have them sing a simple song as they pass the lunchbox. When the song is finished, have the child holding the lunchbox remove a cookie. Read the question aloud and encourage students to provide the answer. Continue until each cookie has been pulled.

Kathy Ginn

Who are the characters in the story?

Do you think pets should be allowed in school? Why or why not?

A Splendid Setting
Identifying the story setting

Help students understand that the setting of a story is where the story takes place. Then encourage each youngster to draw the setting of this story on a sheet of paper. When she is finished, have her add a mouse by making a gray thumbprint and fingerprints on the paper in the arrangement shown. Then help her add mouse details to the prints.

Tracy Shaner, The King's Academy, Woodstock, GA

If you took a mouse to school, what do you think would happen?

TEC42050

Who are the characters in the story?

TEC42050

Do you think this is a real story or a pretend story? Why?

TEC42050

What does Mouse forget when he leaves school?

TEC42050

What does Mouse need after his science experiment?

TEC42050

Do you think pets should be allowed in school? Why or why not?

TEC42050

Mouse packs chocolate chip cookies in the lunchbox. What is your favorite type of cookie?

TEC42050

How would you convince Mouse to stay home instead of going to school?

TEC42050

What is your favorite part of the story?

TEC42050

Leaf Man

by Lois Ehlert

Leaf Man floats in the wind past ducks, pumpkins, orchards, and rivers. Where will he end up next? No one knows!

Where Is Leaf Man?
Positional words

During this class activity, a Leaf Man look-alike builds youngsters' positional vocabulary. Assemble leaf cutouts (or real leaves) so they resemble a leaf man. While students make noises that mimic the sounds of whooshing wind, gracefully move the prop around the room. Each time you signal students to sit quietly, guide the prop to a temporary resting point. Ask, "Where is Leaf Man now?" A volunteer answers the question using a positional word phrase, such as *on the desk, under the table,* or *beside the trash bin.* 💻

adapted from an idea by Robyn Pryor, Prestonwood Christian Academy, Plano, TX

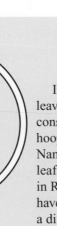

A   B

Looking at Leaves
Sorting by attribute

In advance, ask each child to bring a real leaf to school. If real leaves are not available, have each child tear a leaf shape from construction paper. To begin, have students gather around two hoops (or yarn rings) with their leaves. Label the rings "A" and "B." Name an attribute, such as a color, a size, or a kind. If a student's leaf has the attribute, he puts it in Ring A. If it does not, he puts it in Ring B. Invite students to talk about the results of the sort. Then have the youngsters remove their leaves so they can re-sort them by a different attribute.

Robyn Pryor

In the Wind
Contributing to a class story

A new adventure for Leaf Man is about to unfold! Copy the title and rebus story starter on chart paper. Invite students to tell places where Leaf Man travels. Write each child's idea on the paper, adding pictures as possible for later reading. Continue adding to the story until Leaf Man's adventure is complete.

In the 🌬️

The 🌬️ blew 🍃 away. The last time I saw 🍃...

He was floating over a 〰️. He said hello to the 🐟. *Abby*

He blew over a ⛰️. He got stuck, and then he got loose. *Isaac*

Duck at the Door

By Jackie Urbanovic
One snowy night, Irene and her pets open the door to find one very chilly duck! Max the duck makes himself at home, learning to cook, using the remote control, and annoying Irene's other animals. But when Max finally leaves, he is sorely missed.

Who's at the Door?

Writing a story innovation

Max is the surprise visitor in this story, but your youngsters are sure to come up with other interesting guests! Program a door pattern as shown and make a class supply. Have each student cut out a copy of the door and glue its left edge to a sheet of paper to make a flap. When the glue is dry, have her fold back the door and draw a picture of a different guest in the doorway. Beneath the picture, encourage her to write about the guest and what Irene and her animals do when they open the door. 💻

Who could be knocking at the door?

It is a pig! The pig is smelly. It has to stay outside.

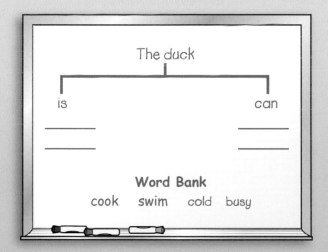

The duck

is   can

_____

_____

Word Bank

cook   swim   cold   busy

Ducky Information

Writing sentences

On the board, draw the graphic organizer and write the words shown. Help youngsters read the words in the bank and write them in the appropriate blanks. Next, encourage students to make a sentence from the organizer, such as "The duck can cook." Write the sentence on the board. Then have students stand and pantomime the sentence. Continue with each remaining sentence. 💻

Angie Kutzer
Garrett Elementary
Mebane, NC

Does It Migrate?

Investigating animal behavior

Help youngsters identify other migrating creatures with this activity! Cut out a copy of the cards on page 250 and put them in a bag. Place the headings shown in a pocket chart. Have a child take a card from the bag and identify the animal. Help the youngsters decide whether the animal migrates (see the chart for answers) and place the card in the chart. If the animal does migrate, prompt students to stand and quickly "migrate" to a designated point in the room and then back to their seats. Continue with each card. 💻

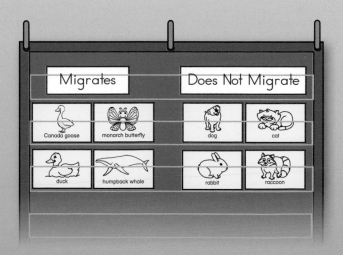

Migrates		Does Not Migrate	
Canada goose	monarch butterfly	dog	cat
duck	humpback whale	rabbit	raccoon

Picture Cards

Use with "Does It Migrate?" on page 249.

Canada goose

TEC42052

dog

TEC42052

cat

TEC42052

monarch butterfly

TEC42052

rabbit

TEC42052

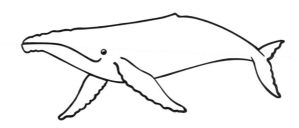

humpback whale

TEC42052

duck

TEC42052

raccoon

TEC42052

McDuff Moves In

Written by Rosemary Wells
Illustrated by Susan Jeffers

When a little white dog escapes from a dogcatcher's truck, he looks for a house where he can find something to eat and a warm place to sleep. He finds the home of Fred and Lucy, who decide to name him "McDuff" after a biscuit brand name!

ideas contributed by Lynn Wagoner, Greensboro, NC

So Many Feelings!

Drawing conclusions

McDuff feels many different emotions during his adventure! In advance, draw a happy face, a sad face, and a scared face on your board. Name one of the events from the book (see the suggestions given). Have a child point to the appropriate face with a pointer to identify the pup's emotion during that event. Then prompt youngsters to chime in with happy dog barks or with sad or frightened whines to match the emotion. Continue with each remaining suggestion, calling on a different youngster each time.

Suggestions:

McDuff doesn't know where he is.
The cat says, "Hiss."
The owls hoot.
It starts to rain.

Lucy asks McDuff to come in.
Lucy feeds McDuff.
Fred says, "We can't keep him."
McDuff gets a name.

From Truck to Home

Retelling story events in sequence

Give each child a long paper strip and a blank card. On the card, have him draw a picture of McDuff. On the strip, direct him to draw and label the dogcatcher's truck on the left and Lucy and Fred's house on the right (leaving the center of the strip blank). After rereading the story, ask each child to draw and label story events, in order, on the strip. Then invite each youngster to move McDuff down the strip as he retells the story.

truck   tulips   cat   owl   rain   house

Story Biscuits

Writing

How can youngsters make connections with the story? Try these no-calorie story biscuits! Cut out a class supply of the story biscuits on page 252 and place them in a tin (or box). Cut out a copy of the tin label on page 252 and attach it to the tin. Have each child choose a story biscuit and glue it to her writing paper. Then help her complete the prompt or answer the question. Have students illustrate their work.

If I found a dog... I would not let him in. My cat would not like him.

McDuff's Story Biscuits

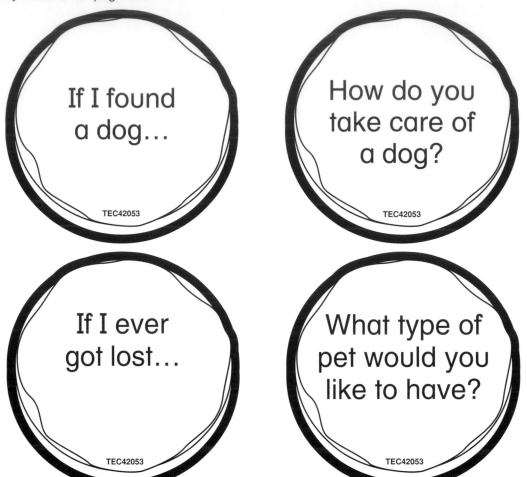

If I found a dog…

TEC42053

How do you take care of a dog?

TEC42053

If I ever got lost…

TEC42053

What type of pet would you like to have?

TEC42053

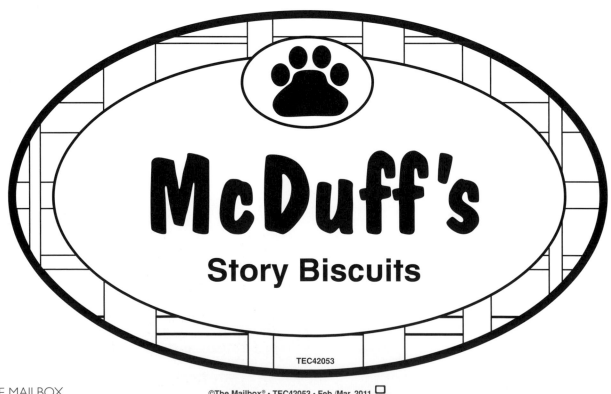

McDuff's
Story Biscuits

TEC42053

Froggy Plays T-ball

Written by Jonathan London
Illustrated by Frank Remkiewicz

Froggy's very excited about his first T-ball game, but the game doesn't go as smoothly as planned! Froggy has a tough time hitting the ball and misunderstands his job in the outfield. Fortunately, Froggy has a spectacular home run at the end of the game. Now that deserves a reward of a hot dog with fly relish!

ideas contributed by Lynn Wagoner, Greensboro, NC

On a Roll
Retelling a story

Youngsters retell the story with the aid of a ball similar to the one Froggy hits! Seat students in a circle and say, "Froggy has a dream that he is playing T-ball." Roll a softball (or a similar ball) to a student and encourage her to name the next event in the story, using the book as an aid if needed. Next, prompt her to roll the ball to a classmate to name the next story event. Continue until the end of the story.

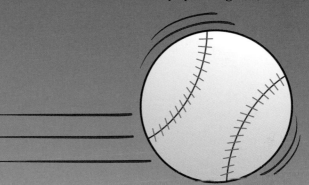

Flop, Whack, Zap!
Listening responsively

Explain that there are many words in the story that sound like sounds, such as *zap*, *zwish*, and *bonk*. Reread the story, prompting students to raise their hands when they hear one of these special words. Pause briefly and write the word on the board. Encourage youngsters to say the word using great dramatic flair. Then continue reading. If desired, sprinkle other examples of onomatopoeia throughout your day, such as saying "skritch, skritch" as students write or "blam, blam, blam" when a visitor knocks on the classroom door.

Fabulous Flies
Writing

Ask students if they notice anything unusual about the foods that Froggy eats, prompting them to notice that the foods involve flies! Surely your youngsters can come up with some appetizing fly recipes that Froggy is sure to enjoy! Give each child a copy of page 254. Encourage her to write a tasty recipe that uses flies as an ingredient. Then have her illustrate her work. 🖥

Name Anna

Mmmm, Flies!

This is fly macaroni and cheese. It has lots of flies and cheese. It needs lots of salt.

Mmmm, Flies!

_____

_____

_____

_____

Note to the teacher: Use with "Fabulous Flies" on page 253.

Down by the Bay

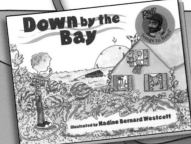

Written by Raffi
Illustrated by Nadine Bernard Westcott
Two children take turns singing verses of this traditional song until they run out of rhyming phrases!

ideas contributed by Barbara Mason Worobey, Deposit Elementary, Deposit, NY

Does It Rhyme?
Recognizing rhyming pairs

At the end of the story, the little girl attempts to make a rhyme but does not succeed. Try this whole-group activity to help little ones recognize successful rhymes! Label simple watermelon cutouts with word pairs, most of which rhyme. Scatter the watermelons on your floor and set out containers labeled as shown. Direct a child to "pick" a watermelon and help her read the words aloud. Encourage each student to give a signal, such as a thumbs-up or a thumbs-down, to show whether the words rhyme. Then have her place the watermelon in the appropriate container. Continue for each remaining watermelon. **To generate rhymes,** read the words on the watermelons from the "Do Not Rhyme" box and have youngsters name words that make successful rhymes. 💻

Rhyme

Do Not Rhyme

pin
fin

fan
fit

ham
jam

dog
log

That's Nonsense!
Changing initial phonemes

You're sure to hear oodles of giggles with this rereading of the story! Turn to the page that shows the goose. Have students say the word *goose*. Then tell them to change the /g/ to /t/ and say the resulting nonsense word. Write the new word on a sticky note and attach it to the page. Continue with other words in the story—such as *whale*, *fly*, *bear*, and *llamas*—having students create other nonsense words. Finally, read the story aloud, inserting the new word options!

New Sights
Creating rhymes, writing

Your young authors create new rhymes for this class book! Write several animal names on chart paper as shown. Encourage students to create new verses for *Down by the Bay*, using the animals provided. Write each verse on the chart paper. Next, prompt each child to draw a picture to match one of the new verses. Help him write the verse on his page. Then bind the completed pages together and place the book at your reading center. 💻

cat—Did you ever see a cat wearing a hat?
goat—Did you ever see a goat eating a coat?
frog—Did you ever see a frog dancing on a log?
pig—Did you ever see a pig wearing a wig?
dog—Did you ever see a dog si
fox—Did you ever see a fox h
duck—Did you ever see a duck
mouse—Did you ever see a mo

Did you ever see a frog dancing on a log?

Wonderful Watermelon

✂ Cut.

🍶 Glue the pictures in order.

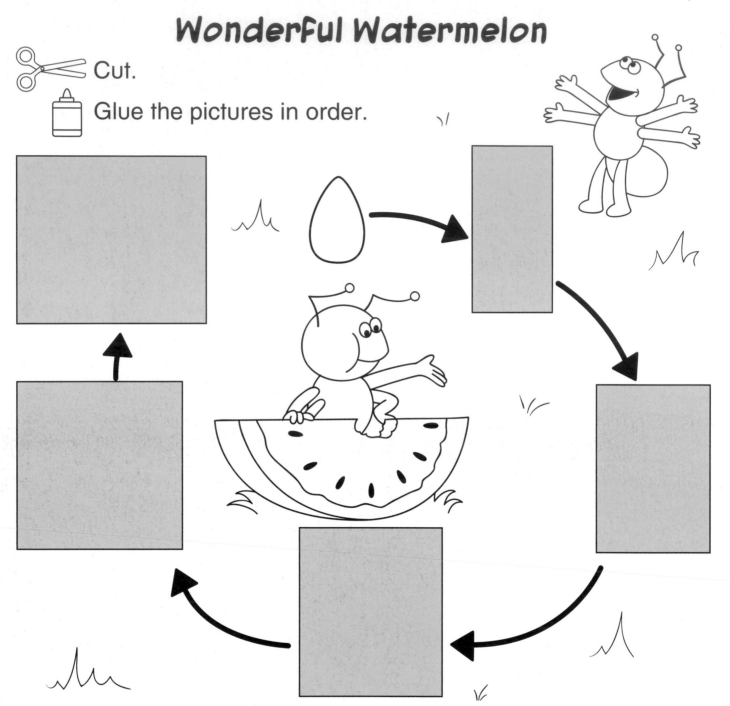

Bonus: Write to tell about how a watermelon grows.

MATH UNITS

Nutty About Numbers

Incorporate the fall season with this collection of number-sense ideas that are just right for your kindergartners!

ideas contributed by Gerri Primak, Charlotte, NC

Treetop Treats
Counting sets

For this group-time activity, cut out a copy of the acorn cards on page 260. Draw the outline of a large tree on the board. Place the acorn cards and Sticky-Tac adhesive nearby. To begin, attach some acorns to the tree and invite youngsters to count them. Then lead students in reciting the rhyme shown, inserting the number of acorns where indicated. While saying the third line of the rhyme, pretend to be a squirrel and remove some acorns from the tree. Then guide youngsters in counting the remaining acorns. To play again, place a different number of acorns on the tree. 💻

[Number] little acorns
In a tree.
Along comes a squirrel—
Now how many do you see?

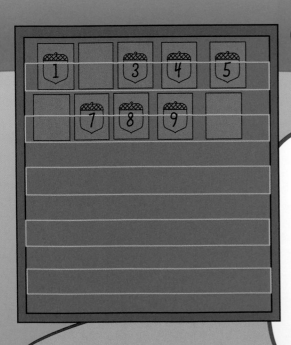

Squirrel Says
Writing numbers

Youngsters follow Squirrel's directions in this small-group game. To prepare, number a copy of the acorn cards on page 260 from 1 to 10 and place them in order in a pocket chart. To begin, give each student a whiteboard and marker. Then say a command such as "Squirrel says, 'Write the number five.'" Using the acorns as a reference, have each child write the announced number on his board. After checking students' work, turn over the matching number card and have youngsters wipe off their boards. Then continue for each remaining number. 💻

Collecting Nuts
Ordering numbers through ten

To prepare this center, cut out a copy of the acorn cards on page 260 and number them from 1 to 10. Also glue a copy of a squirrel card on page 260 to a craft stick. Place the resulting squirrel puppet at a center along with the acorn cards. A child puts the acorns in order and then "walks" the squirrel by each acorn while practicing counting. 🖥

One, two, ...

So Many Squirrels
Matching numbers to sets

Youngsters are sure to go nutty for this version of lotto! To prepare, stack ten squirrel cards (cards on page 260) facedown in a pocket chart. Give each child ten game markers and an uncut copy of the acorn cards on page 260 to use as a lotto board. Instruct each youngster to write a different number from 1 to 10 in each acorn. To play, flip a desired number of squirrel cards. Lead the group in counting the squirrels. Then have each child cover the matching space on his board. When a child has five spaces covered in a row, he announces, "Nutty numbers!" Continue until each number has been covered. 🖥

Acorns Aplenty
Comparing sets

Place at a center a set of number cards from 1 to 10, a brown washable ink pad, paper strips, and brown markers. A child takes two cards and copies the numbers on a paper strip as shown. Next, she makes a corresponding number of fingerprints next to each number and uses a marker to add acorn details to each print. Then she circles the set of acorns with more. 🖥

Acorn Cards

Use with "Treetop Treats" and "Squirrel Says" on page 258 and "Collecting Nuts" and "So Many Squirrels" on page 259.

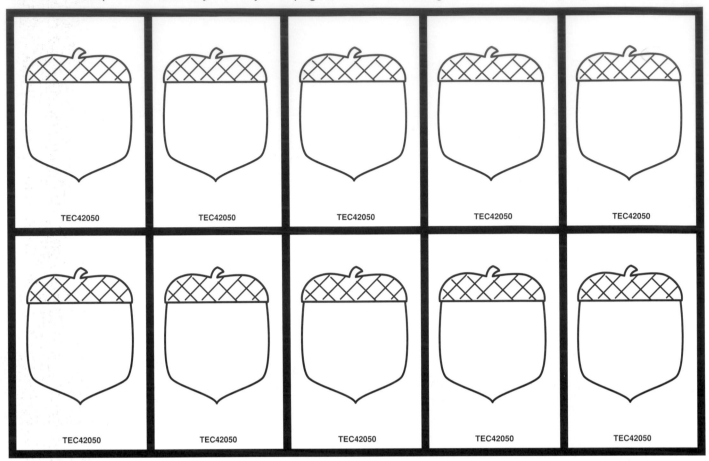

Squirrel Cards

Use with "Collecting Nuts" and "So Many Squirrels" on page 259.

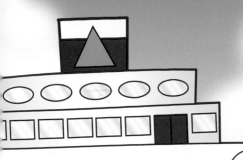

"Ship-Shape" Math

Watch your little sailors cruise through shape experiences with these nautical ideas.

ideas contributed by Jennie Jensen, North Cedar Elementary, Lowden, IA

Out at Sea

Identifying shapes

To prepare for this whole-group activity, choose one card set from page 263. Make enough copies to have one card per child plus one complete set. Color the complete set and then cut out all the cards.

Begin by seating students in a circle. Stack the set of colored shapes facedown inside the circle and give each child one of the remaining cards. Invite a volunteer to stand inside the circle and play the role of the sailor. Lead the group in chanting the rhyme. Then ask the sailor to take a card from the stack, show the card to his classmates, and name its shape. Each child who has a matching shape holds up her card. Repeat the activity with different sailors until each shape is named at least one time. 💻

> A happy sailor went to sea
> To find a shape for you and me.
> [He/She] looked high and [he/she] looked low
> To find a shape that we all know!

A 3-D Shipment

A box (shipment) of blocks, balls, and cones are all you need to review these skills!

Sorting: Have students unload the shipment and sort its contents by shape.

Patterning: Have students use the objects to make *AB* or *ABC* patterns. If desired, have youngsters copy and extend the patterns on paper.

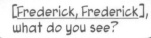

Speech bubble: [Frederick, Frederick], what do you see?

Speech bubble: I see a [rectangle] looking at me!

On the Lookout

Recognizing shapes in the environment

How does a crafty telescope support math skills? It's the perfect tool to search for shapes! To make a telescope, glue construction paper to cover a cardboard tube. Have a child look through the telescope to find a shape-related object while you lead youngsters in chanting the first line of this familiar rhyme. The child with the telescope names the shape he sees as he recites the second line of the rhyme. Then challenge your little sailor-sleuths to determine what object he sees. Continue with more rounds as time permits.

Find That Shape!

Choose a set of cards from page 263. Then follow the directions below to review shapes with one or both of these game ideas! 🖥

Lotto: Cut out a copy of the cards to make caller's cards. Also give each child a copy of the card set and a copy of page 264. Have her cut out the cards and glue each card to a randomly chosen board space. Then lead students to play the game like traditional lotto.

Three in a Row: For this two-player game, make two copies of the card set and one copy of page 264. Cut apart the cards and glue a different card to each board space. Stack the remaining cards facedown. Set out game markers in two colors. To take a turn, a player takes a card, names the shape, and puts his color of game marker on the matching board space. Play continues until one player marks three shapes in a vertical, horizontal, or diagonal row or until the board is covered.

A Colorful Fleet

Creating patterns

To make these shapely ships, give each child three paper shapes: a trapezoid (ship's main body), a rectangle, and a square. Also set out two colors of paper circles sized so six or eight fit on the paper rectangle. A youngster uses the circles to make an *AB* color pattern on his rectangle. Then he glues the circles in place, glues his three shapes together to make a ship like the one shown, and adds desired crayon details. Post the ships with the title "A Fleet of Fine Patterns!" 🖥

Editor's Tip: Use two colors of sticky dots for the patterning activity.

set 1

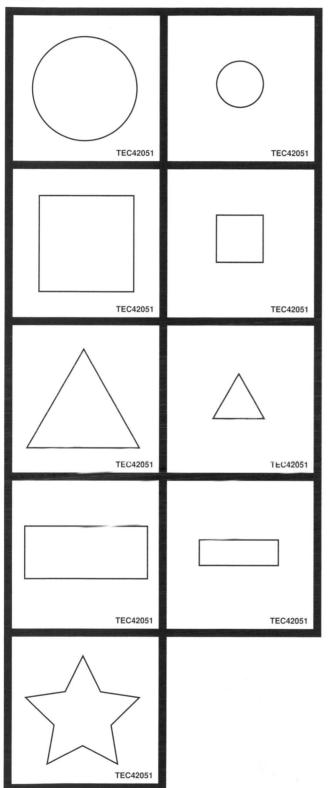

set 2

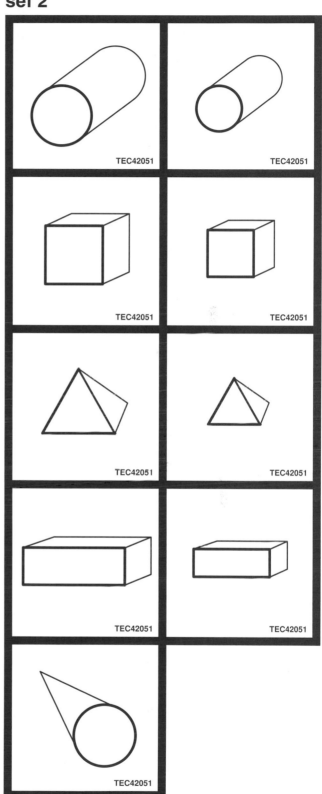

Toot, Toot!

SS Math

Note to the teacher: Use with "Find That Shape!" on page 262.

Diving Into Money Skills

From naming coins to counting money, you and your students can dive right into this stash of ideas!

In the Bank

Naming coins and their values

This call-and-response chant is sure to be valuable when introducing coins. Post a large piggy bank cutout and place enlarged coin cutouts nearby. To begin, attach a penny to the piggy bank. Then lead youngsters in the chant shown. Repeat the chant using other coins. 🖥

Teacher: Do you see the [penny] on our piggy bank?
Students: Yes, we see the [penny] on our piggy bank.
Teacher: It's worth…
Students: [One cent!]
Teacher: How much?
Students: [One cent!]

Shelley Scoggins, Bethesda United Methodist Preschool, Lawrenceville, GA

This is a quarter.

It's worth twenty-five cents.

Find a Partner

Identifying coins and their values

Here's a whole-group game that gets students up and moving! Put enough pairs of imitation coins in a small bag so that there is one coin for each child. (Plan to participate if you have an odd number of students.) Invite each child to take a coin from the bag. On your signal, have each youngster find and hook arms with another student who has the same coin. Once students are paired, ask each twosome, in turn, to name its coin and its value. **For a more advanced version,** have students match imitation coins and cards programmed with the matching values.

Janet Dobbins
Stolley Park Elementary
Grand Island, NE

Lots of Links

Comparing coin values

To prepare this "cent-sational" center, laminate large coin cutouts and punch a hole near the bottom of each coin. Place the coins and a supply of plastic links at a center. A child attaches to each coin the number of plastic links equal to the coin's value. Then she compares the lengths of the chains and orders the coins from the smallest value to the largest value. 🖥

Jodi Darter, Cabool Elementary, Cabool, MO

Take a Step

Identifying coins and their values

This partner activity is right on the money! Begin by attaching masking tape start and finish lines to the floor, several feet apart. Then give each twosome a small bag containing several imitation pennies, nickels, and dimes. One child holds the bag and stands at the finish line. Her partner stands behind the starting line. The child holding the bag removes a coin and names it. The other child names the coin's value and takes the matching number of steps toward the finish line. The pair continues in this manner until both students are at the finish line. Then the partners switch roles and play again.

Allison Pratt
Onalaska Kindergarten Center
Onalaska, WI

Coin Grab

Counting money

Provide a wealth of coin counting practice with this independent or small-group activity. For each child, place in a resealable plastic bag nine pennies and either a nickel or a dime. Give each child a bag and a copy of either the star border recording sheet on page 267 (if using a nickel) or the square border recording sheet (if using a dime). Have each student grab some coins from her bag. Then direct her to sort the coins and record, on the first section of her paper, the number of each coin. Next, assist each youngster in counting the total value of her coin set; then ask her to write it on her paper. After checking her work, direct her to return the coins to the bag and continue until the recording sheet is complete. 🖥

Jennifer Hafer
Camp Lejeune, NC

Name _____ Recording sheet

☆ ☆ ☆ ☆ ☆ ☆ ☆ **Coin Grab** ☆ ☆ ☆ ☆ ☆ ☆ ☆

Number of nickels   **Number of pennies**

A. _____   _____   total _____¢

B. _____   _____   total _____¢

C. _____   _____   total _____¢

D. _____   _____   total _____¢

©The Mailbox® • TEC42052 • Dec./Jan. 2010–11

- -

Name _____ Recording sheet

 Coin Grab

Number of dimes   **Number of pennies**

A. _____   _____   total _____¢

B. _____   _____   total _____¢

C. _____   _____   total _____¢

D. _____   _____   total _____¢

©The Mailbox® • TEC42052 • Dec./Jan. 2010–11

Note to the teacher: Use with "Coin Grab" on page 266.

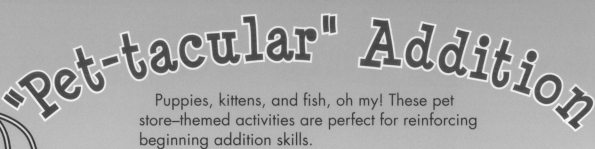

"Pet-tacular" Addition

Puppies, kittens, and fish, oh my! These pet store–themed activities are perfect for reinforcing beginning addition skills.

ideas by Ada Goren
Winston-Salem, NC

At the Pet Store

Solving picture problems

You can count on these pets to provide practice with the concept of addition! Cut out several copies of the pet cards on page 270. Then draw a rectangle on the board and label it as shown. To begin, tape a desired number of each of two different kinds of pet cards to the board. Then lead youngsters in the rhyme shown, inserting the names and numbers of the displayed pets. Direct the class in counting the pets to find the sum. Repeat the activity with different card groupings. 💻

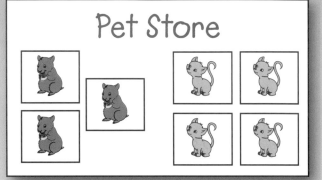

Pet Store

Look inside the pet store.
There are pets, big and small.
[Three hamsters] and [four cats]—
How many pets are there in all?

Doggy Treats

Adding using manipulatives

Students serve up dog bones at this "paws-itively" fun center. To prepare, program cards with different addition problems. Place at a center the cards, a dog bowl cutout, dog bone cutouts, and paper. A child places a card on the dog bowl and uses the bones to solve the problem. Then she writes the problem and sum on a sheet of paper. She repeats the activity with each remaining card. **For added fun,** place a stuffed dog and a plastic dog bowl at the center. Have students place the bone cutouts in the bowl. 💻

Casey
5 + 5 = 10

5 + 5 =

Noisy Pets
Solving addition sentences

Oh no! Tell your students that some pets have gotten loose, and it's up to them to determine how many animals are missing. Make a pet sound a desired number of times as students count the sounds aloud. Write the number on the board. Repeat with a different pet sound. Then enlist students' help in solving the corresponding addition sentence. If desired, invite student volunteers to make the animal sounds.

Meow, meow!

$2 + 2 = 4$

Squawk, squawk!

9

9
2 and 7
4 and 5

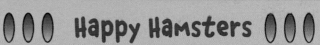

Happy Hamsters
Modeling addition combinations

With this center, students determine different ways to make one sum. Label ten paper circles (hamster wheels) with a different number from 1 to 10. Place at a center the wheels, paper, and ten brown and ten black pom-poms (hamsters). A youngster takes a wheel and labels a sheet of paper with the featured number. Then she places hamsters of each color on the wheel to make the number. After writing the combination on her paper, she repeats the activity with the same wheel, using a different combination of hamsters. **For an easier version,** draw circles on each wheel to match the number.

A Full Tank
Writing addition sentences

Display several of these fish tanks to showcase math facts. To make a fish tank, a child draws a waterline across the top of a sheet of paper. Then he rolls two number cubes. He uses the numbers rolled to write an addition problem above the waterline. Next, he makes two different-colored sets of fingerprints to illustrate the number sentence and uses a fine-tip marker to add fish features. Finally, he counts the fish and writes the sum.

$3 + 5 = 8$

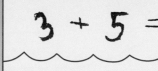

Pet Cards

Use with "At the Pet Store" on page 268.

TEC42053

TEC42053

TEC42053

TEC42053

TEC42053

TEC42053

©The Mailbox® • TEC42053 • Feb./Mar. 2011

Build the Hives

Small group

These honeycomb hives are sure to keep your worker bees buzzing! Cut out a copy of the honeycomb patterns and bee cards on page 274. Write a different number (difference) on each honeycomb (hive starter). Write subtraction problems that correspond with the differences on additional honeycomb shapes. To build three honeycomb hives, group members use the bee cards, as needed, to solve problems and put each honeycomb by its matching hive starter. Then encourage youngsters to buzz like bees as you confirm each hive's accuracy. 🖳

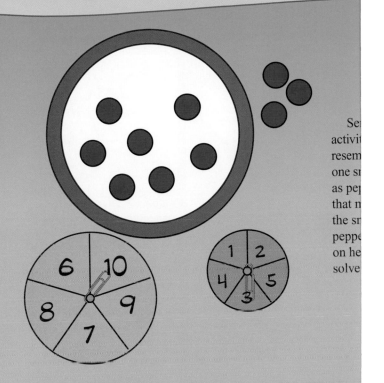

Fun With Fish!

Whole group

What do fish, water, and dice have in common? Subtraction! Have each child trim the top of a sheet of blue paper to resemble wavy water. Then give her 12 fish-shaped crackers. Invite a youngster to roll a pair of jumbo dice and have each student put the matching number of fish on her water. Then have a child roll one die to find out how many fish swam away. Guide youngsters to move the matching number of fish and solve the problem. Continue as time permits. **For added fun**, lead youngsters to solve a final problem, 12 minus 12 equals zero, by eating their fish. Yum!

See page 275 for a subtraction **practice page**.

More Seeds, Please!

Add. Use the counters to help you.

🖍 Color the 🪶 by the code.

$3 + 3 =$ _____

$6 + 1 =$ _____

$4 + 4 =$ _____

$2 + 3 =$ _____

$6 + 2 =$ _____

$2 + 5 =$ _____

$5 + 1 =$ _____

$1 + 7 =$ _____

$4 + 1 =$ _____

$3 + 4 =$ _____

$5 + 3 =$ _____

$2 + 4 =$ _____

Bonus: Write four addition problems with a sum of 5.

Seeds

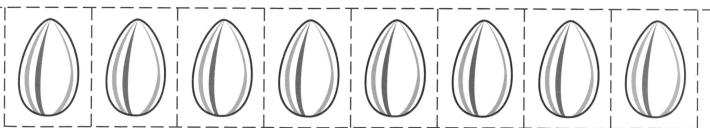

Tee Off With S

These fun-filled ideas are sure to help
make a hole-in-one with subtraction skil

ideas contributed by Kathy Gin
Wa

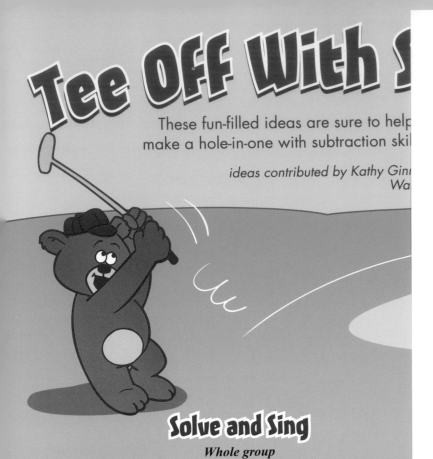

Solve and Sing

Whole group

Help students understand the parts of a subtraction problem with th
sing-along activity. Set out manipulatives or cutouts that match a desire
theme. Then say a theme-related story problem. Invite a child to use th
manipulatives to act out the story problem. When the problem is solve
write the corresponding number sentence on the board. Then lead stud
in singing the song below. **For ongoing practice**, write several story
problems on separate cards and store the cards in a file box for a ready
use daily activity at your fingertips!

> *(sung to the tune of "If You're Happy and You Know It")*
>
> [Five] minus [three] equals [two].
> [Five] minus [three] equals [two].
> Well, you start with [five], and you take [three] away.
> [Five] minus [three] equals [two].

Claire
10 – 3 = 7

Honeycomb Patterns and Bee Cards
Use with "Build the Hives" on page 273.

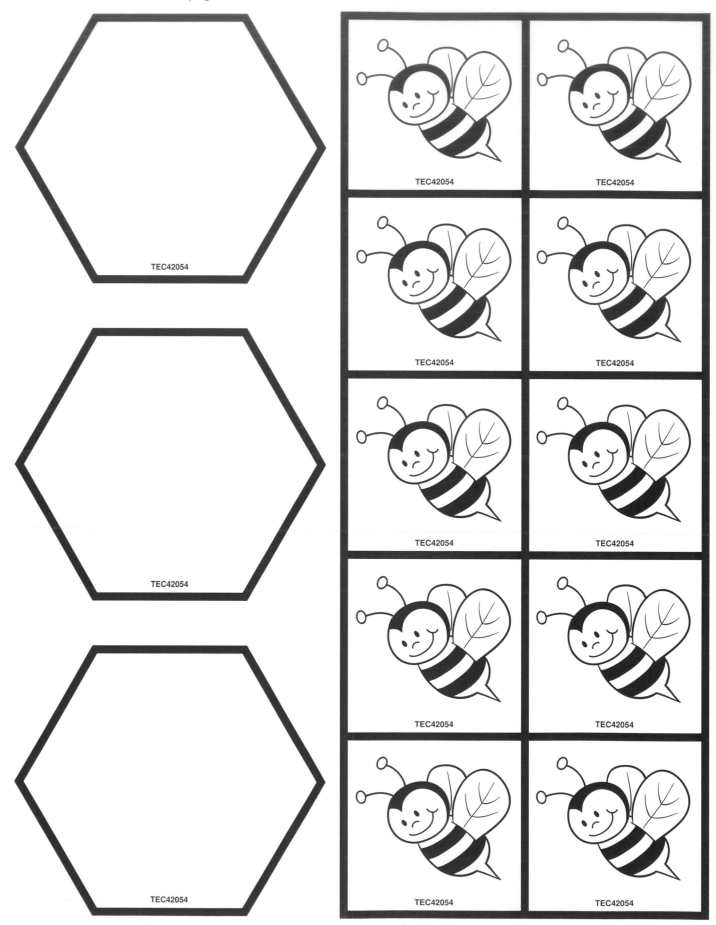

Putt It In!

 Cut.

Subtract.

Use the counters to help you.

4 – 3 = _____

6 – 6 = _____   10 – 4 = _____

8 – 3 = _____   9 – 1 = _____

7 – 4 = _____   10 – 3 = _____

9 – 5 = _____   10 – 6 = _____

8 – 0 = _____   10 – 1 = _____

Bonus: Draw a picture that shows 10 – 5. Solve. Write the number sentence.

Name _____

ide-and-See

✏️ Write the numbers in order.

10 9 8

8, 9, ___, ___

10 12 11

___, ___, ___

6 5 7

___, ___, ___

23 21 22

___, ___, ___

24 26 25

___, ___, ___

14 12 13

___, ___, ___

17 16 15

___, ___, ___

30 29 28

___, ___, ___

19 21 20

___, ___, ___

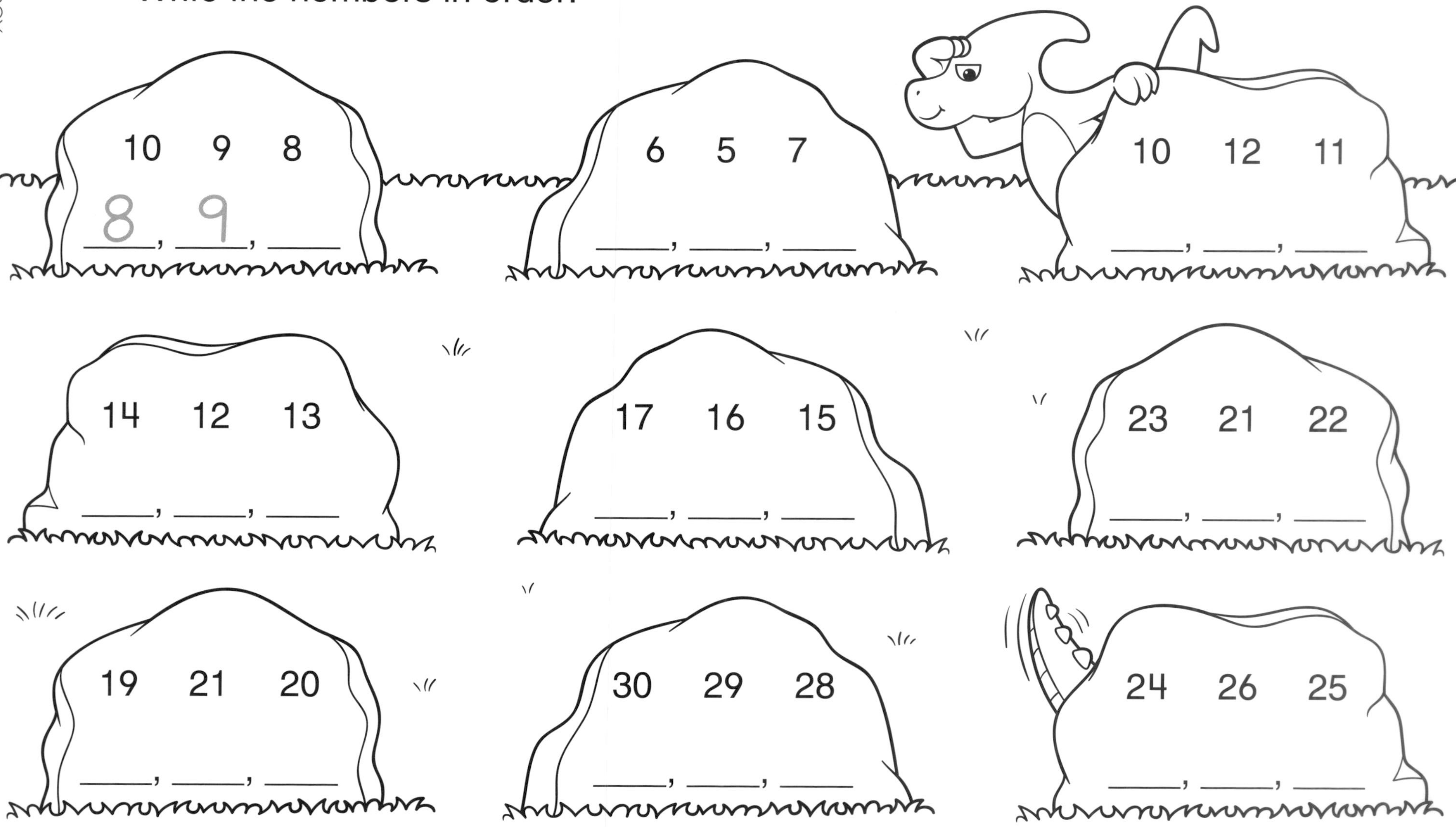

Bonus: Write the numbers in order. 28, 30, 25, 29, 27, 26

SEASONAL UNITS

Favorite Back-to-School Themes

Looking for a fun way to add flair to your classroom? You can't go wrong with one of these engaging themes! 💻

Pick of the Crop

ideas contributed by Gerri Primak, Charlotte, NC

Classroom Decorations

- Mount on the classroom door a large basket cutout with the title "Pick of the Crop." Then write each student's name on a separate apple cutout and display the apples above the basket.
- Post a large apple tree. On each apple, write a different theme or subject that students will be learning during the year.

Classroom Labels

- Write each child's name on a red, green, or yellow apple cutout and attach it to her desk or table space. Use the apple colors to assign groups.
- To make a job chart, write each classroom job on an apple cutout. Write each child's name on a leaf cutout. To assign jobs, simply attach a leaf to each apple.

First-Day Activity

Gather students in a circle and give one child an apple to hold. Then lead students in saying the chant shown as they pass the apple around the circle. The student holding the apple at the end of the chant stands up and says, "Hi, my name is [child's name]." Continue play until each child has introduced himself.

Apple, apple of my eye,
It is your turn to say, "Hi!"

Sam

Line Leader

Math Center

Art Center

Kindergarten Is Out of This World!

ideas contributed by Gerri Primak

Classroom Decorations

- Cover the classroom door with black paper. On a large rocket cutout write "Stars in [your name]'s Kindergarten." Label yellow star cutouts with student names and display them around the rocket.
- Tape a large star cutout to the floor to show the line leader where to stand.
- Use space-themed gift wrap as the background paper for a bulletin board.

Classroom Labels

- On a supply of star and planet cutouts, use glitter pens to write the different classroom areas or classroom rules.
- To make a job chart, write each classroom job on a planet cutout. Write each child's name on a small rocket cutout. To assign jobs, attach each rocket to a planet.

First-Day Activity

Draw a simple rocket ship on the board. Write a student's name on the rocket. When a child sees her name, she stands up and says, "Blast off!" Then erase the name and continue until each child has had a turn.

A Colorful Kindergarten

ideas contributed by Ada Goren, Winston-Salem, NC

Classroom Decorations
- Outside the classroom door, post a large rainbow with a cloud at each end. Label one cloud with your name and the other with the room number.
- Use colorful strips of crepe paper as bulletin board border.

Classroom Labels
- To make nametags, write each child's name on a white cloud cutout. Use a length of colorful crepe paper as the necklace.
- To make a job chart, label rainbow cutouts with jobs. Label cloud cutouts with student names. To assign jobs, attach a cloud to each rainbow.

First-Day Activity
Take youngsters on a color scavenger hunt! In advance, draw and color a large rainbow; then cut each band apart. Place each band at a different school location. Take students on a school tour, collecting the bands as you go. When you return to the classroom, enlist students' help in assembling the rainbow.

Mary

Door Holder

Cierra

A "Bear-y" Good Year!

ideas contributed by Ada Goren

Classroom Decorations
- Display on the classroom door an enlarged bear cutout (pattern on page 283) and the title "A 'Bear-y' Merry Welcome." Around the bear post bear paw cutouts (patterns on page 283) programmed with student names.
- Use brown bulletin board paper to make a bear cave in your reading area. Provide teddy bears for students to read to at the bear cave.

Classroom Labels
- Label a bear paw cutout (patterns on page 283) for each student. Use the paws to label student cubbies or desks.
- Label an index card for each classroom area or center. At each area, place a teddy bear holding the label.
- To make a job chart, label paper cave shapes with jobs. Label bear cutouts (pattern on page 283) with student names. To assign jobs, attach a bear to each cave.

First-Day Activity
Have each child color a copy of the bear pattern from page 283. Then ask each child to sit with a partner and introduce himself. Have the partners determine one thing that is the same and one thing that is different about their bears. Then ask them to find one similarity and one difference between themselves. Invite each student pair to share its findings with the class.

More Themes!

Choose from these ideas to jump-start your classroom theme!

Welcome to the Kindergarten Jungle

To set up a jungle in your classroom, display jungle animal paper plates and brown paper vines on a bulletin board. Use outstretched grass skirts to cover shelves. To show students around the school or classroom, take them on an imaginary safari. *Sharron Posey, Double Springs Elementary, Double Springs, AL*

Kindergarten Is "Dino-mite!"

Choose a dinosaur species to act as your class mascot. Use cutouts of the chosen dinosaur to label the different areas of the classroom. For a display, post an enlarged dinosaur cutout and a large volcano with the title "Learning Is a Blast!" If desired, carry the theme throughout the grade level by inviting the other classrooms to choose different dinosaur mascots. *Stacey Tatum, Glennville Elementary, Glennville, GA* 🖥

Reading Center

A Kindergarten Campout

A mock campfire is a great way to help students get acquainted. To make a campfire, glue red, yellow, and orange tissue paper to empty paper towel tubes. Make a roasting marshmallow by gluing a white paper square to a craft stick. Gather students around the fire and hand one child the marshmallow. Encourage her to introduce herself and then pass the marshmallow to the next child. *Peggy Carty, Tot Spot Childcare, Conroe, TX*

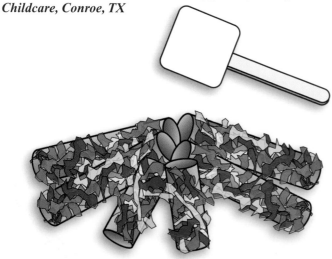

Back-to-School Roundup

To make a lasso, have each child glue a length of thick yarn to a paper square, as shown. When it's dry, write his name in the lasso. Attach the lasso cards to the door and add the title "Look Who's Rounded Up in Kindergarten!" For a school tour, have each child color a horse pattern and then glue it to a craft stick. Line up students and their horses and take them on a "trail ride" through the school. *Angie Inman and Lisa Meeks, Chalybeate Elementary, Walnut, MS* 🖥

Quinn

TEC42050

TEC42050

TEC42050

A "Paws-itively" Perfect Open House

Prepare for open house with this selection of ideas to use before, during, and after the big day!

Guess Who!

Prior to open house, have students help prepare this **parental involvement** activity! Have each child fold a sheet of construction paper in half and write on the outside flap "Guess who likes…" Next, ask her to draw and label, with your help, three things that she likes. Tell each child to consider including a favorite animal, color, food, game, movie, or book. Then have her open the paper and write her name on the inside. Collect the finished projects.

On the day of open house, display the folded projects on a table so they are standing upright. When parents enter the classroom, encourage them to find their child's project. Invite parents to take the projects home as a kindergarten keepsake. 🖥

Randi Austin, Gasconade C-4, Falcon, MO

Guess who likes…

Welcome to Ms. Pawsly's Kindergarten

A Sunny Welcome

This bright **display** not only gives students and their parents a warm welcome but also can be used for a class activity! Display an extra large sun with one ray for each student in your class. Title the sun as desired. During open house, invite each family to write their child's name and their names on a ray. To use the display after open house, encourage each student, in turn, to point to his ray and share some information about his family.

Katie Zuehlke, Bendix Elementary, Annandale, MN

A Guided Tour

Youngsters take their parents on a **classroom tour** with this idea! Before open house, give each child a sheet of paper divided into three sections and numbered and titled as shown. Have her write her name on the line. Then ask her to draw and label each of three areas of the room that she would like to show to her family during open house. (Be sure that each classroom area is clearly labeled.) Collect the papers.

When each child and her family arrives at open house, give the child her list. Encourage her to act as a tour guide, taking her family to the three places on the list and telling a little about each area. 🖥

Kelly A. Lu, Berlyn School, Ontario, CA

Tour guide: Violet

1. Book Nook
2. Writing Center
3. My Desk

Violet

Editor's Tip:
If you do not have photo software, add the digital photos to your screen saver's slideshow option instead.

Picture-Perfect Kindergarten

A digital camera and a computer are all you need to make a **presentation** of a day in your classroom. Take photos throughout the day of students involved in different activities. (Be sure that each child is represented.) Then use photo software to make a slideshow. If the software allows, add a caption to each picture. During open house, continuously play the slideshow on the computer and invite parents to see their youngsters in action!

Peggy Campbell-Rush, Washington, NJ

Take and Make

Recruit **parent volunteers** during open house! In advance, gather materials for several projects—such as bulletin board displays, art samples, centers, and games—that you will need prepared this school year. Place each set of materials, along with directions, in a gallon-size resealable plastic bag. Label each bag with a title and due date. Also make a checklist with each title.

During open house, place the bags and checklist on a table. Encourage parents to preview the projects on the table, choose a bag, and sign the checklist. Parents who are not able to help in the classroom are sure to appreciate this opportunity to help from home! 🖥

Krista Crates Miller, Findlay, OH

Apple Bulletin Board
Due: September 15

Directions

Seasonal Skill Practice
Apples and Pumpkins

Students are sure to have bushels of fun with these science, math, and literacy ideas!

From Seed to Pumpkin

This crafty mobile makes it easy to picture how a pumpkin grows! First, give each student a simple pumpkin pattern and a copy of page 288. Then talk about the growth of a pumpkin and lead students to color their patterns as follows: brown seed, green leaves, yellow flower, orange pumpkin.

Then, to make a mobile, a child cuts out his patterns and word cards. He glues the seed cutout and its label to a three-inch brown paper square; then he glues each remaining word card to its corresponding cutout(s). Next, he tapes the card and cutouts to a 15-inch length of green yarn (vine) to show the sequence in which a pumpkin grows. To complete the mobile, he tapes the seed card to a hanger. *Changes and growth of a pumpkin* 💻

Ada Goren, Winston-Salem, NC

Crops to Compare

For this center activity, set out a container with ten red pom-poms (apples), a container with ten orange pom-poms (pumpkins), a bag holding ten cards numbered from 1 to 10, paper, and crayons. A child makes two columns on her paper. She draws a red apple at the top of one column and an orange pumpkin at the top of the other. Next, she pulls two cards from the bag. She copies each number in a different column and uses the pom-poms to determine which number is larger. Then she circles the larger number and returns the pom-poms and cards. She repeats the activity with other number pairs as time permits. *Counting, comparing sets of objects* 💻

Ada Goren

Fall Favorites

Write the poem shown on strips for pocket chart use. Then try these activities! 🖥

Print awareness: For a pointer, glue one end of a craft stick between an apple cutout and a pumpkin cutout. Then have individuals guide the class in reciting the poem, flipping the pointer when needed to show the matching fruit or vegetable.

Rhyming: Help students identify rhyming word pairs in the poem.

High-frequency words: Write high-frequency words from the poem on apple and pumpkin cutouts. Slide the cutouts in front of the matching words. Have students take turns picking apples and oranges. To pick one, a child reads the word and then drops the cutout in a basket.

Ada Goren, Winston-Salem, NC

Apples, apples on a tree.

Apples, apples—good for me!

I like apples; yes, I do!

Big and red for me and you!

Pumpkins, pumpkins on a vine.

Pumpkins, pumpkins look so fine!

I like pumpkin; yes, I do!

Big and orange for me and you!

LITERACY AND MATH

Where's My Stem?

Use this whole-group game to practice a variety of skills! Cut out orange circles (pumpkins) for half your students and the same number of green rectangles (stems). Label the pumpkin and stem pairs to practice a skill, such as uppercase and lowercase letters, addition facts and answers, or color dots and color words. Then give each child a cutout. To play, youngsters work together to correctly pair each pumpkin with its stem. **For an independent activity,** place the prepared pumpkins and stems at a center. *Skill practice* 🖥

Laurie Gibbons, Huntsville, AL

LITERACY

A Treetop Family

For this small-group activity, write a word family ending on the trunk of a large tree cutout. Also program several apple cutouts with onsets that form words when paired with the rime. Put the apples on the tree. Have students take turns picking apples and reading the words they make. **For a writing connection,** have each child draw a tree outline on paper and copy the word family ending on the trunk. Each time a word is made, ask him to write it on the treetop. *Word families* 🖥

See page 289 for a **practice page** on nonstandard measurement.

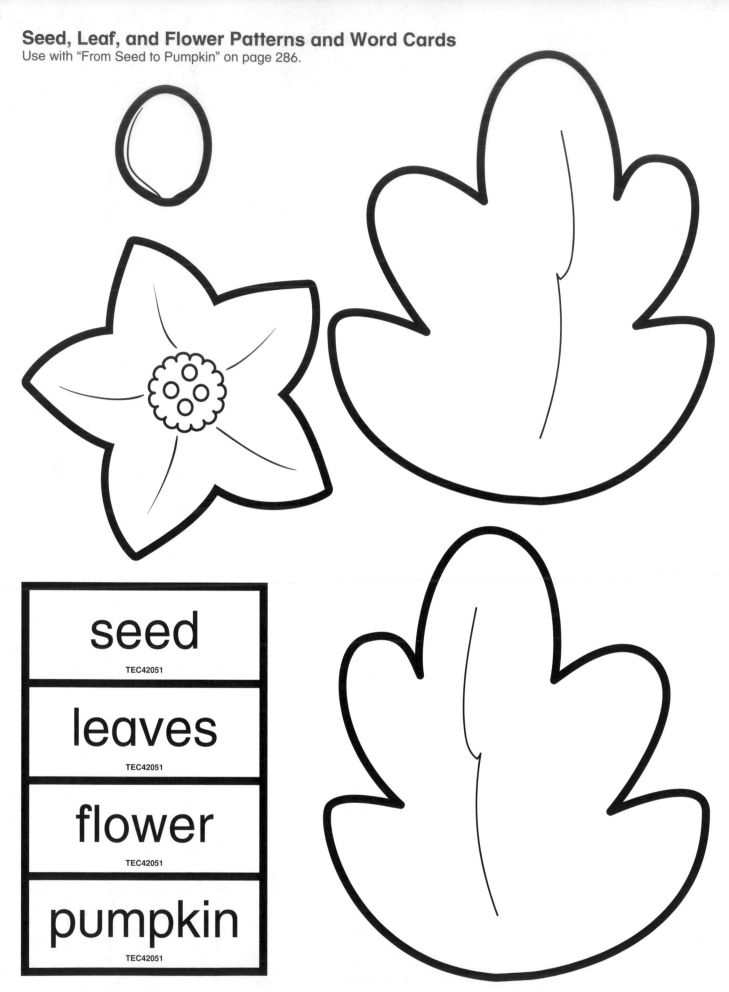

seed

TEC42051

leaves

TEC42051

flower

TEC42051

pumpkin

TEC42051

How Many Seeds?

✂ Cut. Measure.

✏ Write.

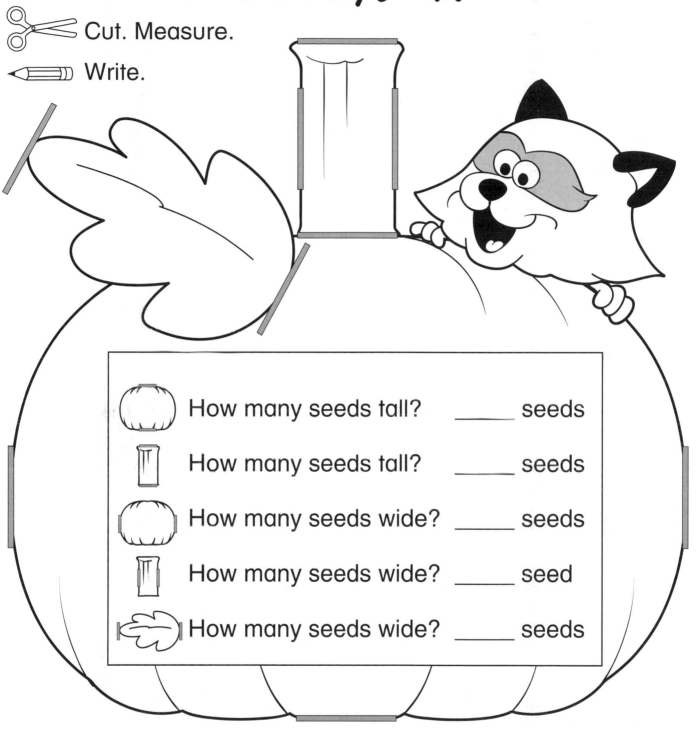

How many seeds tall?   ____ seeds

How many seeds tall?   ____ seeds

How many seeds wide?   ____ seeds

How many seeds wide?   ____ seed

How many seeds wide?   ____ seeds

Winter Celebrations

Festive Five-Minute Filler

Tuck cards (or die-cuts) labeled with numbers, letters, or sight words inside a holiday stocking. Students take turns pulling a card from the stocking. A student either reads the card for his classmates or asks his classmates to read the card for him! *Carrie Johnson, Stone Elementary, Crossville, TN*

Adding Holiday Touches

- Store center activities in holiday-themed gift bags.
- Use holiday-themed rubber stamps when grading papers.
- Keep a supply of sharpened holiday pencils handy. Pass out the pencils to give select written activities extra holiday flair.

Math Masterpieces

Deck the halls with math! A child colors a holiday shape using an assigned pattern. Showcase the artwork with a matching rhyme. *Melodie Smith, Weeden Elementary, Florence, AL* 💻

Did you know? Can you see? My candy cane's pattern Is AB!

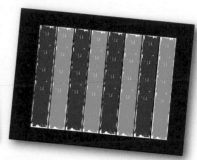

The Joy of Giving

Warm the hearts of residents at a local care facility. To make a placemat, a student glues a border of precut paper squares to a large sheet of construction paper. She copies a holiday greeting on the mat and then glues one or more holiday cutouts to her project. Laminate the mats before delivery. *Tammy Lutz, George E. Greene Elementary, Bad Axe, MI* 💻

Storytime Surprise

Cover a large box and lid with seasonal gift wrap. Hide your daily reading selection inside the box until storytime. Then introduce the book with great fanfare. Add excitement to a math lesson, writing activity, or art project in a similar manner.

Seasonal Skill Practice
Frosty Fun

These science, math, and literacy ideas are just in time for wintry weather!

adapted from ideas contributed by Laurie K. Gibbons, Huntsville, AL

SCIENCE
Chilly Changes

Is the temperature dropping? Do your students feel a chill in the air? Ask youngsters about the changes they see, smell, hear, taste, and feel during the transition from fall to winter. Write each student's response on a white paper circle (snowball) and display the snowballs one above the other to form a tall snowpal body. Then top the body off with a snowpal head. **To extend the activity,** have youngsters use the display to help them write about and illustrate winter-related scenes. *Recognizing seasonal changes* 🖥

LITERACY
No School?

If the seasonal conditions closed your school for a day, your students would surely keep busy! Sing this short tune to prompt a discussion of what youngsters might like to do on a snow day. Following the discussion, have each child write to complete the sentence "On a snow day, I would…" Then have her draw a picture to match her writing. *Writing* 🖥

On a snow day, I would go sledding at the park!

(sung to the tune of "Do Your Ears Hang Low?")

If you hear "no school," what would you do that day?
Would you stay inside or go outside to play?
Blankets, boots, and scarves—comfy things that keep you warm
If you hear "no school."

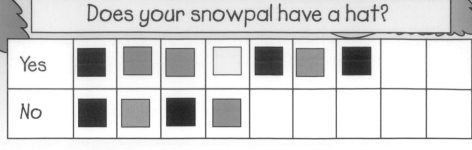

Yes	■	■	■	□	■	■	■		
No	■	■	■	■					

MATH
Take a Look

Here's a cute craft that results in daily math practice. Give each child an outline of a snowpal. Encourage him to cut it out and add details as desired. Then post a question of the day, such as "Is your snowpal smiling?" Invite each youngster to put a sticky note or paper square on a simple graph to respond yes or no. Discuss the results as time allows. To change the graph, simply remove the squares and post a different question. *Graphing* 🖥

Super snowpal! "My" is the winning word.

	my		
	my	see	
the	my	see	can
the	my	see	can

LITERACY
Super Snowpal!

Your kindergartners are sure to be eager to read and write words at this partner center. In advance, secure a paper clip and brad to a tagboard copy of the spinner pattern on page 293. At a center, put the spinner, a copy of the recording sheet from page 293 for each child, and pencils.

To play, a child spins the spinner and writes the word in the matching column on her recording sheet. Then her partner takes a turn. When a player writes the same word three times, she says, "Super snowpal!" and announces the winning word. If desired, have the twosome continue until one player fills her paper. *High-frequency words* 🖥

MATH OR LITERACY
Pockets Full of Snow

These snowpals include storage pockets! For each skill you would like to review, glue a half circle to a snowpal cutout to make a pocket; then label the snowpal's hat with the skill. Next, write on white paper circles (snowballs) numbers, letters, or words, or draw pictures or shapes that correspond with the skill. Slide the snowballs in the snowpal's pocket. If desired, place matching-color dots or stickers on the back of each snowpal and its snowballs for easy sorting. Now it's ready-to-use and easy to transport! *Skill practice* 🖥

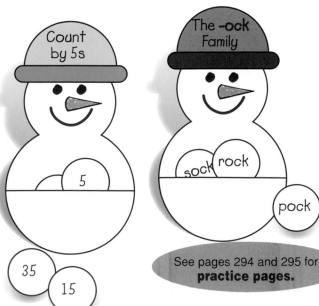

See pages 294 and 295 for **practice pages.**

the | my | see | can

TEC42052

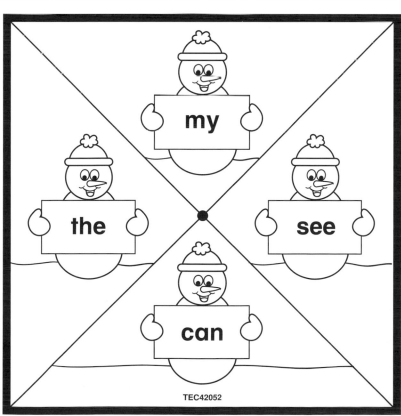

my

the | see

can

TEC42052

Super Sledder

Name _____

✋ **Count by 10s.**

✂️ Cut. 🧴 Glue.

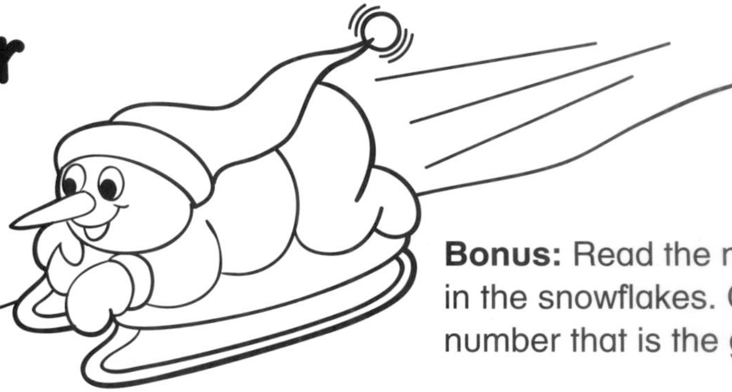

Bonus: Read the numbers in the snowflakes. Color the number that is the greatest.

❄️ 40 ❄️ 60 ❄️ 70

❄️ 20 ❄️ 50 ❄️ 60

✋ **Count by 10s.**

✏️ Write.

10, ____, ____, 40, 50, ____, 70, ____

❄️ 90 ❄️ 50 ❄️ 10 ❄️ 30 ❄️ 40 ❄️ 70 ❄️ 100 ❄️ 80

©The Mailbox® • TEC42052 • Dec./Jan. 2010–11

Wintry Fun

Change the first letter in each word to name the picture.

 Write.

 Cross out the matching letter.

t	m	b	n
s	x̶	h	f

 log

dog

 **cat**

 bun

 pin

 jet

 pen

10

 tag

cap

Just for Valentine's Day!

♥ How Many Hearts?

Candy hearts add festive flair to nonstandard measurement. Make available a supply of candy hearts and several small classroom items. Encourage each youngster to use the hearts to measure each item. Then have him record his measurements on a sheet like the one shown. *adapted from an idea by Rebecca L. Mueller, Clay Road Baptist School, Houston, TX*

Name Scott	
What I measured	♥ hearts
[crayon]	8
[hand]	6
[block A]	3

♥ Valentine Headbands

After each student opens her valentines, ask her to choose five of her favorites. Have her glue the chosen cards to a construction paper headband. Invite students to wear their headbands during Valentine's Day celebrations. *Joe Appleton, Durham, NC*

♥ Sight Word Placemats

To make a placemat, have each child write a different word on each of ten heart cutouts. Then direct him to glue the hearts to a 12" x 18" sheet of construction paper labeled with his name. Laminate the resulting placemats for durability. If desired, invite students to use the placemats when eating Valentine's Day treats. *Felice Kestenbaum, Goosehill Primary, Cold Spring Harbor, NY*

♥ Heart Lotto

For this game, give each child a paper strip, five different-color crayons, and five game markers. Have him write "HEART" on his strip, using a different color for each letter. In a bag, place a set of the crayons and letter cards to spell "HEART." To play, remove a crayon and a letter from the bag. If a child has the matching set on his card, he covers it with a marker. Return the items to the bag and play until a child covers all five letters and announces, "I have heart!" *adapted from an idea by Brenda Pritchett, Columbus, MS*

♥ Party Game

Have students sit in a circle. Then stand in front of a child and say, "Oh, sweet friend of mine, will you be my valentine?" as you hand the child a heart cutout. After the child responds, "Yes, I will be your valentine!" the youngster trades places with you. Then she repeats the process with another student. *Marla Cobb, Barhitte Elementary, Burton, MI*

♥ A Happy Hunt

Label a class supply of red and pink heart cutouts each with a different number. Secretly hide the hearts around the classroom; then invite each child to find one. After the hunt, use the hearts to reinforce a math skill such as ordering numbers, comparing numbers, or patterning. *Milisa McDaniel, Eshelman Avenue Elementary, Lomita, CA*

Hooray for Dr. Seuss!

Delightful, charming, entertaining, and just plain silly—Dr. Seuss books are pure fun! Use these ideas to inspire youngsters to read here, there, and everywhere!

Tap That Hat!

Rhyming

Does the Cat in the Hat have a favorite hat? Of course he does! So add a fun twist to your rhyming review by encouraging youngsters to wear their favorite hats. Have each child bring a hat of her choice to school. (Glue a tagboard copy of the hat pattern on page 299 to a paper headband for each student who does not have a hat.) After reading a Dr. Seuss story aloud, lead students in one of the options below.

Recognizing rhymes: Name pairs of words from the story, most of which rhyme. Instruct each child to touch his hat when he hears two words that rhyme.

Generating rhymes: Name a real or nonsense word from the story. Then invite youngsters, in turn, to produce rhyming words. For each correct word, have each child tap her hat!

Reading -*at* words: Write -*at* on chart paper. Then name words, some of which end with the featured rime. For each matching word, instruct students to tap their hats. Then solicit student help to write each matching word on the chart. For each rhyming word added, read the rhyming word list.

Gerri Primak
Charlotte, NC

-at
hat
cat
mat

Fish.

one   fish
two   here
red   there
blue   everywhere
black   some

See the **practice sheets** on pages 300 and 301.

Look in a Book

High-frequency words

Dr. Seuss books are not only fun but they also include many words your kindergartners can read! In advance, post a list of high-frequency words from a selected story on a large book cutout. For added interest, have youngsters make Seuss-style characters to embellish the display. Then encourage each child to look and listen for the posted words as you read the story aloud. Each time a word is recognized, have him form silly glasses around his eyes with his fingers. **For a writing activity,** have each youngster write three words from the display and then draw a smiley face next to the corresponding word each time he sees it in the book. 🖥

Gerri Primak

So Many Stripes!

Word families

On a wall? In the hall? Show your enthusiasm for reading and writing with these Seuss-style hats! Give each youngster a red copy of the hat pattern on page 299 and four 1" x 6" white paper strips. Assign each student a rime and have him write it on his hat rim. Then, on each strip, instruct him to write a different word that corresponds with the rime. When his words are approved, have him glue the strips to his hat. Then display the completed hats with the rhyme shown.

> We can spell! Yes, it's true!
> Read the words we wrote for you!

Steven Lamkin, Salisbury Christian School, Salisbury, MD

How Many Feet?

The Foot Book is easy to adapt for a variety of math and literacy skills. Try one or all of these activities after reading this popular story aloud.

Nonstandard measurement: Set out manipulatives, such as counters, Unifix cubes, and paper clips. Have each child tape a 12-inch length of string to a sheet of paper. Then direct him to choose a manipulative and measure how many it takes to equal one foot. Have him record the information on his paper. Then encourage him to measure with different objects as time permits.

adapted from an idea by Amanda Bangert, Trinity Lutheran School Grand Island, NE

Counting by fives and tens: Invite youngsters to stand for a Seuss-stomp! Discuss with youngsters how one foot has five toes and two feet have ten toes. Then have students count by fives as they stomp, one foot at a time, around the room. For the next round, have students hop on both feet as they count by tens.

Reading fluency: Set out different-color paints and help each youngster make her footprints on a sheet of paper. Then have her write on her paper to complete the sentence "[Student name] has [color] feet." When the pages are dry, bind them together between construction paper covers and put the book in your reading area.

So Funny!

Responding to a story

Silly Seuss scenes are sure to prompt some laughter! Before reading a Dr. Seuss book aloud, tell students that, at the end of the story, you will ask them to name the funniest parts of the story. Remind youngsters to listen carefully and look closely at the illustrations. After reading, invite each student to tell which part she thought was the silliest. Then have her write a sentence similar to the one shown and draw a picture to match. **To make a class book,** bind the pages between construction paper covers and add the title "So Funny!" Then invite each youngster to read her page aloud.

Gerri Primak, Charlotte, NC

Seasonal Skill Practice
Just Hatched!

Crack into science, literacy, and math skills with these "egg-ceptional" ideas!

SCIENCE

The Chicken and the Egg

A supersize egg is the perfect background for this life-cycle activity. Following a discussion about the changes of a growing chick, guide each child in making this craft using the suggestions below for each of the four stages. **For a more advanced version**, have students label each arrow to tell about each stage. *Life cycle of a chicken*

- **Nest:** A student uses brown and tan paper scraps to make a nest and glues a white oval (egg) in the nest.
- **Inside the egg:** A student draws an irregular shape on an oval (egg) to represent a window. Then she colors the inside of the window yellow and draws eyes and a beak to represent a growing chick.
- **Chick:** A student uses craft supplies and paper scraps to glue two eyes, an orange beak, wings, and orange legs to a yellow paper oval.
- **Chicken:** A student uses paint to make a handprint on the left side of the egg background. When it is dry, she draws details such as wings, legs, eyes, a wattle, a comb, and a beak.

Laurie K. Gibbons, Huntsville, AL

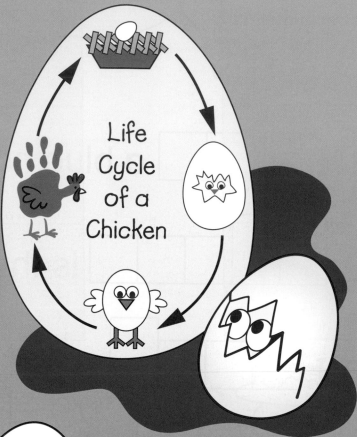

Life Cycle of a Chicken

butter

butterfly

fly

LITERACY

Match That Chick!

Students match compound words and their word parts to pair these chicks with their cracked egg halves. Cut out several copies of the chick and egg patterns on page 304 to have one pattern for each student. For each set, write a compound word on the chick and write each matching individual word on an egg half. Give each youngster an egg half or a chick. On your signal, encourage youngsters to match each chick to its egg halves. When all the chicks are matched, invite each group to share its word parts and the compound word. *Compound words*

Laurie K. Gibbons

MATH

Add Those Eggs!

What fits perfectly in a nest? Why, eggs do, of course! For each student, staple several white paper ovals between two brown construction paper ovals to make a booklet. Have each child write a title and draw nest details on the front cover. Then have her roll two number cubes and use the numbers to form an addition problem on the first page. Provide ink pads for her to make fingerprint eggs in two different colors to match the numbers. Then have her count the eggs and solve the problem. Instruct her to write different addition problems in this manner on each remaining page. *Addition using objects* 🖥

Laurie K. Gibbons, Huntsville, AL

Katie's Nest

$4 + 2 = 6$

This animal has three body parts, six legs, and two eyes.

Animals that hatch from eggs:

salamander	ladybug
caterpillar	spider
frog	bird
toad	ant
turtle	alligator
earthworm	crocodile
platypus	penguin

SCIENCE

Hatchling Predictions

Students learn that chicks are not the only creatures that hatch from eggs with this riddle activity. In each of ten plastic eggs, put a picture or small plastic toy of an animal that hatches from an egg. Number the eggs from 1 to 10 and jot down each number and the name of its corresponding animal. To play, select an egg and give animal-related riddles leading youngsters to name the animal hidden in the egg. When a student is correct, invite him to crack open the egg and reveal the contents. Continue with each remaining egg. *Animal characteristics* 🖥

Sheli Gossett, Sebring, FL

MATH

Eggs! Eggs! Eggs!

To prepare this center activity, set out a supply of plastic eggs in three different sizes and colors. When a child visits the center, she takes six eggs and then decides whether she will sort them by size or color. She colors the matching smiley face on a copy of the recording sheet on page 304. Next, she draws or writes to label the bottom row of the graph and then completes the graph to record her egg collection. If desired, have each child repeat the activity at a later time using the other criterion. *Graphing* 🖥

Kaye Sowell, Pelahatchie Elementary
Pelahatchie, MS

Name *Rukiya*

Recording sheet

I sorted my eggs by
😊 size.
😊 color.

See page 305 for a reading **practice page**.

Chick and Egg Patterns

Use with "Match That Chick!" on page 302.

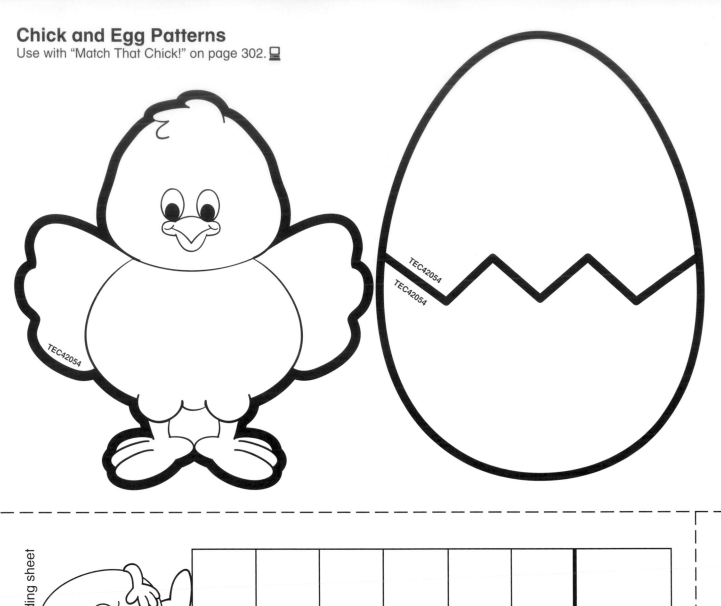

TEC42054

TEC42054

TEC42054

Recording sheet

Name _____

I sorted my eggs by

☺ size.

☺ color.

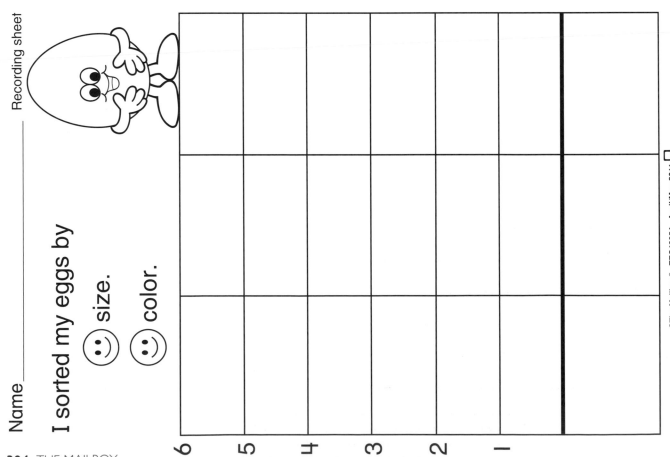

6			
5			
4			
3			
2			
1			

©The Mailbox® • TEC42054 • April/May 2011

Note to the teacher: Use with "Eggs! Eggs! Eggs!" on page 303.

A Bed of Hay

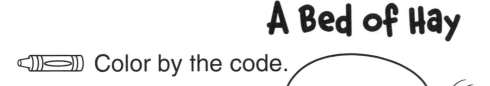

Color by the code.

bed

sled   hay

play   shed   tray

Color Code

-ed as in —yellow   **-ay** as in —orange

Write the **ed** and **ay** words to match.

-ed	-ay
 _____	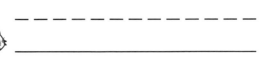 _____
 _____	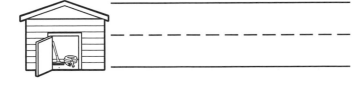 _____
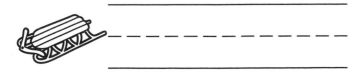 _____	 _____

Bonus: Write five words to make an **at** word family.

©The Mailbox® • TEC42054 • April/May 2011

"Toad-ally" Cool Year-End Ideas

From expressing gratitude to making a summer reading list, students are sure to enjoy hopping toward the last day of school with these activities!

ideas contributed by Laurie K. Gibbons, Huntsville, AL

A "Toad-ken" of Our Appreciation

To: Ms. Mansour
From: Ms. Gibbons' Kindergarten Class

June 2011
Ms. Mansour,
Your dedication to literature and our school library has helped us grow by leaps and bounds! Thank you for all you do!

B.J. liked the way you read the stories.

Green With Gratitude!

Help youngsters express appreciation to support staff and parent volunteers with these **thank-you booklets**! To make one, cut out a green copy of the booklet cover on page 308. Use the front cover as a tracer to make a back cover and a class supply of student pages. Personalize the front cover and share it with your youngsters. Then guide each child to complete a page by drawing and writing about something the recipient did or shared, such as a favorite book from the media specialist, a favorite song with the music teacher, or a skill-related task with a volunteer. If desired, write a thank-you note on an extra page to tell how the person helped your class grow by leaps and bounds this school year. Then bind the completed pages between the covers. 💻

"UN-frog-ettable" Memories

____Katie____'s
Kindergarten Memories
2010–2011

Years from now, preserved kindergarten moments in this **time capsule** are sure to be appreciated. Collect cardboard tubes or canisters to have a class supply. For each child, personalize and sign a copy of the note on page 309. Then guide each student to complete a copy of page 310. Using the options below, prepare other materials to include in each capsule. After each child puts her capsule items in her tube, help her wrap the tube in brown paper so it resembles a log and label it as shown. Then have her use craft materials to make a frog and glue it to her log. Now that's an "un-frog-ettable" keepsake! 💻

Time Capsule Options

Note from the teacher	Writing samples
Kindergarten questionnaire	Artwork
School news	Self-portrait
Class newsletter	Painted handprints
Piece of string that shows child's current height	Class photo

Fashionable Friends

These **class-made T-shirts** not only serve as kindergarten keepsakes but are also perfect for end-of-the-year programs, award ceremonies, and the last day of school! For each student, obtain a plain white or light blue T-shirt and label it with a title and academic year as shown. Put a piece of cardboard inside each shirt to separate the front and back of the shirt. Guide each child to use a permanent marker to write her name in small letters on the front of each shirt. Also have her use green or brown fabric paint to make a fingerprint above her name. When the paint is dry, help each child draw eyes and a mouth to transform her fingerprint into a toad.

Our "Toad-ally" Cool Class

Sarah Isaac Liam Jessica Felipe
Juan Monica Tyler Evan
Peter Matthew Kate Danny Carrie

2010–2011

Editor's Tip:
As an alternative, make one class T-shirt and put it on a stuffed animal to serve as an end-of-the-year mascot.

Getting a Jump on Summer!

Students hop, skip, and jump as they countdown to the last day of school with this **display idea**! Write each number from 1 to 10 on a separate lily pad cutout. On the back of each one, write an exercise of your choice. Display the lily pads on a pond background with the title shown, leaving a space by the last lily pad. On the appropriate day, post a frog cutout by the number 10 lily pad to begin the countdown. Then flip the lily pad and have youngsters perform the programmed action. At the end of the last day of school, post blue tissue paper to represent the frog's splash as it hops into summer! **For a skill-related variation**, program the back of each lily pad with a review question for youngsters to answer. 💻

Splash Into Summer!

10 9 8 7 6 5 4 3 2 1

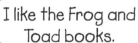

I like the Frog and Toad books.

Ribbit, Read It!

Select an option from the ideas below to promote **summer reading**! 💻

- **Personal reading list:** Make a copy of the recording sheet on page 309. Instruct each child to record ten books he reads (or listens to) over the summer. If desired, offer a small reward, such as a new pencil, for completed papers returned in the fall.

- **Home-school connection:** Invite youngsters to share their favorite book titles and give a brief description of what makes the story appealing. Write each title on a chart. Then lead students to select a top ten list of favorites. Transfer the list to a copy of the recording sheet on page 309 and make a class supply. Encourage each child to share the list with her family and use it to find interesting, age-appropriate books to read during the summer.

A "Toad-ken" of Our Appreciation

From:

To:

TEC42055

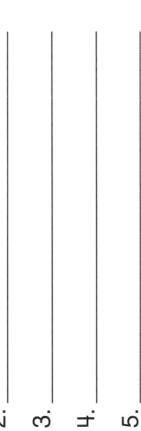

Dear _____,

I still remember greeting you

On your first day of school.

We spent that first week learning

The routines and all the rules.

The months flew by, we learned and laughed,

And we had a lot of fun!

Soon the year was over,

Though it seemed it had just begun.

Congratulations and Best Wishes!

Note to the teacher: Use with "'Un-frog-ettable' Memories" on page 306.

Read It!

Name _____

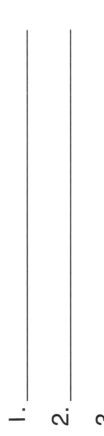 1. _____

 2. _____

3. _____

4. _____

5. _____

6. _____

7. _____

8. _____

9. _____

10. _____

Note to the teacher: Use with "Ribbit, Read It!" on page 307.

Kindergarten Memories

_____ 's

At school, I liked to

_____

_____

_____

_____

Favorite Food

I am glad I learned

_____

_____

_____

Favorite Book

More about me:

_____

_____

_____

©The Mailbox® • TEC42055 • June/July 2011

310   THE MAILBOX   **Note to the teacher:** Use with "'Un-frog-ettable' Memories" on page 306.

INDEX

ISBN 978-161276139-8

9 781612 761398